1 & 2
CHRONICLES

J. Vernon McGee

THOMAS NELSON
Since 1798

NASHVILLE   DALLAS   MEXICO CITY   RIO DE JANEIRO

Published in Nashville, Tennessee, by Thomas Nelson, Inc.

Scripture quotations are from the KING JAMES VERSION of the Bible.

Library of Congress Cataloging-in-Publication Data

McGee, J. Vernon (John Vernon), 1904–1988
    [Thru the Bible with J. Vernon McGee]
    Thru the Bible commentary series / J. Vernon McGee.
      p.   cm.
    Reprint. Originally published: Thru the Bible with J. Vernon
McGee. 1975.
    Includes bibliographical references.
    ISBN 0-7852-1015-6 (TR)
    ISBN 0-7852-1081-4 (NRM)
    1. Bible—Commentaries. I. Title.
BS491.2.M37 1991
220.7'7—dc20   90–41340
ISBN: 978-0-7852-0413-8   CIP

Printed in the United States
19 20 21 22   QG   14 13 12 11 10

CONTENTS

1 CHRONICLES

2 CHRONICLES

PREFACE

The radio broadcasts of the Thru the Bible Radio five-year program were transcribed, edited, and published first in single-volume paperbacks to accommodate the radio audience.

There has been a minimal amount of further editing for this publication. Therefore, these messages are not the word-for-word recording of the taped messages which went out over the air. The changes were necessary to accommodate a reading audience rather than a listening audience.

These are popular messages, prepared originally for a radio audience. They should not be considered a commentary on the entire Bible in any sense of that term. These messages are devoid of any attempt to present a theological or technical commentary on the Bible. Behind these messages is a great deal of research and study in order to interpret the Bible from a popular rather than from a scholarly (and too-often boring) viewpoint.

We have definitely and deliberately attempted "to put the cookies on the bottom shelf so that the kiddies could get them."

The fact that these messages have been translated into many languages for radio broadcasting and have been received with enthusiasm reveals the need for a simple teaching of the whole Bible for the masses of the world.

I am indebted to many people and to many sources for bringing this volume into existence. I should express my especial thanks to my secretary, Gertrude Cutler, who supervised the editorial work; to Dr. Elliott R. Cole, my associate, who handled all the detailed work with the publishers; and finally, to my wife Ruth for tenaciously encouraging me from the beginning to put my notes and messages into printed form.

Solomon wrote, ". . . of making many books there is no end; and much study is a weariness of the flesh" (Eccl. 12:12). On a sea of books that flood the marketplace, we launch this series of THRU THE BIBLE with the hope that it might draw many to the one Book, *The Bible*.

J. VERNON McGEE

The Book of

1 CHRONICLES

INTRODUCTION

The two Books of Chronicles are very similar in many ways. They cover the same historical ground all the way from Saul to Zedekiah. Then are the Chronicles a duplication of Kings? Emphatically, no. Greek translators gave Chronicles the title, "Things Omitted," which is a good title, but not adequate. Chronicles include more than that which is omitted in the other historical books. Actually Chronicles is another instance of the law of recurrence or recapitulation. The policy of the Holy Spirit in giving the Word of God is to give a great expanse of truth, to cover a great deal of territory, then come back and select certain sections which He wants to enlarge upon. It is as if the Spirit of God takes up a telescope, looks out over the landscape for us, then takes a particular portion of it and puts it under the microscope and lets us look at it in detail. This is what is happening in 1 and 2 Chronicles.

We have seen the law of recurrence or recapitulation in operation before. In Genesis, the second chapter goes back over the seven days of creation, and lifts out one thing: the creation of man. For us, that is very important since we are members of Adam's race. Also the Book of Deuteronomy (*Deuteronomy* means a "second law") is more than a repetition of the Law. Rather it is an interpretation of the Law in the light of forty years' experience with it in the wilderness.

Now we will see in the Chronicles that God goes over the ground which He had covered in 1 and 2 Samuel and 1 and 2 Kings in order to add details and to emphasize things which He considers important.

Let me give you some examples of this. The emphasis in 1 Chronicles is David, and the emphasis in 2 Chronicles is David's posterity. The northern kingdom is practically ignored when the division occurs between the northern and southern kingdoms. Chronicles does not record David's sin. Why? Well, God so completely forgave it that He does not even mention it again. When God forgives, He forgets. In Kings the history of the nation is given from the standpoint of the throne; in Chronicles it is given from the standpoint of the altar. In Kings the palace is the center; in Chronicles the temple is the center. Kings gives us the political history of the nation, while Chronicles gives the religious history. Chronicles is the interpretation of Kings. All through the Books of Kings we noted the phrase, "Is it not written in the book of the chronicles of the kings of Israel?" Chronicles, you see, is the interpretation of Kings. Also Kings gives us man's viewpoint while Chronicles gives us God's viewpoint.

Ezra is probably the writer of the Chronicles. There is a striking similarity in style and language to the Books of Ezra and Nehemiah. Evidently Chronicles was written during the Babylonian captivity. The two Books of Chronicles not only constituted one book in the original, but apparently also included Ezra and Nehemiah. This lends support to the Jewish tradition of the authorship of Ezra.

OUTLINE

I. Genealogies, Chapters 1—9

II. Saul's Reign, Chapter 10

III. David's Reign, Chapters 11—29
   A. David's Mighty Men, Chapters 11—12
   B. David and the Ark, Chapters 13—16
   C. David and the Temple, Chapter 17
   D. David's Wars, Chapters 18—20
   E. David's Sin in Numbering People, Chapter 21
   F. David's Preparation and Organization for Building the Temple, Chapters 22—29

CHAPTERS 1—9

THEME: Genealogies

The first nine chapters contain the genealogies, and in many senses this is one of the most remarkable passages of the Word of God.

Notice how it begins:

> Adam, Sheth, Enosh,
> Kenan, Mahalaleel, Jered,
> Henoch, Methuselah, Lamech,
> Noah, Shem, Ham, and Japheth
> [1 Chron. 1:1–4].

These are the names of the men about whom we have read in the first eight chapters of Genesis.

As you read the genealogy, you will notice that the same policy is followed that was used in the Book of Genesis. That is, the rejected lines are mentioned first, then we are given the line that is to be followed through the Scriptures to the Lord Jesus Christ.

Notice that the sons of Japheth are listed, then the sons of Ham, and finally the sons of Shem. Only the line of Shem continues. It leads to Abraham. Then Abraham's posterity is recorded: Ishmael and his sons, also the sons of Abraham by Keturah, and finally Abraham's son Isaac. Then Isaac's line is followed—first listing the descendants of Esau. However, the line which leads to the Lord Jesus will continue through Isaac's other son, Jacob.

Chapter 2 begins the genealogy of Jacob, which continues through chapter 9. Coming to verse 15, we find the posterity of Jesse, and one of Jesse's sons was David. Now we will follow his line, because the Lord Jesus will be a "son" of David.

Chapter 3 records the family of David, and we find that David had

some sons we had not known about before—they were not mentioned
in the Books of Samuel or Kings.

**And these were born unto him in Jerusalem; Shimea,
and Shobab, and Nathan, and Solomon, four, of Bath-
shua the daughter of Ammiel [1 Chron. 3:5].**

Did you ever hear of Shimea and Shobab? We know Solomon, but who
is Nathan? Well, if you go over to the genealogy of the Lord Jesus,
which is recorded in the Gospel of Luke, you will find that the line
goes through Nathan rather than through Solomon. Mary, the mother
of Jesus, traced her ancestry through Nathan, while Joseph's genealogy is traced through Solomon. In Matthew we see that the Lord Jesus
gets His legal title to the throne of David through Solomon, and in
Luke we see that he gets His blood title to the throne of David through
Nathan. This is very important, because in the ancestry of Solomon,
Jeconiah (whom the Lord calls Coniah) appears, and the Lord declares
that ". . . no man of his seed shall prosper, sitting upon the throne of
David, and ruling any more in Judah" (Jer. 22:30). This one man produced a short circuit in the line leading to the Messiah, which is fur-
ther proof that Joseph could not be the father of the Lord Jesus and that
Jesus must be virgin born.

In chapter 4 the posterity of Judah through Caleb and Shelah is
followed, also the tribe of Simeon.

Chapter 5 traces the tribe of Reuben to the captivity.

**Now the sons of Reuben the firstborn of Israel, (for he
was the firstborn; but, forasmuch as he defiled his
father's bed, his birthright was given unto the sons of
Joseph the son of Israel: and the genealogy is not to be
reckoned after the birthright.**

**For Judah prevailed above his brethren, and of him
came the chief ruler; but the birthright was Joseph's:)
[1 Chron. 5:1-2].**

This verse informs us that Reuben's lost birthright was given to Joseph, not to Judah. However, Judah prevailed, and the ruler came from Judah. The record of the tribes of Gad and the half tribe of Manasseh is given until their captivity. The final two verses give the reason for the captivity.

Chapter 6 traces the tribe of Levi (family of the high priests), through the sons Gershon, Kohath, and Merari.

Chapter 7 gives the genealogies of the tribes of Issachar, Benjamin, Naphtali, Manasseh, Ephraim, and Asher. All of these went into Assyrian captivity.

Chapter 8 traces the genealogy of the tribe of Benjamin, with special reference to Saul and Jonathan.

Chapter 9 opens with a tremendous statement relative to the preservation of the genealogies.

> **So all Israel were reckoned by genealogies; and, behold, they were written in the book of the kings of Israel and Judah, who were carried away to Babylon for their transgression [1 Chron. 9:1].**

Apparently the genealogies of each tribe of Israel were on exhibit in the temple. They were registered until the people went away into captivity. However, the genealogies were preserved and brought back to Jerusalem. When the returning remnant rebuilt the temple, the genealogies were there. At the time the Lord Jesus was born, those genealogies were intact, and you may be sure that the enemies of Jesus went in and checked His genealogy. As we have said, the Gospel of Matthew carries Joseph's genealogy, from whom He gets the legal title to the throne, and the Gospel of Luke carries Mary's genealogy, from which He gets the blood title to the throne of David. As far as we know, there never was an attack made upon the genealogy of the Lord Jesus Christ. It was accurate, and it was available for all to see.

When the temple was destroyed by Titus the Roman in A.D. 70, apparently the genealogies were also destroyed. However, the important thing to note is that here in Chronicles the genealogies are traced to the time of the captivity. Then after the return of a remnant of Israel, the genealogies were continued until the time the Lord Jesus Christ came into the world. After His lifetime the record disappeared. Why? Well, God was interested in making it very clear to us that Jesus was "very man of very man." God wants us to know that Jesus Christ came in the line of Adam and that He is the last Adam—there won't be a third one. Jesus heads up the last family here on earth. There are only two families: the family of Adam and the family of God.

Adam's family is a lost family, and you and I were born into it. We were born sinners, alienated from God, with no capacity for God. This alienation is obvious as we look around the world today. The entire human family is in Adam's family—and "in Adam all die." It is a very dismal prospect that we have in Adam.

However, we have hope in Christ, the last Adam. He heads the other family, the family of God. He is called the second man because the Lord is going to make a whole lot of other men in this new family. And that genealogy goes right back to the One who is born of the Spirit. If you today can say, "I came to Christ and trusted Him. He is my Savior, and the Spirit of God has made Him real to me," then you belong to the last Adam's family. In this family there is life. The Lord Jesus said that is what He brought. In fact He said, "I am the life." He also said, "I am come that they might have life, and that they might have it more abundantly" (John 10:10). He makes life more than mere existence or an exciting trip on drugs or alcohol. The trip with Him will eventuate in a trip to heaven—into His very presence.

The remainder of chapter 9 is an emphasis upon the tribe of Levi.

Now the first inhabitants that dwelt in their possessions in their cities were, the Israelites, the priests, Levites, and the Nethinims [1 Chron. 9:2].

It means that the first of the Israelites was of the tribe of Levi—first the priests, those who had the service of God, then the Levites. You see, not all of the tribe of Levi served in the priesthood. The family of Aaron served as priests. The others were more or less custodians of the temple.

Then the Nethinims are mentioned. The word *Nethinims* means "servants." They could have been slaves. There is a question as to whether or not Israel had slaves. I think they did, but not of their own brethren. Essentially that is what the Gibeonites had become. They were used in the service of the temple—probably swept out the place, polished the brass, and things like that.

Let me point out another interesting verse from this chapter.

> **And these are the singers, chief of the fathers of the Levites, who remaining in the chambers were free: for they were employed in that work day and night [1 Chron. 9:33].**

There was a great deal of singing going on, which was directed by certain Levites. (If I were an Israelite, I would certainly know I didn't belong to the tribe of Levi, because I can't sing.) In Israel music was developed to a very high degree. You may recall that David was very much interested in music. In fact, he was called the sweet psalmist of Israel, and the majority of the psalms came from his pen.

The chapter concludes with the genealogy of the family of Saul. It follows through Saul and his son Jonathan, which is quite remarkable.

Chapter 9 concludes the genealogy of Chronicles. It is the longest genealogy in Scripture, and there is nothing like it in the literature or history of the world. It begins with Adam and goes to Jesus Christ. It beings with the first Adam and goes to the last Adam. It is the greatest genealogical table in existence. It tells us that all of us are in the same family. Of course no one can trace his genealogy back to Adam in our day, because the genealogies were destroyed when Titus the Roman burned the temple in A.D. 70. Nevertheless, we can tell the general route by which we came from Adam. Many of us go back through Japheth, some of us go back through Ham, some of us go back through Shem, but we all go back to Adam.

It is interesting and important to note the glaring omissions in the genealogies recorded here in Chronicles. For example, Cain and his family are not even mentioned. Didn't Adam have a son by the name of Cain? Yes, but he is not listed here because his line ended. It was destroyed in the Flood as recorded in Genesis 7. Also I think there are omissions in all of the genealogical tables—even in Genesis. This may throw a light on the very important question of the age of man. How old is mankind? It is my personal opinion that mankind is older than 6000 years. I think he has been on this earth a long time. However, when God created him, he was Adam, a *man*, not a monkey!

Perhaps you have seen the satirical cartoon directed at the theory of evolution and man's vaunted civilization and so-called progress. It pictures a scene of devastation. All the atomic bombs have been exploded, and man has at last destroyed himself. The last vestige of life has disappeared—with two exceptions. There are two monkeys sitting on a tree which is stripped of all its leaves and most of its limbs. There they sit, surveying this scene of desolation. All human life has disappeared. The caption of the cartoon reads, "Now we're going to have to do it all over again!"

Of course the Scriptures assure us that mankind will not commit suicide. But what about man's progress? He has been on this earth a long time since the days of Adam.

Psychology attempts to tabulate and classify man according to his I.Q. It is a rather mechanical device, of course, and it classifies him mechanically according to his achievements and his aptitudes. On one end of the scale is "subnormal," on the other end is "supernormal" or "genius," and somewhere in between is "normal." However, God's tests are different. All must come under His classification. Do you know what God says? God says none of them are normal—". . . all have sinned, and come short of the glory of God" (Rom. 3:23).

There are three universal facts in relationship to man which are true without exception:

1. Adam and all his children must die. In the beginning, God said to Adam, "In the day that thou eatest thereof thou shalt surely die" (Gen. 2:17). However, God did not create man to die. Scripture tells us that ". . . by *man* came death, and death passed upon all men . . ." (Rom. 5:12, paraphrased). It also says, ". . . in Adam all die . . ." (1 Cor. 15:22). And, ". . . it is appointed unto men once to die . . ." (Heb. 9:27). This earth on which you and I live is nothing but a great big

graveyard. David said on his deathbed, "I go the way of all the earth" (1 Kings 2:2). All the freeways today eventually lead to the cemetery. "Though I walk through the valley of the shadow of death" (Ps. 23:4) is the picture of man going through life. Like a monster, death stalks this earth.

There are three kinds of death: physical death, spiritual death, and eternal death. Adam did not die physically until about 900 years after he ate the prohibited fruit. But he died spiritually instantly. Death means separation. Physical death is separation of the spirit from the body. Spiritual death means the separation of man from God. And eternal death means the separation of man from God. Eternal death is separation from God eternally. That is what hell will be—a place where God never goes, my friend. There is no blessing, nor mercy, nor love of God there.

2. Another universal fact is that Adam and all his children are sinners. God says of us, "All have sinned." The proof of this statement is that all die—"in Adam all die." All sinned in Adam.

Abraham was a good man, but Abraham sinned—Ishamel is an evidence of that. Caleb was a good man and outstanding, but he had his concubine. And sin has driven contemporary man away from God. He is in open rebellion against God. He has gone out, as did Cain, from the presence of the Lord.

Chapter 59 of Isaiah is a chapter everyone ought to read. Let me quote just one verse: "But your iniquities have separated between you and your God, and your sins have hid his face from you, that he will not hear" (Isa. 59:2). Adam and his children are sinners, separated from God. Sin is a scourge, a sickness, a plague, which has infected the race. My friend, a heart condition is bad, but only a few of the human family have heart trouble. Cancer is terrible—I know it from personal experience—but a small percentage has cancer. However, all have sinned. Of course there is one grand exception to this: the Lord Jesus Christ didn't have to die because He did not sin. He challenged His enemies, "Which of you convinceth me of sin? . . ." (John 8:46). No one did. He said, "No man taketh it [my life] from me, but I lay it down of myself. I have power to lay it down, and I have power to take it again . . ." (John 10:18). The Lord Jesus is the exception to the universality of sin. However, He is the *only* exception. The rest of us have sinned.

3. The third universal fact is that Adam and all his children have obtained mercy. Enoch was saved. How? By faith. Noah was a good man, but he wasn't saved because of that. It was by *faith* that Noah prepared an ark to the saving of his house. Abraham was a good man, but he sinned. Abraham believed God, and *that* was counted unto him for righteousness. Actually that is the problem in the Near East today. Is it possible that Abraham's sin is the cause of continual fighting between Israel and the Arab countries? Absolutely. If he, through that little Egyptian maid Hagar, had not brought Ishamel into the world, the Arabs wouldn't be over there today. David also was a great man of God, but we all agree that David sinned. And, my, God was certainly merciful to him! God is rich in mercy. Paul said to the Ephesians, "But God, who is rich in mercy, for his great love wherewith he loved us, Even when we were dead in sins, hath quickened us together with Christ, (by grace ye are saved;)" (Eph. 2:4–5). And Peter said, "Blessed be the God and Father of our Lord Jesus Christ, which according to his abundant mercy hath begotten us again unto a lively hope by the resurrection of Jesus Christ from the dead" (1 Pet. 1:3). Our God has made it possible for the children of Adam to obtain mercy.

Have you received mercy from the hand of God yet? It is there for you.

This glorious truth is only part of the message that we find here in the genealogies of the first nine chapters of 1 Chronicles. It is the genealogy of the family of Adam, and you and I are in it. We all belong to the same race. We are all fallen in nature. We are all on an equality; we are born equal in the sense that we all have sinned and come short of the glory of God. And salvation today is for all mankind.

CHAPTER 10

THEME: Saul's Reign

H ere we can see the distinction that God is making between the Books of Samuel and Kings and the Books of Chronicles. In the Books of Samuel we find a great deal about King Saul. In fact, his entire history is given there. When we come to Chronicles and see God's viewpoint, we find only one chapter given. The rest of 1 Chronicles is all about David, and it goes on into 2 Chronicles with the history of David's family. David is the subject, not Saul. Down here from the human viewpoint Saul occupied a prominent place. That is why it is amazing here to find only one chapter devoted to Saul.

Now what is the subject of this chapter? Did the Lord pick out some outstanding performance of Saul? No. Works do not commend a person to God. The chapter is not about Saul's works. It is about his death and how he was slain.

I am of the opinion that a great many men and women who have occupied a large place in human history will not get much of a write-up in heaven. This is certainly true of Saul!

You will recall that when we were studying 1 and 2 Samuel, we attempted to determine who had slain Saul. Who was the one that was responsible for his murder? Or did he commit suicide? The record in those books goes something like this: Saul was mortally wounded in the battle with the Philistines. Then he told his armorbearer to kill him because he didn't want the disgrace of being killed by a Philistine. The armorbearer refused to take his sword to kill the king. So Saul fell on his own sword. Was Saul physically able to kill himself? Did he commit suicide? That has always been a question. Then a young man of the Amalekites told David that when he came upon the scene, Saul was still alive and that Saul had asked him to kill him. The young Amalekite claimed that he was the one who had slain King Saul, and he brought Saul's crown and bracelet to David to prove his story. King David had the Amalekite slain, saying, ". . . Thy blood be upon thy head; for thy mouth hath testified against thee, saying, I have slain the LORD's anointed" (2 Sam. 1:16). Now who is responsible for the death of King Saul? We almost need to call in the FBI. But actually it won't be necessary to call them into the case, because we will have a confession here from the one who is responsible for Saul's death.

> Now the Philistines fought against Israel; and the men of Israel fled from before the Philistines, and fell down slain in mount Gilboa.
>
> And the Philistines followed hard after Saul, and after his sons; and the Philistines slew Jonathan, and Abinadab, and Malchi-shua, the sons of Saul.
>
> And the battle went sore against Saul, and the archers hit him, and he was wounded of the archers [1 Chron. 10:1–3].

He was wounded by the Philistines, but he did not die from that wound.

> Then said Saul to his armour-bearer, Draw thy sword, and thrust me through therewith; lest these uncircumcised come and abuse me. But his armour-bearer would not; for he was sore afraid. So Saul took a sword, and fell upon it.
>
> And when his armour-bearer saw that Saul was dead, he fell likewise on the sword, and died.
>
> So Saul died, and his three sons, and all his house died together.
>
> And when all the men of Israel that were in the valley saw that they fled, and that Saul and his sons were dead, then they forsook their cities, and fled: and the Philistines came and dwelt in them [1 Chron. 10:4–7].

I assume from this record that when that Amalekite came along, Saul was already dead. The Amalekite knew that David and Saul had been enemies, so he went into the presence of David and took credit for the slaying of Saul. The motive which he had was the hope that David would bestow some honor upon him and give him some reward for the slaying of Saul. He didn't dream that David would react as he did. David executed him on his own confession—David said that he was condemned out of his own mouth. However, it appears that the young man was lying, and that he really did not slay the king.

> And it came to pass on the morrow, when the Philistines came to strip the slain, that they found Saul and his sons fallen in mount Gilboa.

> And when they had stripped him, they took his head, and his armour, and sent into the land of the Philistines round about, to carry tidings unto their idols, and to the people.

> And they put his armour in the house of their gods, and fastened his head in the temple of Dagon [1 Chron. 10:8–10].

The Philistines did this terrible dishonor to Saul's body. The temple of Dagon was in Ashdod. You remember that Samson had pulled down the pillars in the temple of Dagon when they were making sport of him there. Now this is where the Philistines brought the head and the armor of Saul.

> And when all Jabesh-gilead heard all that the Philistines had done to Saul,

> They arose, all the valiant men, and took away the body of Saul, and the bodies of his sons, and brought them to Jabesh, and buried their bones under the oak in Jabesh, and fasted seven days [1 Chron. 10:11–12].

Does this close the case? No, we still haven't been told who really killed King Saul. But the final verses of this chapter will give us the confession we have been waiting for.

> **So Saul died for his transgression which he committed against the LORD, even against the word of the LORD, which he kept not, and also for asking counsel of one that had a familiar spirit, to inquire of it;**
>
> **And inquired not of the LORD: therefore he slew him, and turned the kingdom unto David the son of Jesse [1 Chron. 10:13–14].**

Now, who was it that slew Saul? It says that he inquired not of the Lord; therefore He slew him. Who is he? The Lord is the One who took his life. It is as Job said, ". . . the LORD gave, and the LORD hath taken away; blessed be the name of the LORD" (Job 1:21). The Lord takes the responsibility.

God says that He removed Saul. God executed him. Do you wish to find fault with the Lord? Can God be arrested for murder? My friend, God has taken many a person. By the way, that is the reason God says you and I are never to take a human life. The Lord gave and the Lord hath taken away. Until you and I can give life, we have no business in taking life. Only God can give life; so God can take away life, and for Him it is not murder. For you and me it is murder to take a life, and we must surrender our own lives when we do it. This is the reason David executed the Amalekite when he claimed he had murdered King Saul.

Why was Saul executed? He died "for his transgression which he committed against the LORD, even against the word of the LORD, which he kept not, and also for asking counsel of one that had a familiar spirit"—Saul turned to Satan for advice. For these reasons God took his life. In the New Testament we find that God took the lives of Ananias and Sapphira. A great many people give Simon Peter the credit (or the blame) for that. I believe that Simon Peter was the most surprised person there that day. God was the One responsible for their deaths. And Saul died because of his transgression. Many times God reaches in and takes a human life because of that.

I have lived long enough now so that I can look back and see that many times God has put a man aside. He can put a man on the shelf by putting him out of His service. He can remove him from an office. God moves in the affairs of men. God has not abdicated today. He is still running the universe. It is His universe and He will run it His way. If He wants to remove someone, that is His business, not yours or mine. He is not accountable to us, but we are accountable to Him. He is the One who calls the shots. He is the One who is the umpire, and He will make the decisions.

By the way, to whom are you listening today? Do you hear God's voice? Or are you listening to man's voice, even to Satan's voice? This is the sin that causes God to move into the affairs of men.

What a chapter this is! It throws heaven's light on a very moot subject.

CHAPTERS 11 AND 12

THEME: David's Reign

We have now come to the third major division of 1 Chronicles. The first nine chapters recorded the remarkable genealogies. The second division, only one chapter, was on the reign of King Saul.

From God's viewpoint Saul did not make anywhere near the splash that many of the people in his day thought he had. He did not impress God. The Lord records his death and the reason for it but gives us nothing about the accomplishments of Saul.

Now we come to the section which deals with the reign of King David. First we will see David's mighty men (chs. 11—12), then David and the ark (chs. 13—16), David and the temple (ch. 17), David's wars (chs. 18—20), David's sin in numbering the people (ch. 21), and David's preparation and organization for building the temple in chapters 22—29.

The remainder of this book is about David and David's reign. In fact, the genealogy that is given in the first chapters brings us up to David, and beyond into the family of David. The next book, 2 Chronicles, will follow the story of the line of David. There is practically no attention given to the northern kingdom after it rebelled and withdrew from the reign of David's family.

It is also well to note as we go along how God puts the emphasis on certain things in David's life and plays down others. You will notice that I called chapter 21 "David's Sin." It has nothing to do with his sin with Bathsheba, which is the sin which immediately comes to the minds of men when they speak of David. Rather, God records his sin in numbering the people. In God's sight this was the greatest sin.

I believe there is a tremendous lesson for us in this. Many Christians consider certain things as sin, and other things they don't consider sin at all. I believe that when we get into God's presence we will find that we have had some false notions in this connection. What they thought was a great sin may not have been one and, what they thought was slight and unimportant, God put down as sin.

In David's life everyone could point the finger at him relative to his sin with Bathsheba. And God punished him for that sin—it was a terrible sin. But God forgave him of that because he came in confession to the Lord. Although this matter of numbering the people may seem insignificant to us, we shall see that it was rather important as far as God was concerned—and we'll see why.

This should cause all of us to get a different perspective of what sin really is. We need to recognize sin not only in the sense of acts—things to do and not to do—but also sins of the thoughts and intents. We need to study the Word of God in order to understand God's perspective of sin.

> **Then all Israel gathered themselves to David unto Hebron, saying, Behold, we are thy bone and thy flesh [1 Chron. 11:1].**

You will recall back in Samuel, which covered this period of history, we were told that for seven years David reigned over the two tribes in the south, Judah and Benjamin, and his capital was Hebron. That is all passed over in Chronicles. Why? Because God looks at Israel as one nation of twelve tribes. From God's perspective, David really became king when he became the king over all of Israel and all twelve of the tribes of Israel accepted him, and said, "We are thy bone and thy flesh."

> **And moreover in time past, even when Saul was king, thou wast he that leddest out and broughtest in Israel: and the Lord thy God said unto thee, Thou shalt feed my people Israel, and thou shalt be ruler over my people Israel [1 Chron. 11:2].**

They were acknowledging the hand of God in this. David did not become king until the people accepted him as being God's choice, which was seven years after he began to reign over Judah and Benjamin.

> **Therefore came all the elders of Israel to the king to Hebron; and David made a covenant with them in Hebron before the LORD; and they anointed David king over Israel, according to the word of the LORD by Samuel [1 Chron. 11:3].**

Now he is made king over all twelve tribes. From God's viewpoint, this is when David began his reign.

> **And David and all Israel went to Jerusalem, which is Jebus; where the Jebusites were, the inhabitants of the land [1 Chron. 11:4].**

David had inspected that land. I think that he had been over that land with a fine-toothed comb and probably knew it better than the spies that had been sent in by Joshua. He knew a great deal about it, and Jerusalem was the city that he had chosen to become the capital. It was the place where the temple was to be built. It was David's choice, and it was the Lord's choice.

A great deal is said in the Word of God about the city of Jerusalem. Of course it is not the city of Jerusalem as we see it today. Many of you have visited Jerusalem or seen pictures of it. Excavations in recent years have revealed that the wall in early times went the opposite direction from the way it goes today. The city of David was down below, and they always looked up to the temple. Later on, when the walls were moved, and built up on Mount Zion and higher up, one looked down to the temple area. It is this way today. A great deal of the city of Jerusalem is above the temple area.

The temple area is located on Mount Moriah, which goes like a ridge right through Jerusalem today. And over there, outside the wall, on that ridge is where Golgotha is located, the place of the skull where Jesus was crucified. This is the place David chose.

**And the inhabitants of Jebus said to David, Thou shalt
not come hither. Nevertheless David took the castle of
Zion, which is the city of David [1 Chron. 11:5].**

David took the castle of Zion, and it was there that he built his palace.
Mount Zion was very precious to David.

**And David said, Whosoever smiteth the Jebusites first
shall be chief and captain. So Joab the son of Zeruiah
went first up, and was chief [1 Chron. 11:6].**

Joab is the number one man in the service of David. He was an adviser
to David, and he was the number one man who led the army. He belonged to the mighty men of David. You will recall that we were told
something about his exploits when he first came to David, incidents
of how he led the army and how he fought for David. This man became the captain. You might say that he was the one in charge of the
Pentagon in David's day. He had command of all the brass—the army
and navy, and whatever else they might have had. He had charge of it
all.

**And David dwelt in the castle; therefore they called it
the city of David [1 Chron. 11:7].**

The "city of David" is actually the Mount Zion area. Apparently it was
here that David's palace was constructed. David loved Mount Zion.

**And he built the city round about, even from Millo
round about: and Joab repaired the rest of the city
[1 Chron. 11:8].**

Joab was not only in charge of David's military, he was in charge of the
urban renewal program.

**So David waxed greater and greater: for the LORD of
hosts was with him [1 Chron. 11:9].**

David brought Israel up to the place where it was a great kingdom and had tremendous influence throughout the world. David laid the foundation on which Solomon was able to bring a witness to the world of that day.

DAVID'S MIGHTY MEN

David's mighty men are those who came to him during the time of his rejection. Now that he has been elevated to the place of kingship, these men are elevated also.

There is a corollary here that we cannot pass by. Today the Lord Jesus Christ is calling out a people to His name; they are His "mighty men." And these are the days of Christ's rejection. His own people said, "We will not have this man rule over us." He has not assumed His position on the throne as King of kings and Lord of lords. David also was a rejected man, although he had been anointed king of Israel. Saul was still reigning—God gave him every opportunity to make good, but he did not. During those years, David was fleeing for his life; it was the period of his rejection. And there came to him from every side men who put themselves under his command. They became David's mighty men. In our day, Christ is rejected by the world. I don't have to labor to make that point. If we can't see that, we can't see anything. You and I live in a world where the Lord Jesus Christ is rejected. But during this period He is calling out a people to His name. He is our Savior, our Lord and Master today, so we will have to wait until He comes to the place of Kingship. Then, we are told, we are to reign with Him.

Since our Lord is rejected, I don't know why in the world some believers attempt to become the most popular people in town. They cannot be. The Lord Jesus said that since the world hated Him, it would hate us also.

If you are popular with the world today, it is time to take a long look at yourself. The late Dr. Bob Schuller used to say, "I judge a man not by the friends he has but by the enemies he has. If you have the right kind of enemies, you are all right." My friend, if you are a true believer in the Lord Jesus Christ, then the devil's crowd will be your enemies. We are living in the period of Christ's rejection, and He is calling out His mighty men.

The three men who were singled out as being the mightiest were the men who brought water from the well of Bethlehem to David. This is a tremendous story.

> Now three of the thirty captains went down to the rock to David, into the cave of Adullam; and the host of the Philistines encamped in the valley of Rephaim.
>
> And David was then in the hold, and the Philistines' garrison was then at Beth-lehem.
>
> And David longed, and said, Oh that one would give me drink of the water of the well of Beth-lehem, that is at the gate!
>
> And the three brake through the host of the Philistines, and drew water out of the well of Beth-lehem, that was by the gate, and took it, and brought it to David: but David would not drink of it, but poured it out to the LORD,
>
> And said, My God forbid it me, that I should do this thing: shall I drink the blood of these men that have put their lives in jeopardy? for with the jeopardy of their lives they brought it. Therefore he would not drink it. These things did these three mightiest [1 Chron. 11:15–19].

David had been brought up in Bethlehem. That was his hometown. There was a well at the entrance there and, many a time after he had been out with his sheep, he had come back thirsty and had stopped at that well to get a drink. Now the Philistines have him holed up and he cannot get to that well. He said, "I sure would like to have a drink from that well." It was just a wish, not a command. These three men broke through the lines of the Philistines and got the water and brought it to David. The interesting thing is that he would not drink it, but he poured it out as a drink offering to God.

There are some analogies we can make from this. Jesus was born at Bethlehem, and He is that Water from Bethlehem; He is the Water of Life. There are many of the mighty men of Jesus Christ who down through the centuries have taken this Water to a thirsty world. I think of Livingstone, Judson, Henry Martin, and other wonderful missionaries of the past. Then there are all the missionaries today. I have visited them in Mexico, South America, Africa, Asia, and Europe. These are the ones who have left everything to penetrate barriers in order to get the Word of God to a thirsty world. The Lord takes note of them, my friend. They are listed among the mighty men.

Notice how David's men responded when he merely expressed a wish—he would never have given such a command. Yet our Lord has commanded us to take the Water of Life to the whole world. And what have we done with it? Are you obeying His orders?

Notice what David did with the water that was brought to him at such tremendous risk. David was unselfish—no wonder his men loved him. They were willing to suffer for him because he was willing to suffer with them. He wouldn't take that drink because his men didn't have water, and he chose to take his place with them.

Pslam 22:14 tells us that when the Lord Jesus died on the cross He said, "I am poured out like water. . . ." He poured His life out like water on the ground. He took His place down here as one of us— ". . . unto us a child is born, unto us a son is given . . ." (Isa. 9:6). He took our hell that we might share His heaven.

And, my friend, if we are to be rewarded by Him, we are to make a sacrifice for Him.

There is another incident in this chapter that I have always appreciated.

Benaiah the son of Jehoiada, the son of a valiant man of Kabzeel, who had done many acts; he slew two lionlike men of Moab: also he went down and slew a lion in a pit in a snowy day [1 Chron. 11:22].

I love that. He slew a lion. Did you notice when he did it? He did it on a snowy day. Our Lord took note of that. I also think the Lord takes note of faithful people who will come to church rain or shine.

Now in chapter 12 there is only one incident which I would like to call to your attention.

There were some men of the tribe of Gad who came to David during the time of his rejection. This is what is recorded of them:

> **These were the sons of Gad, captains of the host: one of the least was over an hundred, and the greatest over a thousand.**
>
> **These are they that went over Jordan in the first month, when it had overflown all his banks; and they put to flight all them of the valleys, both toward the east, and toward the west.**
>
> **And there came of the children of Benjamin and Judah to the hold unto David.**
>
> **And David went out to meet them, and answered and said unto them, If ye be come peaceably unto me to help me, mine heart shall be knit unto you: but if ye be come to betray me to mine enemies, seeing there is no wrong in mine hands, the God of our fathers look thereon, and rebuke it.**
>
> **Then the spirit came upon Amasai, who was chief of the captains, and he said, Thine are we, David, and on thy side, thou son of Jesse: peace, peace be unto thee, and peace be to thine helpers; for thy God helpeth thee. Then David received them, and made them captains of the band [1 Chron. 12:14–18].**

Here is a group of men who came to David. They swam the Jordan River at flood time. They were just about to give up and David went down to meet them. He didn't know whether they were friends or enemies and he said in effect, "If you mean to harm me, I'll destroy you." They said, "Oh no, David, we have come over to be on your side." They wanted to live for David. They wanted to be on his side and in his service.

Too many Christians who want to be in the service of the Lord think that it is just a matter of being busy. However, the point is: do you want to live for Christ? That is what these men from Gad were saying to David. "We want to be on your side, David. We want to yield ourselves to you and live for you."

We can carry this spiritual application a step further. Christ has brought you over "Jordan" by His death and resurrection, and He has blessed you with all spiritual blessings. But you have to return to the world to live the Christian life. The Lord Jesus prayed for His own, "I pray not that thou shouldest take them out of the world, but that thou shouldest keep them from the evil" (John 17:15). We are to live the Christian life here and now. My friend, the only place you ever will have an opportunity to live the Christian life is right down here on this earth. And to do this, you will have to yield to Christ. This idea today that living the Christian life is a cheap sort of thing, that it is compromise and hypocrisy, is dead wrong. You will have to swim the water. It will cost you something. You will have to go to the One who is greater than David—to the Lord Jesus—and surrender to Him. Oh, what joy it is to be in His service!

CHAPTERS 13—16

THEME: David and the ark

In this section we see God's viewpoint of David's first attempt to bring the ark of the covenant to Jerusalem. During the period of the judges, you may recall, the ark had been captured in war by the Philistines. Because it had caused them no end of trouble, they placed it on a new cart and sent it back to Israel (1 Sam. 6). From that time to this, the ark had remained in the house of Abinadab at Kirjath-jearim. Now David makes an attempt to bring the ark to his capital, which is Jerusalem. God took note of this because it pleased Him that David was putting an emphasis on spiritual matters.

However, David starts off on the wrong foot, as we shall see.

And David consulted with the captains of thousands and hundreds, and with every leader [1 Chron. 13:1].

David now is Israel's new king. As he comes to the throne, he has tremendous plans, he has great vision, and he wants to bring the ark to Jerusalem. So he consults with "every leader." I feel that David made a mistake in consulting all these men. God was leading him and giving him direction; he didn't need human advice.

As I see it, there is a serious problem developing in many churches today because there are too many men who want to have their fingers in the pie. That is, they (especially the boards of churches) want to make the decisions. The problems arise because many of those men are not spiritually equipped to make decisions. Many times their wrong decisions hurt the cause of Christ.

It seems to me that David made a mistake by consulting with all of these leaders. He got into trouble by listening to everybody.

And David said unto all the congregation of Israel, If it seem good unto you, and that it be of the LORD our God,

let us send abroad unto our brethren every where, that
are left in all the land of Israel, and with them also to
the priests and Levites which are in their cities and suburbs, that they may gather themselves unto us:

And let us bring again the ark of our God to us: for we
inquired not at it in the days of Saul [1 Chron. 13:2-3].

This is a sidelight on the days of Saul. During that period the worship
of God in the tabernacle was entirely omitted. As a result, the entire
tabernacle organization was broken up. The Levites were scattered.
Now word is sent throughout the entire land that David wants to bring
up the ark.

And all the congregation said that they would do so: for
the thing was right in the eyes of all the people [1 Chron.
13:4].

The decision is unanimous. They all want the ark brought to Jerusalem.

So David gathered all Israel together, from Shihor of
Egypt even unto the entering of Hemath, to bring the ark
of God from Kirjath-jearim [1 Chron. 13:5].

In 1 Samuel 7 we have the record of the ark being taken to Kirjath-
jearim and left there because they had had a bad experience with it.

And David went up, and all Israel, to Baalah, that is, to
Kirjath-jearim, which belonged to Judah, to bring up
thence the ark of God the LORD, that dwelleth between
the cherubims, whose name is called on it [1 Chron.
13:6].

Of course, God did not live in the ark, nor between the cherubims, but
that is the place He designated as His meeting place with the people of
Israel. His presence was there.

Now they will make their big mistake. As someone has put it, this is doing a right thing in a wrong way. It was right to bring the ark up to Jerusalem, but the method of doing it was wrong.

> **And they carried the ark of God in a new cart out of the house of Abinadab: and Uzza and Ahio drove the cart [1 Chron. 13:7].**

God had given explicit directions as to how the ark was to be carried. Other parts of the tabernacle could be transported on carts, but not the ark. Notice what God had said to Moses: "And when Aaron and his sons have made an end of covering the sanctuary, and all the vessels of the sanctuary, as the camp is to set forward; after that the sons of Kohath shall come to bear it: but they shall not touch any holy thing, lest they die. These things are the burden of the sons of Kohath in the tabernacle of the congregation" (Num. 4:15). The ark was never to be carried on a wagon. It was to be borne on the shoulders of the sons of Kohath. Why? Well, the ark speaks of Christ, and He is to be carried, even today, by individuals.

A lot of people would like to do it the easy way. My friend, it will require work to get out the Word of God. Many people complain about the expense. I deplore the expense myself, but I want to tell you that it will cost us to get out the Word of God. We can't put it on a wagon. We must carry it. Each one needs to shoulder his own pack. So let's get it out. Paul says, "For every man shall bear his own burden" (Gal. 6:5). That is another way of saying that each one must shoulder his own pack.

In other words, all of us have to put our shoulders to the wheel to get the Word of God out to a world that desperately needs it. God doesn't write the gospel in the sky; it has to be passed along by His children.

> **And David and all Israel played before God with all their might, and with singing, and with harps, and with psalteries, and with timbrels, and with cymbals, and with trumpets [1 Chron. 13:8].**

David was a great musician, and this was an occasion of real joy. But it was all interrupted very suddenly.

> And when they came unto the threshingfloor of Chidon, Uzza put forth his hand to hold the ark; for the oxen stumbled.
>
> And the anger of the LORD was kindled against Uzza, and he smote him, because he put his hand to the ark: and there he died before God [1 Chron. 13:9–10].

Why? Because they were doing it wrong. They were not giving the right testimony. "But," you may say, "this was certainly a severe sort of thing—a man just put his hand on it!" Well, to begin with, the ark should not have been on that cart. And the ark did not need Uzza to steady it.

Today there are many folk who are putting their hands in the Lord's work where they should not be putting them. They are interfering with the Lord's work. I could tell you of many instances of men, probably meaning well, but not doing it God's way. As a result, blessing does not come. Just so in the case of the ark—the man who interfered was put out of the way.

> And David was displeased, because the LORD had made a breach upon Uzza: wherefore that place is called Perez-uzza to this day [1 Chron. 13:11].

David was displeased by it, as much as you would be, and as much as the critic is today.

> And David was afraid of God that day, saying, How shall I bring the ark of God home to me? [1 Chron. 13:12].

Oh, how often we attempt to do things our own way, and then when we fail, we blame it on God! We say, "How am I going to do this for the

Lord?" Well, do it God's way. Turn it over to Him. That is what David finally had to do.

> So David brought not the ark home to himself to the city of David, but carried it aside into the house of Obed-edom the Gittite.

> And the ark of God remained with the family of Obed-edom in his house three months. And the LORD blessed the house of Obed-edom, and all that he had [1 Chron. 13:13–14].

This concludes the episode. The ark is not going to be brought up to Jerusalem at this time. God is blessing the family that has it now, but David is going to turn his attention to something else.

THE PROSPERITY OF KING DAVID

In chapter 14 we see that God is prospering David and that his fame is spreading.

> Now Hiram king of Tyre sent messengers to David, and timber of cedars, with masons and carpenters, to build him an house [1 Chron. 14:1].

David and Hiram were great friends. We are told elsewhere that Hiram loved David. Here at the beginning of David's reign, Hiram wants to help him build his house, his palace.

> And David perceived that the LORD had confirmed him king over Israel, for his kingdom was lifted up on high, because of his people Israel.

> And David took more wives at Jerusalem: and David begat more sons and daughters [1 Chron. 14:2–3].

Now perhaps you are saying, "And God permitted this!" Yes, God permitted a multiplication of wives, but God did not approve of it. In fact, this will eventuate in God judging him, and it will bring sorrow to him for the rest of his life. It is wrong. This record is not given to us because God approved of it. But God wants us to know that this is exactly what happened. This is a historical record, and as we follow it we will discover God's attitude.

At one time, during the time of David's rejection, the Philistines thought he had become their man (1 Sam. 27). Now that he has returned to his own people and has been crowned as their king, the Philistines are out to get him.

> And the Philistines came and spread themselves in the valley of Rephaim.

> And David inquired of God, saying, Shall I go up against the Philistines? and wilt thou deliver them into mine hand? And the LORD said unto him, Go up; for I will deliver them into thine hands.

> So they came up to Baal-perazim; and David smote them there. Then David said, God hath broken in upon mine enemies by mine hand like the breaking forth of waters: therefore they called the name of that place Baal-perazim.

> And when they had left their gods there, David gave a commandment, and they were burned with fire [1 Chron. 14:9-12].

This was a great victory for David over the Philistines. And Israel hadn't had many victories over these people.

> And the Philistines yet again spread themselves abroad in the valley.

> Therefore David inquired again of God; and God said unto him, Go not up after them; turn away from them,

**and come upon them over against the mulberry trees
[1 Chron. 14:13–14].**

David could have said, "Well, here are the Philistines back again to
fight against me. I had victory before, so I'll go out against them
again." No, he inquired of God, and God said he shouldn't do it. He
told David to retreat and to draw the Philistines to the mulberry trees.
There David would have the advantage.

There are a great many Christians who actually tempt the Lord.
They don't trust Him; they actually tempt Him. They enter into some
sort of a business, or an agreement, or they try to do something and, as
the saying goes, they bite off more than they can chew. They claim to
be doing it because they "trust the Lord." Well, what makes them
think the Lord told them to do it that way?

My friend, God expects you and me to use sanctified common
sense. I have known folk who say they are acting on faith, when it is
not faith but presumption. They call it trusting the Lord but, actually,
they do these things when the Lord never indicated to them that they
should.

God wants us to use sanctified common sense and to wait for His
leading. Everything that is called faith is not actually faith. I have seen
folk make shipwreck of faith in that way.

A dear lady came to the church where I served in Pasadena years
ago. She said she was going to a faith healer and I advised her not to. I
thought she should go to a doctor. She said, "Oh, Dr. McGee, you are
so wrong. God is going to heal me. You think I ought not to go to this
faith healer but I am going and I will be healed." She went and she was
not healed. She couldn't understand it. She thought God was going to
heal her. The whole affair made shipwreck of that woman's faith and
she got to the place where she completely turned her back upon God.
She said, "He let me down." No, He didn't. He doesn't want us to do
something very foolish. He wants us to use good old sanctified common sense. She should have gone to a doctor. Her foolishness eventu-
ated in her death.

My friend, of course we need to trust the Lord. But we need to make sure we are getting our directions from Him. Sometimes we are to go out and do battle, and sometimes we are to withdraw.

And it shall be, when thou shalt hear a sound of going in the tops of the mulberry trees, that then thou shalt go out to battle: for God is gone forth before thee to smite the host of the Philistines [1 Chron. 14:15].

A pastor friend of mine came to tell me about a church he was going to serve; and, because I knew things about the church, I advised him not to go. He asked, "Why?" I answered, "You had better wait until you hear the 'sound of going in the tops of the mulberry trees' before you go there." You see, there are times when you and I are simply to wait until there is no doubt that God is preparing the way for us. This talk of stepping out on faith may not be faith at all. It may be presumption. Instead of trusting God, we may be tempting God. We need to wait for the Lord to give the signal, for that sound in the tops of the mulberry trees. We need to be careful that what we call stepping out on faith isn't simply a foolish move. Sometimes we are tempting God instead of trusting Him.

David therefore did as God commanded him: and they smote the host of the Philistines from Gibeon even to Gazer.
And the fame of David went out into all lands; and the LORD brought the fear of him upon all nations [1 Chron. 14:16-17].

This is why I said that David was one of the great world leaders. His kingdom was one of the great world kingdoms at that particular time. God was with this man. That little nation in that insignificant land became a great world power. This should not strike us as strange. There have been other instances like it in the history of the world. Venice, the city of Venice, ruled the world at one time—and it was just a city. So it is not a surprise that a little nation like Israel could be a world power. We are told the reason for it. Verse 2 told us that David perceived that the Lord had confirmed him king over Israel, and verse 17 tells us that the Lord brought the fear of him upon all nations. It was God who brought David to world power.

As we have seen, chapters 13—16 are devoted to David and the ark—that is, of his bringing the ark up to Jerusalem to the place he had chosen. This is quite interesting in view of the fact that these chapters could be giving us a report of the business of the state, some of the many decisions that David made, treaties he signed with the surrounding nations, wars he fought, even accounts of state dinners and other state functions. It could be very much like a newscast we would see on television today. Instead these chapters tell us about the moving of the ark.

There is a lesson in this for us. It helps us to see what is the important matter in the sight of God. We get the news and a lot of propaganda on our newscasts. What do you think would be God's viewpoint of the news today? Would the emphasis be where we find it on CBS or NBC or XYZ? Where does God put the emphasis? We should learn from this attention to the moving of the ark that God is interested in the worship of His people. The ark was the very heart and center of the worship for Israel. This is where God puts the emphasis.

History itself should teach us that all too often we put the emphasis on passing things. Once there was a busy staff in the palace of Napoleon in Paris. Today it is a museum. There are no important decisions being made there today. We think of Versailles and how beautiful it is. How important it was in the past. Great decisions were made there, but now it is just a showcase. It is something for tourists to visit—that is all. It would have been well to have known what God thought was important during those years.

Another question arises. What happened to the tabernacle? My feeling is that it was worn out. After all, it was a tent, made largely of cloth. The golden boards, the brass pillars, and the silver bases were probably taken by the Philistines. There is no record of what happened to the tabernacle other than the ark. The important thing was the ark. Why? Because crowning the ark was the mercy seat. That is the place where God met the people of Israel.

The important thing for you and for me is to have a place where we can receive mercy from God. All of us need God's mercy. God is prepared today to extend mercy because He has a mercy seat for us. "My little children, these things write I unto you, that ye sin not. And if any man sin, we have an advocate with the Father, Jesus Christ the righteous: And he is the propitiation for our sins: and not for ours only, but also for the sins of the whole world" (1 John 2:1–2). That word *propitiation* means "mercy seat." Christ is the mercy seat for our sins. Now this is important to God. Actually, it is not what you and I hear on television that is really important, and it is not the decisions made in Washington (although I do not belittle them), but the important decisions are God's decisions.

As we have seen, David attempted to bring the ark to Jerusalem. Although that was the proper thing to do, he did it in the wrong way. Not only had David chosen Jerusalem as the place for the ark, but God had chosen that same place. So it was important that the ark be brought to Jerusalem. The problem was that David tried to do it in the wrong way. God had given instructions in the Book of Numbers that the ark was to be carried on the shoulders of the Kohathites of the tribe of Levi. There could not be an easier way or any kind of short-cut method used.

My friend, getting out the Word of God today is not easy. Too many people think that the work of the Lord should be some kind of picnic and something very delightful. It is delightful to know one is doing His will out of love for Him—that always makes it a thrilling experience—but it does not make it easy.

God's Word needs to be carried by God's people. "So then faith cometh by hearing, and hearing by the word of God" (Rom. 10:17). God blesses the proclamation of His Word. Paul goes on to say that they have to hear, but how are they going to hear without a preacher? Paul also tells us: "For the preaching of the cross is to them that perish foolishness; but unto us which are saved it is the power of God" (1 Cor. 1:18). God wants the human family to hear His Word through human means. He doesn't write it in the sky. He expects us to preach it, my friend.

As we look around us, we see a restlessness. The church, having departed from the Word of God, is in as much disarray as any other institution. The theology of both Roman Catholicism and Protestantism is a shambles, my friend. Why? Because both got away from the Word of God, and as a result they are not doing it God's way. My firm conviction is that the most important matter is to get the ark of God on the move, by which I mean get the gospel going out, get the Word of God moving out to the human family. Let's put the emphasis where God puts it.

Now here in chapter 15 David is going to move the ark in the right way.

> **And David made him houses in the city of David, and prepared a place for the ark of God, and pitched for it a tent [1 Chron. 15:1].**

God considers the preparation of a place for the ark—not David's housing project—the important matter. "David made him houses in the city of David" *was* a housing project, and I'm sure that was considered important by a great many people.

> **Then David said, None ought to carry the ark of God but the Levites: for them hath the LORD chosen to carry the ark of God, and to minister unto him for ever [1 Chron. 15:2].**

My question is: David, why didn't you do this the first time? Why did you have to go through that sad experience before you did it the right way?

Well, that's the way most of us learn. The old cliché is accurate: hindsight is better than foresight. It is easy for me to tell David he should have done it right in the first place, and then McGee turns right around, and the next step I take, I do it wrong. Then I have to learn to do it God's way. I have a notion that is the experience of most of us.

> **And David gathered all Israel together to Jerusalem, to bring up the ark of the LORD unto his place, which he had prepared for it [1 Chron. 15:3].**

Do you remember that in days gone by when America faced a crisis our national leaders called for a day of prayer? We don't do that any more. Instead we get the brain trust together and expect them to solve the problems. We have seen that the decisions of the brain trust in the past have been as foolish as though they had been made by children; yet we don't change our method. That is the tragedy of America in this dark hour in which we are living.

David thought it was important to gather all Israel together to bring up the ark of the Lord. And God thought it was important. This is the reason He recorded it in Chronicles, which is His viewpoint of this historical period.

Now David prepares to move the ark the right way.

> **And David assembled the children of Aaron, and the Levites [1 Chron. 15:4].**

Then he gives the chief of each family and the number of men each would furnish.

> **And David called for Zadok and Abiathar the priests, and for the Levites, for Uriel, Asaiah, and Joel, Shemaiah, and Eliel, and Amminadab,**
>
> **And said unto them, Ye are the chief of the fathers of the Levites: sanctify yourselves, both ye and your brethren, that ye may bring up the ark of the LORD God of Israel unto the place that I have prepared for it [1 Chron. 15:11–12].**

David had prepared a place for the ark, but we are not told exactly where it was. Was it the threshing floor of Araunah? Later on he bought that place for the site on which the temple was to be built. This is on the ridge called Mount Moriah, the place where Abraham offered Isaac. The ridge goes right through Jerusalem; and Golgotha, the place on which Christ was crucified, is located on this same ridge. I am of the opinion that the place David prepared for the ark was on Mount Moriah.

> For because ye did it not at the first, the LORD our God made a breach upon us, for that we sought him not after the due order [1 Chron. 15:13].

You will recall that David blamed God at first; he thought He was wrong in taking the life of Uzza, but then he discovered he himself was the one who was wrong, and he is confessing that.

> So the priests and the Levites sanctified themselves to bring up the ark of the LORD God of Israel [1 Chron. 15:14].

Have you noticed the repetition of the expression "the ark of the Lord God of Israel"? We get the impression that the ark is very important to God.

> And the children of the Levites bare the ark of God upon their shoulders with the staves thereon, as Moses commanded according to the word of the LORD [1 Chron. 15:15].

He is referring to God's explicit instructions in the fourth chapter of Numbers.

David, we know, was a musician, and he wanted music with all of this.

> And David spake to the chief of the Levites to appoint their brethren to be the singers with instruments of mu-

> sic, psalteries and harps and cymbals, sounding, by lift-
> ing up the voice with joy [1 Chron. 15:16].

David wanted the brass band, the orchestra, and all the choirs. It was
to be a great day when the ark of God was brought to Jerusalem. This
was the high point of David's coming to Jerusalem. God does not even
record David's coming to Jerusalem to capture it from the Jebusites,
nor does He record the great building project that David launched.
God puts the emphasis upon the spiritual, and I hope we get the message.

> So David, and the elders of Israel, and the captains over
> thousands, went to bring up the ark of the covenant of
> the LORD out of the house of Obed-edom with joy
> [1 Chron. 15:25].

Oh, this was a great day!

> And it came to pass, when God helped the Levites that
> bare the ark of the covenant of the LORD, that they offered
> seven bullocks and seven rams [1 Chron. 15:26].

All of these sacrifices pointed to Christ.

> And David was clothed with a robe of fine linen, and all
> the Levites that bare the ark, and the singers, and
> Chenaniah the master of the song with the singers:
> David also had upon him an ephod of linen.
>
> Thus all Israel brought up the ark of the covenant of the
> LORD with shouting, and with sound of the cornet, and
> with trumpets, and with cymbals, making a noise with
> psalteries and harps [1 Chron. 15:27-28].

What a day this was!
I have always wanted a big orchestra, but I never did have it in any

church I served. I guess the Lord just didn't want me to have one. I believe one of the reasons the church service is so dead and the reason the world passes it by is that there is no evidence of joy. Look at people going to any church today and see if they look happy.

Look at a newscast of a crowd at a baseball game, and you don't see a sad face in the whole lot. Even those who are losing don't seem to be sad. They all seem to be having a good time. The tragedy of the hour is that God's people don't seem to be having a good time. We ought to be!

I think the world in that day heard about David bringing up the ark to Jerusalem. I think there were visitors from other countries who went home and said, "You should have been in Jerusalem with me. It was a great day, a great day!"

Have you noticed that there is nothing in the newscasts, nothing on the front pages of the newspapers, which is spiritual or which shows the joy of the Lord? They will publish a freak sort of thing, an oddball news item about religion, or something about some religious nut. Today that which is spiritual and joyful has disappeared from the life of America. That is when we as a nation have begun to die, by the way.

Now, however, we see that not everybody was in accord with David in this celebration.

And it came to pass, as the ark of the covenant of the LORD came to the city of David, that Michal the daughter of Saul looking out at a window saw king David dancing and playing: and she despised him in her heart [1 Chron. 15:29].

Michal was the daughter of King Saul and the first wife of David. She looked at him showing his enthusiasm and joy in serving the Lord, and she thought in her heart, *He is a religious fanatic!*

Oh, how we need men like David in our day. It does not have to be fanaticism, but we do need the underlying river of joy flowing through the hearts and lives of God's people. That is the great message in chapter 15.

THE ARK IS SETTLED IN ITS PLACE

In chapter 16 we find that the ark is placed in the tent David had prepared for it, and David provides for its perpetual care.

> So they brought the ark of God, and set it in the midst of the tent that David had pitched for it: and they offered burnt sacrifices and peace offerings before God.
>
> And when David had made an end of offering the burnt offerings and the peace offerings, he blessed the people in the name of the LORD.
>
> And he dealt to every one of Israel, both man and woman, to every one a loaf of bread, and a good piece of flesh, and a flagon of wine [1 Chron. 16:1-3].

It was an occasion of great joy on the part of the people of Israel.

Then "they offered burnt sacrifices." As we saw in our study of Leviticus, the burnt sacrifices typified what God sees in Christ. The burnt offering ascended to the presence of God. Also they offered "peace offerings" which speak of the fact that Christ made peace by the blood of His Cross. Everything is right between God and us when we come God's way through Christ.

The exaltation of the Person of Christ and the fact that He shed His blood is the gospel right here in the Old Testament.

> And he appointed certain of the Levites to minister before the ark of the LORD, and to record, and to thank and praise the LORD God of Israel [1 Chron. 16:4].

We need to get so involved in the Word of God that we become enthusiastic. Anyone who is enthusiastic and excited about a football game is called a *fan*, but a person who feels that way about religion is called a fanatic! Well, we don't need fanatics, but we do need believers who get involved in the Word of God to the extent that they feel like thanking and praising the Lord God!

David had this organized. Asaph was the chief, and next to him was Zechariah—then a whole list of them. My, what a group of musi- cians he had there.

Now we see David's glorious psalm of thanksgiving.

Then on that day David delivered first this psalm to thank the LORD into the hand of Asaph and his brethren [1 Chron. 16:7].

We'll see this psalm again because it is Psalm 105. "O give thanks unto the LORD; call upon his name: make known his deeds among the people. Sing unto him, sing psalms unto him: talk ye of all his won- drous works" (Ps. 105:1-2). My friend, we need to talk about God and get His Word out. Unfortunately, many Christians today know more about the things advertised on television than they do about the Word of God. Also there are preachers among us who know more about the baseball clubs than they know about the Bible. In this computerized age we all are being pressed into a little form. My Christian friend, for God's sake get into the Word of God and learn what liberty is in Christ!

Give thanks unto the LORD, call upon his name, make known his deeds among the people [1 Chron. 16:8].

God has been moving in the past, and He is still moving today. He is not through with this little world and I think that His hand can be seen in the affairs of the world today.

Sing unto him, sing psalms unto him, talk ye of all his wondrous works [1 Chron. 16:9].

Singing is an important way in which to praise God. Although I can't sing, I can make a "joyful noise unto the Lord." I don't attempt to sing in public, but when I get in the car by myself, I really let go with a song. It doesn't sound good even to me, but I like to praise God.

Glory ye in his holy name: let the heart of them rejoice that seek the LORD.

Seek the LORD and his strength, seek his face continually [1 Chron. 16:10–11].

James 4:8 tells us, "Draw nigh to God, and he will draw nigh to you. . . ." All we must do for salvation is to come to Christ and trust Him as our Savior. God has promised that we shall be saved. However that doesn't ensure fellowship with God. We have to follow through with "Seek the Lord and his strength, seek his face continually."

Do you seek His face continually? What is the first thing you think about when you wake up in the morning? When you go to bed at night, what is the last thing you think about? Do you think about God all during the day? Or do you just leave God behind when you go to work or go to school or go to a social gathering?

Remember his marvellous works that he hath done, his wonders, and the judgments of his mouth [1 Chron. 16:12].

We were in the Hawaiian Islands, and one evening there was a glorious sunset. I called attention to it and said, "My, look at what God has done." God does things in such a magnificent way. He had plenty of light, a great big sun, a lot of sky, and big mountains. He let that sun go down and put a lot of color in it just so we could enjoy it. David calls attention to God's wonderful creation. He calls attention to God's works.

O ye seed of Israel his servant, ye children of Jacob, his chosen ones.

He is the LORD our God; his judgments are in all the earth [1 Chron. 16:13–14].

God made judgments in all the earth at that time. I think that He is making judgments today. His hands are moving in the affairs of men. Oh, I know that Satan is the god of this world. I know that God has given him a certain amount of rope in the present age and that he is going to be turned loose in the Great Tribulation period. That does not mean that God is not in control. God is finally going to close in on Satan and all his works because He is the God of judgment.

> **Be ye mindful always of his covenant; the word which he commanded to a thousand generations;**
>
> **Even of the covenant which he made with Abraham, and of his oath unto Isaac;**
>
> **And hath confirmed the same to Jacob for a law, and to Israel for an everlasting covenant [1 Chron. 16:15–17].**

There are many people who would like to minimize the covenant that God made with Abraham. Well, my friend, David doesn't minimize that covenant. David says, "Let's talk about it." God's covenants are still important today. God made a covenant with Abraham and He hasn't gone back on it. God promised Abraham that He would give to him and to his offspring the land we call the Holy Land, and God is going to do it. When they get that land given to them from the hand of God, they will not need to fear the Egyptians or the Arabs or the Russians. They won't need to fear anyone because every man is going to dwell under his own vine and under his own fig tree in peace. In other words, people will own their own property. All the land belongs to God, and God will give it to them in His time.

Just as God made a covenant with Abraham and with his offspring, so God has also made covenants with us. He has promised us all spiritual blessings in Christ Jesus.

It is apparent that David understood that God had made a covenant with him regarding the land.

> **Saying, Unto thee will I give the land of Canaan, the lot of your inheritance;**
>
> **When ye were but few, even a few, and strangers in it.**
>
> **And when they went from nation to nation, and from one kingdom to another people;**

> He suffered no man to do them wrong: yea, he reproved
> kings for their sakes,
>
> Saying, Touch not mine anointed, and do my prophets
> no harm [1 Chron. 16:18–22].

God had His protecting hand on the patriarchs as they moved about. This has primary reference, I am sure, to Abraham, Isaac, and Jacob, but it has application for us as well. We need to be very careful about laying a hand or a *tongue* on God's anointed. Before you criticize your pastor, ask yourself if you are hurting or helping the work of God.

> Sing unto the LORD, all the earth; shew forth from day to
> day his salvation.
>
> Declare his glory among the heathen; his marvellous
> works among all nations.
>
> For great is the LORD, and greatly to be praised: he also
> is to be feared above all gods [1 Chron. 16:23–25].

Today all creation is groaning in pain waiting for the redemption of the sons of God. There is a day coming when all creation will be released. Then, my friend, we shall hear music the like of which we have never heard before.

> For all the gods of the people are idols: but the LORD
> made the heavens [1 Chron. 16:26].

The word *idol* is the Hebrew *elil*, meaning "a thing of naught." Idols are nothings. They are just a piece of wood, or stone, or metal. They can be animal, vegetable or mineral. In contrast, the Lord God is identified as the *Creator*.

> Glory and honour are in his presence; strength and
> gladness are in his place.

> Give unto the LORD, ye kindreds of the people, give unto
> the LORD glory and strength.
>
> Give unto the LORD the glory due unto his name: bring
> an offering, and come before him: worship the LORD in
> the beauty of holiness [1 Chron. 16:27–29].

This does not simply mean to worship Him in a beautiful church. It
means to worship Him in the beauty of holiness, all that He is in His
person. Most of us don't even know what it is to worship God. Right
now as we read this psalm, don't you really feel like just saying a little
"Amen" or a "Glory to God" or a "Praise the Lord"—not as little
Christian clichés but from the depth of your heart? How wonderful He
is!

> Fear before him, all the earth: the world also shall be
> stable, that it be not moved.
>
> Let the heavens be glad, and let the earth rejoice: and let
> men say among the nations, The LORD reigneth
> [1 Chron. 16:30–31].

That day is coming!

> Let the sea roar, and the fulness thereof: let the fields
> rejoice, and all that is therein.
>
> Then shall the trees of the wood sing out at the presence
> of the LORD, because he cometh to judge the earth
> [1 Chron. 16:32–33].

The trees are going to sing. I'm waiting for that day. Someone asks,
"How do you think they'll sing?" Well, I don't know. But when we get
to that day, you and I will both know. It will be wonderful. It will all be
to the praise of God.

> O give thanks unto the LORD; for he is good: for his
> mercy endureth for ever [1 Chron. 16:34].

God is not short on mercy. Mercy is what I need. Mercy is what you
need. He has plenty of it. Why don't you go to Him today? He has
what you need.

> And say ye, Save us, O God of our salvation, and gather
> us together, and deliver us from the heathen, that we
> may give thanks to thy holy name, and glory in thy
> praise.

> Blessed be the LORD God of Israel for ever and ever. And
> all the people said, Amen, and praised the LORD.

> So he left there before the ark of the covenant of the LORD
> Asaph and his brethren, to minister before the ark con-
> tinually, as every day's work required:

> And Obed-edom with their brethren, threescore and
> eight; Obed-edom also the son of Jeduthun and Hosah to
> be porters:

> And Zadok the priest, and his brethren the priests, be-
> fore the tabernacle of the LORD in the high place that was
> at Gibeon.

> To offer burnt offerings unto the LORD upon the altar of
> the burnt offering continually morning and evening,
> and to do according to all that is written in the law of the
> LORD, which he commanded Israel [1 Chron. 16:35–40].

They kept the way open to God. Apparently there had not been a continuation of the sacrifices and of worship during the reign of Saul.
David now organizes it. The ark is in Jerusalem, and he designates
those who shall minister before the ark continually.

It is interesting that we are not told who was his secretary of state,
or his secretary of the treasury, or his representative at the United Na-

tions, but we are told who were the ones who took care of the ark and who worshiped before God and carried on the spiritual matters of his kingdom.

> And with them Heman and Jeduthun, and the rest that were chosen, who were expressed by name, to give thanks to the Lord, because his mercy endureth for ever [1 Chron. 16:41].

This is the reason we are to give thanks to God—"his mercy endureth forever."

> And with them Heman and Jeduthun with trumpets and cymbals for those that should make a sound, and with musical instruments of God. And the sons of Jeduthun were porters.

> And all the people departed every man to his house: and David returned to bless his house [1 Chron. 16:42–43].

CHAPTER 17

THEME: David and the temple

David's desire to build God a house so delighted the Lord that He repeats the entire episode as recorded in 2 Samuel 7.

> Now it came to pass, as David sat in his house, that David said to Nathan the prophet, Lo, I dwell in an house of cedars, but the ark of the covenant of the LORD remaineth under curtains [1 Chron. 17:1].

I think it rained the night before, and as David heard the pitter-patter of the rain on his palace, he thought of the ark of God out there in a tent. Now David says to Nathan, "I want to build God a house."

> Then Nathan said unto David, Do all that is in thine heart; for God is with thee [1 Chron. 17:2].

Nathan said what he thought was right. I am very sympathetic with Nathan. However, here is a case when a prophet of God was wrong. God will have to straighten him out.

> And it came to pass the same night, that the word of God came to Nathan, saying,
>
> Go and tell David my servant, Thus saith the LORD, Thou shalt not build me an house to dwell in:
>
> For I have not dwelt in an house since the day that I brought up Israel unto this day; but have gone from tent to tent, and from one tabernacle to another [1 Chron. 17:3–5].

God always identifies Himself with His people, which is the reason He took upon Himself our humanity, my friend. Back in the Old Testament He met with His people in a tent because they lived in tents.

> **Wheresoever I have walked with all Israel, spake I a word to any of the judges of Israel, whom I commanded to feed my people, saying, Why have ye not built me an house of cedars? [1 Chron. 17:6].**

Now when the people of Israel moved into the Promised Land and built permanent homes, there was no permanent temple built. And God says that He didn't say to them, "Why haven't you built Me a house of cedars?" But this desire has come into the heart of David.

> **Now therefore thus shalt thou say unto my servant David, Thus saith the LORD of hosts, I took thee from the sheepcote, even from following the sheep, that thou shouldest be ruler over my people Israel:**
>
> **And I have been with thee whithersoever thou hast walked, and have cut off all thine enemies from before thee, and have made thee a name like the name of the great men that are in the earth [1 Chron. 17:7-8].**

God told Nathan to deliver a message to David. God said to David, in effect, "I don't want you ever to forget your humble beginning. I went down and picked you up, a little shepherd boy, and I made you king over My people." God made David great like the great men in the earth. David stands as one of the great men of history.

> **Also I will ordain a place for my people Israel, and will plant them, and they shall dwell in their place, and shall be moved no more; neither shall the children of wickedness waste them any more, as at the beginning [1 Chron. 17:9].**

God says the day will come when *He* will put Israel in that land, and then they will have peace. They will turn to Jehovah God in that day—they are still far from that. There is quite a division in Israel today as to whether or not they should even follow the orthodox viewpoint.

> **And since the time that I commanded judges to be over my people Israel. Moreover I will subdue all thine enemies. Furthermore I tell thee that the LORD will build thee an house [1 Chron. 17:10].**

Isn't this just like our God? David had said, "I want to build God a house." God said, "David, you can't do it. You are a bloody man, and I can't let you build the temple. But I will build *you* a house." It was in David's heart to build God a house, and God gave him credit for it.

> **And it shall come to pass, when thy days be expired that thou must go to be with thy fathers, that I will raise up thy seed after thee, which shall be of thy sons; and I will establish his kingdom.**

> **He shall build me an house, and I will stablish his throne for ever [1 Chron. 17:11–12].**

Who is this One? Notice God's message to the Virgin Mary: "And, behold, thou shalt conceive in thy womb, and bring forth a son, and shalt call his name JESUS. He shall be great, and shall be called the Son of the Highest: and the Lord God shall give unto him the throne of his father David: And he shall reign over the house of Jacob for ever; and of his kingdom there shall be no end" (Luke 1:31–33). The great covenant which God made with David is to be fulfilled in Jesus Christ.

> **I will be his father, and he shall be my son: and I will not take my mercy away from him, as I took it from him that was before thee:**

> **But I will settle him in mine house and in my kingdom for ever: and his throne shall be established for evermore [1 Chron. 17:13–14].**

God means this. God will build a Kingdom on this earth, and Jesus Christ is coming to establish that Kingdom.

> **According to all these words, and according to all this vision, so did Nathan speak unto David [1 Chron. 17:15].**

As we have said, this entire incident was recorded in 2 Samuel 7. And here in Chronicles He goes over it again because He considers it important.

> **And David the king came and sat before the LORD, and said, Who am I, O LORD God, and what is mine house, that thou hast brought me hitherto? [1 Chron. 17:16].**

Notice the reaction of David. "I just don't understand your goodness, your grace, and your mercy." My friend, I am another one who can say the same thing. Why has God been so good to me? Why has God been so good to you? Our God is not short on mercy, is He? Oh, to come to Him and have a personal communication with Him—we have a communication from Him, His Word.

> **And yet this was a small thing in thine eyes, O God; for thou hast also spoken of thy servant's house for a great while to come, and hast regarded me according to the estate of a man of high degree, O LORD God [1 Chron. 17:17].**

That is a remarkable statement. They were looking for One to come. He was to be of the seed of the woman. He was to be from Abraham; He was to come from the tribe of Judah; now we are told that He will be in the family of David. David is overwhelmed by the fact that the Messiah will be in his line.

> **What can David speak more to thee for the honour of thy servant? for thou knowest thy servant [1 Chron. 17:18].**

Have you ever poured out your heart to God until you didn't have anything left to say? This is David's state here. He had poured out his heart and is empty. He is just sitting there before God.

> O Lord, for thy servant's sake, and according to thine own heart, hast thou done all this greatness, in making known all these great things [1 Chron. 17:19].

Did God do all of this for David because he was a nice boy? No, he wasn't always a nice boy. Neither did God save you and me before we were nice folk. He saved us because of His marvelous, infinite grace. He does so many special things for us, not because of our goodness, but because of *His* goodness. David is overwhelmed by what God has told him. It is no wonder he could sing those beautiful psalms.

> O Lord, there is none like thee, neither is there any God beside thee, according to all that we have heard with our ears [1 Chron. 17:20].

My, what a privilege to have a God like this!

> And what one nation in the earth is like thy people Israel, whom God went to redeem to be his own people, to make thee a name of greatness and terribleness, by driving out nations from before thy people, whom thou hast redeemed out of Egypt?

> For thy people Israel didst thou make thine own people for ever; and thou, Lord, becamest their God [1 Chron. 17:21–22].

David reviews and marvels at God's grace to the nation Israel.

> Therefore now, Lord, let the thing that thou hast spoken concerning thy servant and concerning his house be established for ever, and do as thou hast said.

Let it even be established, that thy name may be magnified for ever, saying, The LORD of hosts is the God of Israel, even a God to Israel: and let the house of David thy servant be established before thee [1 Chron. 17:23-24].

David believed and rested upon what God had promised.

For thou, O my God, hast told thy servant that thou wilt build him an house: therefore thy servant hath found in his heart to pray before thee.

And now, LORD, thou art God, and hast promised this goodness unto thy servant:

Now therefore let it please thee to bless the house of thy servant, that it may be before thee for ever: for thou blessest, O LORD, and it shall be blessed for ever [1 Chron. 17:25-27].

CHAPTERS 18—20

A t this point somebody is going to say, "You have been emphasizing that Chronicles is God's viewpoint. How can wars be fitted into this interpretation?" Because that is a question in the minds, I am sure, of many folk, let me make some preliminary statements.

In the New Testament James, in a very practical manner, asked the question: "From where do wars come?" He not only asked the question, but he gives the answer: "From whence come wars and fightings among you? come they not hence, even of your lusts that war in your members? Ye lust, and have not: ye kill, and desire to have, and cannot obtain: ye fight and war, yet ye have not, because ye ask not" (James 4:1–2). In other words, the background of war is the sinful heart of man. It is very easy to protest wars, but we will never get rid of wars by protesting. Protesting may bring a single war to an end, but another one is sure to start, because the basic problem is in the sinful heart of man.

The Lord Jesus came into our world and this is what He said, "When a strong man armed keepeth his palace, his goods are in peace: but when a stronger than he shall come upon him, and overcome him, he taketh from him all his armour wherein he trusted, and divideth his spoils" (Luke 11:21–22). Why did He say that? Because there are enemies abroad. We do not live in an ideal situation. The Millennium has not come yet—nor is man able to produce it. The Prince of Peace is the only One who will bring peace to this earth. Until He comes, we will do well to keep our powder dry.

Immediately after man sinned, God said to Satan, "And I will put enmity between thee and the woman, and between thy seed and her seed . . ." (Gen. 3:15). Friend, you cannot remove that.

There are going to be wars until sin is removed from this earth, until all wickedness is removed. Wars are the symptom. The disease is sin. It is sin that is the problem.

David is becoming a man whom God has blessed and as a result there are enemies round about. As long as he was a little petty king, a tribal king, they paid very little attention to him. God lets us know that He took note of the fact that even David's kingdom was in a world where there was war. Since you and I live in that kind of a world also, we do well to keep locks on our doors. Crime at home and abroad is the result of sin in the heart of man.

Now let's look at David's wars. The nations mentioned here were the perpetual enemies of Israel and always attacked when the nation was weak.

> Now after this it came to pass, that David smote the Philistines, and subdued them, and took Gath and her towns out of the hand of the Philistines.
>
> And he smote Moab; and the Moabites became David's servants, and brought gifts.
>
> And David smote Hadarezer king of Zobah unto Hamath, as he went to stablish his dominion by the river Euphrates.
>
> And David took from him a thousand chariots, and seven thousand horsemen, and twenty thousand footmen: David also houghed all the chariot horses, but reserved of them an hundred chariots [1 Chron. 18:1-4].

Why did David get rid of the horses? Because God had told His people that their king was not to multiply horses or wives. Later on, his son Solomon really went into the horse business, but David did not.

These were the spoils of war. I think by the time David died, Israel had cornered the gold market. The gold was there in Jerusalem.

> And David took the shields of gold that were on the servants of Hadarezer, and brought them to Jerusalem.
>
> Likewise from Tibhath, and from Chun, cities of Hadarezer, brought David very much brass, wherewith Solo-

> mon made the brasen sea, and the pillars, and the ves-
> sels of brass [1 Chron. 18:7–8].

You see, the materials out of which Solomon constructed the temple
were accumulated by David.

Then we see that the king of Hamath sent gifts of appreciation to
David for his victory over a mutual foe.

> **Them also king David dedicated unto the LORD, with the
> silver and the gold that he brought from all these na-
> tions; from Edom, and from Moab, and from the chil-
> dren of Ammon, and from the Philistines, and from
> Amalek [1 Chron. 18:11].**

David is given the victory over all of these old enemies of Israel which
had fought against them when they were weak. You see, in order to
become a king over that land, there were enemies to be driven out.

The child of God in our day has enemies also. In Ephesians 6:11
we are told to "Put on the whole armour of God. . . ." Our enemy
doesn't happen to be a flesh and blood enemy. Our enemy is a *spiritual* enemy. That is the point Paul is making in Ephesians 6:12: "For
we wrestle not against flesh and blood, but against principalities,
against powers, against the rulers of the darkness of this world,
against spiritual wickedness in high places." This is the situation in
which you and I find ourselves.

This idea that the Christian can sit down and twiddle his thumbs,
that he can compromise with everything that comes along, is entirely
wrong. As Christians, we need to stand for what is right. I once heard
a country preacher down in Georgia say, "A lot of people, instead of
standing on the promises, are sitting on the premises." Unfortunately,
that is true. We have spiritual enemies that must be overcome.

WAR WITH AMMON AND SYRIA

Chapter 19 records an incident that reveals God has a sense of humor.
It also suggests that David was a hotheaded fellow, but that he did try
to live in peace.

> Now it came to pass after this, that Nahash the king of
> the children of Ammon died, and his son reigned in his
> stead [1 Chron. 19:1].

Ammon was an enemy of Israel. David didn't want to make war.
David is on the defensive as he was most of his life, as we have seen—
God's man will usually find himself on the defensive.

As we mentioned in the previous chapter, we are told to put on the
whole armor of God. What is it for? To march? No, we are to put it on
to *stand*. That is the important thing. The tragedy of the hour is that so
few of God's people will stand.

Wanting to repay an old kindness, David sent a message of comfort
to Hanun upon the death of his father.

> And David said, I will shew kindness unto Hanun the
> son of Nahash, because his father shewed kindness to
> me. And David sent messengers to comfort him concern-
> ing his father. So the servants of David came into the
> land of the children of Ammon to Hanun, to comfort
> him [1 Chron. 19:2].

Now notice what happened.

> But the princes of the children of Ammon said to
> Hanun, Thinkest thou that David doth honour thy
> father, that he hath sent comforters unto thee? are not his
> servants come unto thee for to search, and to overthrow,
> and to spy out the land [1 Chron. 19:3].

This is a very serious charge made by these men—apparently young
men—who are around the king. They say, "David is not your friend.
He wasn't a friend of your father's. These men he has sent are spies!"
Now notice what they did to David's ambassadors.

> Wherefore Hanun took David's servants, and shaved
> them, and cut off their garments in the midst hard by
> their buttocks, and sent them away [1 Chron. 19:4].

They shaved them, which was a disgrace for a Jew—he was told not to even trim his beard. Then for their complete humiliation, they cut off their uniforms. You can imagine how these fellows felt. That was not a day of nudism, and they were greatly embarrassed. Of course it was an insult that could not be ignored, and David was a hotheaded fellow.

> **Then there went certain, and told David how the men were served. And he sent to meet them: for the men were greatly ashamed. And the king said, Tarry at Jericho until your beards be grown, and then return [1 Chron. 19:5].**

Since these men were too humiliated to return to Jerusalem, David went down to Jericho to meet with them. David told them to stay in retirement until their beards were grown out again. And, of course, they would be given new uniforms.

Word got back to the people of Ammon what David had said when he heard how his ambassadors had been treated.

> **And when the children of Ammon saw that they had made themselves odious to David, Hanun and the children of Ammon sent a thousand talents of silver to hire them chariots and horsemen out of Mesopotamia, and out of Syria-maachah, and out of Zobah [1 Chron. 19:6].**

Instead of David being the one who wanted to make war, this new king of the Ammonites wanted to. He wanted to demonstrate that he could overthrow David. I am sure this was in his mind when he humiliated David's ambassadors. So he hires an army from Syria to help him overcome David.

When David hears of this, he goes into action.

> **And when David heard of it, he sent Joab, and all the host of the mighty men.**

And the children of Ammon came out, and put the battle in array before the gate of the city: and the kings that were come were by themselves in the field.

Now when Joab saw that the battle was set against him before and behind, he chose out of all the choice of Israel, and put them in array against the Syrians [1 Chron. 19:8-10].

The Syrians had the best army, so Joab chose the best of his forces to put them over against the Syrians. The Syrians were coming from the north and Ammon was coming from the south.

And the rest of the people he delivered unto the hand of Abishai his brother, and they set themselves in array against the children of Ammon.

And he said, If the Syrians be too strong for me, then thou shalt help me: but if the children of Ammon be too strong for thee, then I will help thee [1 Chron. 19:11-12].

His strategy was very good. He told his brother that he would come to his aid if he were to be overcome but his brother should come to his aid in case he were overcome. They were going to concentrate their forces at the place of the most heavy attack. That was good strategy. (It was the strategy which was used by both sides in the American Civil War, by the way.)

Be of good courage, and let us behave ourselves valiantly for our people, and for the cities of our God: and let the LORD do that which is good in his sight.

So Joab and the people that were with him drew nigh before the Syrians unto the battle; and they fled before him [1 Chron. 19:13-14].

Joab was a real army man, a real soldier. He would have been trained under David, and he and David were probably tops as far as military men were concerned.

> **And when the children of Ammon saw that the Syrians were fled, they likewise fled before Abishai his brother, and entered into the city. Then Joab came to Jerusalem [1 Chron. 19:15].**

He came back to Jerusalem to report.

> **And when the Syrians saw that they were put to the worse before Israel, they sent messengers, and drew forth the Syrians that were beyond the river: and Shophach the captain of the host of Hadarezer went before them [1 Chron. 19:16].**

They sent for reinforcements.

> **And it was told David; and he gathered all Israel, and passed over Jordan, and came upon them, and set the battle in array against them. So when David had put the battle in array against the Syrians, they fought with him.**

> **But the Syrians fled before Israel: and David slew of the Syrians seven thousand men which fought in chariots, and forty thousand footmen, and killed Shophach the captain of the host.**

> **And when the servants of Hadarezer saw that they were put to the worse before Israel, they made peace with David, and became his servants: neither would the Syrians help the children of Ammon any more [1 Chron. 19:17–19].**

David did not want to go into battle. Remember we are getting God's viewpoint of the situation, and He makes it very clear that David wanted peace with the Ammonites. He didn't want to fight them. When he had seen an army prepared against him, he had sent Joab on the first campaign and the enemy had fled. But that didn't end the war. The enemy went out to get reinforcements, and with allies on their side they again gathered against Israel. This time David himself went out to lead the battle. May I say to you that when David led Israel into battle, he went into battle to win!

It is a tragedy for any nation to fight a war without the determination to win. How tragic that is. My friend, we are not to fight wars just to fight wars! Our nation has found itself in very tragic circumstances because we have fought wars we did not intend to win. If we had fought to win, we would have spared thousands of lives.

Some people will read this part of the history of Israel and say that God is a bloody God. No, friend, God is not bloody. He knows the way to save human lives. That way is to subdue the aggressor and win the war.

We live in a sinful world, my friend. It is a brutal world. It is a mean world. If you like to quote Browning, "God's in His heaven and all's right with the world," you are not quoting what Scripture teaches. We are getting God's viewpoint here. All is not right with the world.

We live in a day of permissiveness. This is the day of the foul-mouthed. We no longer have personal honesty or personal integrity or human sincerity. We need to face the fact that we are in a world of sin. Laws should be enforced, and criminals should be punished. God says that as long as we are in a world like this, a strong man armed will keep his house. We are getting God's viewpoint here, which is quite interesting.

WAR WITH AMMONITES AND PHILISTINES

Chapter 20 concludes this section on the wars of David.

The constant, persistent, enemies of Israel—and especially of David—were the Ammonites and the Philistines. There was no such thing as compromise between Israel and those enemies.

> And it came to pass, that after the year was expired, at
> the time that kings go out to battle, Joab led forth the
> power of the army, and wasted the country of the chil-
> dren of Ammon, and came and besieged Rabbah. But
> David tarried at Jerusalem. And Joab smote Rabbah,
> and destroyed it [1 Chron. 20:1].

It looks as if Joab was the aggressor in this case. Although he may have been, we need to remember that David had made a friendly gesture to the young king of Ammon, but he was insulted and immediately the new king came against David in warfare. So this is just a continuation of that warfare.

There can be no compromise with the enemy. There can be no compromise with evil.

This idea today that right and wrong can walk together is all wrong. "Can two walk together, except they be agreed?" (Amos 3:3). My friend, if you are walking with evil, it is because you have com-promised with it, you have agreed with the evil. This is something that the world is forgetting. It would be amusing if it were not so tragic that there are so many people who are horrified at war when it is across the ocean but are happy to tolerate lawlessness in our streets. They say we must learn to understand and to appreciate the law-breakers. May I say that there is a hypocrisy in our contemporary cul-ture that is sickening beyond degree. If it is evil across the ocean, it is evil here. Evil must be opposed. Lawlessness must be opposed. Right and wrong are in opposition. There cannot be an agreement between the two.

It is during this campaign that David stayed at Jerusalem, and this is the time that he committed his great sin with Bathsheba. Notice that God doesn't record that sin here. God has said that He forgives our sins and that He will remember our sins no more. He means that.

Now here is another persistent enemy of Israel: the Philistines.

> And it came to pass after this, that there arose war at
> Gezer with the Philistines; at which time Sibbechai the

Hushathite slew Sippai, that was of the children of the giant: and they were subdued.

And there was war again with the Philistines: and Elhanan the son of Jair slew Lahmi the brother of Goliath the Gittite, whose spear staff was like a weaver's beam.

And yet again there was war at Gath, where was a man of great stature, whose fingers and toes were four and twenty, six on each hand, and six on each foot: and he also was the son of the giant [1 Chron. 20:4–6].

In this conflict with the Philistines, three men who were giants were slain by David and his men. David, of course, became famous as a young fellow for slaying the giant Goliath. The Philistines were the unrelenting enemy of Israel all during the life of David.

My friend, the believer has an unrelenting enemy also. We are fighting against spiritual wickedness in high places. If you are a child of God, you are also a soldier of God. That is the reason we are enjoined to "Put on the whole armour of God . . ." (Eph. 6:11). We are not to march against anyone; we are to stand. If you stand for the things of God, you are in a battle. You are in a war whether you like it or not. The wars may cease in Asia and in Africa and in Europe and in the western hemisphere, but there will still be war as long as there is evil in the world. As Paul said to the Ephesian believers, "Wherefore take unto you the whole armour of God, that ye may be able to withstand in the evil day, and having done all, to stand" (Eph. 6:13). This is the message in chapter 20 for you and for me.

CHAPTER 21

THEME: *David's sin in taking a census*

This chapter deals with the greatest sin that David committed, and it has nothing in the world to do with Bathsheba. It is the kind of sin about which folk say, "Well, I can't see why this is such a great sin." Everyone seems to think that the matter of Bathsheba is a terrible sin, and I'm in that number. I agree it was an awful sin. But in this chapter, as in all of Chronicles, we are given God's perspective. God does not record David's sin with Bathsheba in the Book of Chronicles, but He does record this sin of numbering the people because it is on the spiritual level. It won't affect David's salvation one whit, but it certainly is going to affect him and the nation of Israel in their personal relationship with God.

> **And Satan stood up against Israel, and provoked David to number Israel [1 Chron. 21:1].**

Now we have found the real culprit. This was satanic. Satan was in back of this whole incident. This throws light upon David's great sin.

David's sin with Bathsheba was a personal sin, a sin of the flesh. In Psalm 51, he cried, "Have mercy upon me, O God, according to thy lovingkindness: according unto the multitude of thy tender mercies blot out my transgressions" (Ps. 51:1). He was referring to his sin with Bathsheba. But here "Satan stood up against Israel," and moved David to take this census.

> **And David said to Joab and to the rulers of the people, Go, number Israel from Beer-sheba even to Dan; and bring the number of them to me, that I may know it [1 Chron. 21:2].**

You recall that Moses had taken a census of the people on two occasions. In the Book of Numbers we are told that he took a census at the beginning of the wilderness march and then again at the end of the wilderness march. There was nothing wrong with that. At least, God did not find fault with that. But here it is sin. There are those who say that the reason David did this was because he was proud. Well, let's read on.

> And Joab answered, the LORD make his people an hundred times so many more as they be: but, my lord the king, are they not all my lord's servants? why then doth my lord require this thing? why will he be a cause of trespass to Israel? [1 Chron. 21:3].

Here is the first man to oppose the computer. David wanted statistics and there is a sin in statistics. Everything today is being computerized, including all of us, for that matter. Joab opposed getting these statistics because he felt that pride was involved in this. I am of the opinion that although pride did enter into it, pride is not the total explanation of the sin.

"Thus saith the LORD, Let not the wise man glory in his wisdom, neither let the mighty man glory in his might, let not the rich man glory in his riches: But let him that glorieth glory in this, that he understandeth and knoweth me, that I am the LORD which exercise lovingkindness, judgment, and righteousness, in the earth: for in these things I delight, saith the LORD" (Jer. 9:23–24). God was not pleased when David took a census because David was not delighting in the Lord; he was delighting in his own might. So the thing that motivated him to number the people was the awful sin of unbelief. David was trusting numbers instead of trusting God.

> Nevertheless the king's word prevailed against Joab. Wherefore Joab departed, and went throughout all Israel, and came to Jerusalem.

> And Joab gave the sum of the number of the people unto David. And all they of Israel were a thousand thousand and an hundred thousand men that drew sword: and Judah was four hundred threescore and ten thousand men that drew sword.
>
> But Levi and Benjamin counted he not among them: for the king's word was abominable to Joab [1 Chron. 21:4–6].

In Israel he had 1,100,000 men, and in Judah he had 500,000 men. When Moses had taken the census, he had 603,000 men. David has a million more men than Moses had!

What contrast this is to David, the shepherd boy, when he came into the camp and saw the great giant Goliath strutting up and down defying Israel. This little shepherd boy didn't want to take a census; he didn't number the army. He just said, "Let me go out after him." Why did he have the courage to do it? Well, he trusted the Lord. He went out with a sling and five stones! My friend, you don't feel the need of God when you have one million men. When you have only a slingshot and five stones, you know you need Him.

I'm afraid that our nation is in very much this same position today. "The greatest nation on earth"—how often we hear that phrase! I imagine the people in the Roman Empire heard that until they got tired of hearing it. They did the same in Babylon and in Greece and in Egypt. Those kingdoms are long gone as great world empires. Why? Because they trusted in armies. Don't misunderstand me. Every nation needs an army to defend itself in this evil world. We are not to be fools and fanatics who say we need no protection and no army. But that is not where our confidence should be!

Joab protests to David. He says, "David, all these men are yours. You don't need to number them. God has given you all these people, and they will be adequate with God." But David insisted on a census.

Today people think that with our atom bombs and hydrogen bombs we have no need for God. My friend, we do need God. People are trusting the wrong things in our day. David's great sin was unbelief.

I realize this fact does not register with many people. Just as today we point the finger at a church member who would stagger into the church service while he was drunk. But you could walk into our Sunday morning church service in unbelief and no one would be the wiser. And if your unbelief was known, this would not be considered a serious matter. My friend, God is telling us here that he considers unbelief the most serious matter. Satan is always behind unbelief. He puts unbelief into our hearts and minds so that we will not trust God. He is always urging us to put our trust in men, in armies, in money, in anything but God. That is the sin of statistics.

May I say that a great many folk today trust mathematics and not the Maker. They trust the computer and not the Christ. They trust in numbers and not in the name of the Lord.

David learned his lesson. Listen to him: "It is better to trust in the LORD than to put confidence in man. It is better to trust in the LORD than to put confidence in princes" (Ps. 118:8–9). "In thee, O LORD, do I put my trust: let me never be put to confusion" (Ps. 71:1).

We need to ask ourselves these penetrating questions. Do we really trust God? Do we really believe God? "But without faith it is impossible to please him . . ." (Heb. 11:6). The Lord Jesus said that when the Holy Spirit would come into the world, He would convict the world of sin. What kind of sin? ". . . because they *believe not* on me" (John 16:9). Paul writes, ". . . for whatsoever is not of faith is sin" (Rom. 14:23). This is the sin of David, and it is real sin. David soon began to see what a terrible thing he had done.

DAVID CHOOSES HIS PUNISHMENT

And God was displeased with this thing; therefore he smote Israel.

And David said unto God, I have sinned greatly, because I have done this thing: but now, I beseech thee, do

away the iniquity of thy servant; for I have done very foolishly [1 Chron. 21:7–8].

Now the Lord is going to put before David a choice of punishment.

And the LORD spake unto Gad, David's seer, saying,

Go and tell David, saying, Thus saith the LORD, I offer thee three things: choose thee one of them, that I may do it unto thee.

So Gad came to David, and said unto him, Thus saith the LORD, Choose thee

Either three years' famine; or three months to be destroyed before thy foes, while that the sword of thine enemies overtaketh thee; or else three days the sword of the LORD, even the pestilence, in the land, and the angel of the LORD destroying throughout all the coasts of Israel. Now therefore advise thyself what word I shall bring again to him that sent me [1 Chron. 21:9–12].

Now listen to David. This is tremendous. I hope you agree with me by now that David was a great man. Oh, he was human like I am and you are. He stubbed his toe, he committed sins, he had his faults, but he never lost his salvation nor his desire for fellowship with God.

And David said unto Gad, I am in a great strait: let me fall now into the hand of the LORD; for very great are his mercies: but let me not fall into the hand of man [1 Chron. 21:13].

David knew his God. Here is a man who ordered the census because he was trusting in man. He sees now what he has done. I think David is an old man now, and he remembers that little shepherd boy who went out with his slingshot and five smooth stones. How he trusted God, and what a testimony he had then! David was as human as we are; we trust God for salvation, but we don't trust Him for the problems of life. David now looks about at his enemies. Their numbers are great; they are giant nations. David wonders if his army is big enough. He has forgotten for the moment that his God is big enough for all the giants and all the nations that are threatening him. So David takes a census.

How many times have you and I taken a census? We didn't really trust God, and we put our faith in something else.

But David knows his God. He says to Gad, "Don't let me fall into the hand of man. I want to fall into the hands of God." Why? Because David has learned that God is merciful. I am afraid that many of us have not learned that. God has ". . . not dealt with us after our sins; nor rewarded us according to our iniquities. For as the heaven is high above the earth, so great is his mercy toward them that fear him" (Ps. 103:10–11).

God is merciful in salvation. He holds out today salvation to a lost world. On what basis? Christ is the mercy seat. You recall that John puts it this way: "And he is the propitiation for our sins: and not for ours only, but also for the sins of the whole world" (1 John 2:2). What is propitiation? It is the Mercy Seat. He has an abundance of mercy. All you have to do if you want to be saved is to go into court with God, plead guilty, and then ask for mercy. He has plenty of mercy. That is the way He will save you. There is a pardon for you, and you must claim it.

Also there is the mercy of God in providence. I look back upon my life—oh, how good He has been! He is so merciful today, not only to me but to the whole unsaved world. Why didn't He come in judgment last night? Because He is merciful. He will come some day but He is long-suffering, He is merciful, He keeps giving time for repentance. He pities us like a father pities his children. His mercy will extend into the future. We can lean securely on His mercy. It will never cease. It is not just a momentary happy disposition with Him. It is not some development in His character. He didn't just read *How to Win Friends and Influence People* and then decide to be merciful. David could say, "O give thanks unto the Lord; for he is good: for his mercy endureth for ever" (Ps. 136:1). So David casts himself upon God's mercy.

So the LORD sent pestilence upon Israel: and there fell of Israel seventy thousand men.

And God sent an angel unto Jerusalem to destroy it: and as he was destroying, the LORD beheld, and he repented him of the evil, and said to the angel that destroyed, It is enough, stay now thine hand. And the angel of the LORD stood by the threshingfloor of Ornan the Jebusite.

And David lifted up his eyes, and saw the angel of the LORD stand between the earth and the heaven, having a drawn sword in his hand stretched out over Jerusalem. Then David and the elders of Israel, who were clothed in sackcloth, fell upon their faces.

And David said unto God, Is it not I that commanded the people to be numbered? even I it is that have sinned and done evil indeed; but as for these sheep, what have they done? let thine hand, I pray thee, O LORD my God, be on me, and on my father's house; but not on thy people, that they should be plagued [1 Chron. 21:14–17].

Notice this marvelous prayer of David. He takes full responsibility for his sin. I would say that David has changed a great deal. The time when he committed the sin with Bathsheba he wasn't going to say a word about it. He even tried to push the blame for the death of Uriah the Hittite to someone else. David tried to cover up. Now it is different. He has learned his lesson. His soul stands absolutely naked before God. He tells the Lord, "I am responsible. I did this thing. Let the judgment fall upon me."

DAVID BUYS THE THRESHINGFLOOR OF ORNAN

Then the angel of the LORD commanded Gad to say to David, that David should go up, and set up an altar unto the LORD in the threshingfloor of Ornan the Jebusite [1 Chron. 21:18].

When I was in Jerusalem, I walked up and down the site of that threshingfloor. It is located on Mount Moriah, the place where the Mosque of Omar stands today. That is the old temple area. So here we learn that it was not actually David who chose that spot for the temple; God chose it. And David certainly concurred with Him.

> **And David went up at the saying of Gad, which he spake in the name of the Lord.**
>
> **And Ornan turned back, and saw the angel; and his four sons with him hid themselves. Now Ornan was threshing wheat.**
>
> **And as David came to Ornan, Ornan looked and saw David, and went out of the threshingfloor, and bowed himself to David with his face to the ground [1 Chron. 21:19–21].**

Ornan was threshing wheat at his threshingfloor. It is interesting that I was there just at the beginning of harvest season. Every afternoon the wind would come up. I sat in our hotel room and I could look over this area, the temple area, the site of Ornan's threshingfloor. The wind really whistled through there, so much so that we had to close the doors to our room. In the days of David they would wait for that wind to come up, and then they would pitch the grain up into the air. The wind would blow away the chaff and the good grain would fall down upon the threshingfloor.

As I have mentioned before, Mount Moriah is the place where Abraham offered up Isaac. And at the other end of that same ridge is Golgotha, the place of the skull, where God offered up His Son. When I was there, I took a picture of the sheaf of rock which was taken out to make the roadway up to the Damascus gate. The wall of Jerusalem goes up over that ridge. It is very high. After taking that picture, I turned right around, walked ten steps, and took a picture of Golgotha—located on the same ridge, at the same elevation. It was a continuous ridge until they put the roadway through there. You see,

God chose the site of Ornan's threshingfloor on Mount Moriah because that is the place where God told Abraham to offer his son, looking forward to the time of the temple sacrifices and finally to the sacrifice of the Lamb of God which takes away the sin of the world.

> **Then David said to Ornan, Grant me the place of this threshingfloor, that I may build an altar therein unto the LORD: thou shalt grant it me for the full price: that the plague may be stayed from the people.**

> **And Ornan said unto David, Take it to thee, and let my lord the king do that which is good in his eyes: lo, I give thee the oxen also for burnt offerings, and the threshing instruments for wood, and the wheat for the meat offering: I give it all [1 Chron. 21:22–23].**

This man Ornan was very generous. He offered the property, and the wheat that he was gathering in which David could use for a meal offering, also the wood and the oxen for a burnt offering. This man offered the whole thing to David. But now listen to David:

> **And king David said to Ornan, Nay; but I will verily buy it for the full price: for I will not take that which is thine for the LORD, nor offer burnt offerings without cost [1 Chron. 21:24].**

David refused to offer to God that which cost him nothing.

> **So David gave to Ornan for the place six hundred shekels of gold by weight [1 Chron. 21:25].**

David paid the full price for the threshingfloor.

> **And David built there an altar unto the LORD, and offered burnt offerings and peace offerings, and called**

> upon the LORD; and he answered him from heaven by
> fire upon the altar of burnt offering [1 Chron. 21:26].

David now makes a sacrifice to God. The fire from heaven indicated
that God had accepted David's offering.

> And the LORD commanded the angel; and he put up his
> sword again into the sheath thereof [1 Chron. 21:27].

The sword of judgment was sheathed. But at Golgotha, that sword
pierced the side of the Lord Jesus Christ. As someone has said, "I got
into the heart of God through a spear wound."

> At that time when David saw that the LORD had an-
> swered him in the threshingfloor of Ornan the Jebusite,
> then he sacrificed there.
>
> For the tabernacle of the LORD, which Moses made in the
> wilderness, and the altar of the burnt offering, were at
> that season in the high place at Gibeon.
>
> But David could not go before it to inquire of God: for he
> was afraid because of the sword of the angel of the LORD
> [1 Chron. 21:28–30].

I want you to see something very important here. David put this altar
in the place where the temple is to be built, and he offers a sacrifice.
This is the place God met with His people. This is now become the
place of sacrifice. You see, David understood what a lot of church
members today do not understand. David put up this altar, and he
offered on it a burnt offering. That burnt offering speaks of the Person
of Christ. Then he offered a peace offering. This speaks of Christ as
our Peace. Christ made peace by the blood of His Cross. Jesus Christ is
our Peace. He has sprinkled His own blood on the mercy seat for us.
He is our great High Priest. He has ascended into heaven and stands at
the right hand of the Father. There is no access to God except through

the Lord Jesus Christ. David understood this, and he offered the burnt offering and the peace offering to God.

Now remember that there was a plague going on. David has seen the angel with a drawn sword in his hand stretched out over Jerusalem. David offers sacrifices to God and calls on the name of the Lord. What was he asking for? For mercy!

God is a God of mercy, of loving-kindness. But did you know that God doesn't save us by His mercy? God can't just be bighearted. He can't be a sentimental old gentleman. You see, there is a penalty that must be paid. Sin must be dealt with. God is also righteous and He cannot save us simply by His mercy, or by His love. God can't save you by love, friend. He loves you and He will extend mercy to you, but He cannot save you that way. We are saved by *grace* through *faith*. What does that mean? That means that someone had to pay the penalty for our sins. God couldn't just open the back door of heaven and slip us in under cover of darkness. He cannot let down the bars of heaven. Sin must be dealt with. He cannot shut His eyes to sin in order to save us. We are guilty sinners before God, and the penalty must be paid. Jesus Christ came to pay our penalty. He is the propitiation, He is the mercy seat for you and me.

CHAPTERS 22—29

THEME: *David's preparation and organization for building the temple*

From this point through to the end of 1 Chronicles, we have the organization, the gathering of the materials, and the enthusiasm of David for building the temple which God would not allow him to build.

Let me remind you again that Chronicles give God's viewpoint, and to Him the temple is the most important project David had in mind. David had a housing project—we saw that. He built many houses in Jerusalem; it was a great urban development. However, the important thing was the building of the temple. Why? My friend, until an individual or a people are right with Almighty God, all these subsidiary subjects must sink into insignificance. When a right relationship with him is established, then urban development is important. Then a poverty program is very much in order. It looked like David had a poverty program when, after he brought the ark to Jerusalem, he was handing out the groceries. Why? Well, because the spiritual part had been settled.

Today we hear so much about urban development and about poverty programs. The news media puts such emphasis on these things and makes people think that if these material things can be solved then the problems of the world would be solved. My friend, man is far from solving the problems of the world because he hasn't solved the major problem, which is his relationship with God. As a result, there is corruption in urban development; there is corruption in poverty programs.

The temple speaks of that which is spiritual, of a right relationship with God. From God's viewpoint that was the important thing that went on in David's kingdom—rather than the continual wars, the intrigue, the petty politics such as are considered newsworthy in our day.

It is interesting to apply this to more recent history. Great Britain was the nation which ruled the world for many years. There was the saying that the sun never set on the British Empire. Great Britain controlled more of the world than any other nation ever has. They were not perfect, and one can find much to criticize, but it still is true that Great Britain had a tremendous influence for good on the entire world.

The significant factors in her history did not take place at 10 Downing Street. They didn't take place in Parliament under the tower of Big Ben. Probably the most important thing was when a young fellow by the name of John Wesley went upstairs in Aldersgate. When I was there, I had to pause a moment and thank God for that man and his work, because we are still reaping the benefits from it. Down the street from Aldersgate is the place where Wesley began his preaching. There is a graveyard there; and, when the state church put him out, he stood on the tombstones and started preaching. The result was a spiritual movement of such magnitude that even Lloyd George said that John Wesley did more for the British Empire than any Englishman who ever lived.

Probably the newspapers and magazines didn't think Wesley was important; yet he was God's instrument for saving Great Britain from a revolution, and God enabled him to begin a movement which brought civilization throughout the world. We can belittle the colonial policy (and Great Britain bogged down under it with all the wrongs inherent in it), but the important thing is that this was a movement which sent missionaries throughout the world and brought a civilizing Christian influence throughout the world.

Even the most prejudiced person in the world surely must admit that those days were better than the godless age in which we are living—which is getting nowhere.

From God's viewpoint, David's preparations for the temple were more important than anything else David did.

Then David said, This is the house of the Lord God, and this is the altar of the burnt offering for Israel.

And David commanded to gather together the strangers that were in the land of Israel; and he set masons to hew

> **wrought stones to build the house of God [1 Chron. 22:1-2].**

David is determined that the temple is to be built there on the threshingfloor of Ornan.

> **And David prepared iron in abundance for the nails for the doors of the gates, and for the joinings; and brass in abundance without weight;**
>
> **Also cedar trees in abundance: for the Zidonians and they of Tyre brought much cedar wood to David [1 Chron. 22:3-4].**

The Zidonians were, of course, the inhabitants of Zidon (sometimes called Sidon). As we have seen, Hiram, king of Tyre and Sidon, was the one who provided the stone and timber for the construction of the temple.

> **And David said, Solomon my son is young and tender, and the house that is to be builded for the LORD must be exceeding magnifical, of fame and of glory throughout all countries: I will therefore now make preparation for it. So David prepared abundantly before his death [1 Chron. 22:5].**

Notice the word *magnifical!* As we see it from God's viewpoint, David made abundant preparation for the temple. He knew that Solomon was young and inexperienced, and the temple of God must be exceedingly magnificent. This is my reason for saying it should be called David's temple rather than Solomon's temple.

> **Then he called for Solomon his son, and charged him to build an house for the LORD God of Israel.**
>
> **And David said to Solomon, My son, as for me, it was in my mind to build an house unto the name of the LORD my God:**

> But the word of the LORD came to me saying, Thou hast
> shed blood abundantly, and hast made great wars: thou
> shalt not build an house unto my name, because thou
> hast shed much blood upon the earth in my sight
> [1 Chron. 22:6–8].

Although the wars David fought were forced upon him—he was not
the aggressor—God said that he was a bloody man. God is not for
war—His name is not Mars. He is opposed to war. He wants peace,
and His Son is the Prince of Peace who will bring peace to this earth.
God would not allow David to build the temple because he was a man
of war.

> Behold, a son shall be born to thee, who shall be a man
> of rest; and I will give him rest from all his enemies
> round about: for his name shall be Solomon, and I will
> give peace and quietness unto Israel in his days
> [1 Chron. 22:9].

God said that Solomon would be a man of peace and rest because he
would give peace to Israel in his days. But, as we shall see, the peace
was not permanent.

However, there was One who stood before the people of Israel
when the religious rulers rejected Him, and said, "Come unto me, all
ye that labour and are heavy laden . . ." (Matt. 11:28). He didn't actually say, "I will give you rest," as our Authorized Version has it, but "I
will rest you." He will do what Solomon was unable to do. He is great
David's greater Son. It is He who can bring rest and peace, solace and
quietness to the human soul. God is merciful because His Son died for
you. Won't you accept His overture? He has moved heaven and hell to
reach the door of your heart. He won't come any further, but He says,
"Behold, I stand at the door, and knock: if any man hear my voice, and
open the door, I will come in to him, and will sup with him, and he
with me" (Rev. 3:20).

> He shall build an house for my name; and he shall be
> my son, and I will be his father; and I will establish the

> **throne of his kingdom over Israel for ever [1 Chron. 22:10].**

As we have seen, the Lord Jesus Christ is the final fulfillment of this promise.

It is my personal feeling that David was not much interested in having Solomon become king. Solomon was a sissy. Solomon was brought up in the palace, in the women's court. He knew nothing of living and defending himself in the rugged terrain of that land as David his father had done. David and Solomon were far apart, and the explanation, of course, is their backgrounds. In effect, David says to Solomon, "You are going to build the temple. Oh, I want to encourage you and get you enthusiastic about it, because it is the desire of my heart to build a magnifical temple, and God won't let me do it because I am a bloody man."

My friend, let me pause here a moment to remind you that David did not get by with sin. He was not able to do the thing he wanted to do above everything else on this earth, which was to build a temple for God. There is many a man whom God has not permitted to reach the goal he wanted to reach, because of sin in his life. Sin drags us all down. It dragged David down.

> **Now, my son, the LORD be with thee; and prosper thou, and build the house of the LORD thy God, as he hath said of thee [1 Chron. 22:11].**

How David was encouraging this boy—and he knew he needed encouraging! He has been brought up in the court of the women, and he's not a very aggressive fellow.

As we shall see, Solomon reaped the benefits of the reign of David. It can be said truly of him, as the Lord Jesus put it, ". . . other men laboured, and ye are entered into their labours" (John 4:38). Solomon entered into the labors of another, and that was his father David.

> **Only the LORD give thee wisdom and understanding, and give thee charge concerning Israel, that thou mayest keep the law of the LORD thy God [1 Chron. 22:12].**

David is urging his son to follow in God's ways. I think David detected some of his weaknesses, and I am sure Bathsheba detected some of the weaknesses in Solomon. One of those traits was his weakness in the direction of women. This is David's advice to Solomon which we are reading. If you want to read his mother's advice to him, you will find it in the last chapter of Proverbs.

> **Then shalt thou prosper, if thou takest heed to fulfil the statutes and judgments which the LORD charged Moses with concerning Israel: be strong, and of good courage; dread not, nor be dismayed [1 Chron. 22:13].**

David knew that Solomon would get discouraged. He knew that Solomon was a weakling. He tells him to be a man—be strong and courageous.

> **Now, behold, in my trouble I have prepared for the house of the LORD an hundred thousand talents of gold, and a thousand thousand talents of silver; and of brass and iron without weight; for it is in abundance: timber also and stone have I prepared; and thou mayest add thereto [1 Chron. 22:14].**

David told Solomon that he wouldn't have to stint in the building of this temple. He wouldn't have to cut any corners. There would be no shortage of materials. David said that in the days of his trouble, the days in which he had attempted to build up the kingdom with all the labor involved, he had carried on the work of gathering the materials for the temple of God.

God had taken note of that. God had seen what was in the heart of David. That is why David is called a man after God's own heart. God wanted this heart attitude, this emphasis on the spiritual values, above everything else.

My friend, what is really the goal of your life? What ambition do you have? We are told that today we have a generation of young people without any purpose or goal in life. They have been brought up in homes of affluence with no Christian direction. There has been no pointing to something that is worthwhile, something that is glorious and great. They haven't had that direction in their homes, neither have they had direction in their schools. The schools are not doing their job. I may sound like a heretic and a real revolutionary, but I don't think it would hurt to close up many of our schools today. I don't think they are serving their purpose until they give moral training and direction and discipline to our young people.

What is the purpose of living? Why are there so many suicides among our young people? Why are so many of them dissolute vagrants wandering aimlessly all over the world? My heart goes out to them because someone failed. Papa and Mamma have failed. The schools have failed. The churches have failed.

May I say to you that David was giving his son some direction. He told him, "You have a worthy goal—build God a house." Let me pass on to you something that was given to me early in life. The catechism asks the question: "What is the chief end of man?" The answer is: "Man's chief end is to glorify God and enjoy Him forever."

Oh, I wish I could get you enthusiastic—not about baseball or football or any kind of ball, not in the things around you, not even in church work (that may sound revolutionary also)—but in the Lord Jesus Christ. I wish I could get you really interested in His person.

My friend, Jesus Christ has promised me and He has promised you that we shall be with Him forever. Since He is God, His way is going to prevail, not yours or mine. He has something glorious in view. I don't have it because I don't know what is out there, but I am interested in what He has for me. We should all be able to say with Paul, "I press toward the mark for the prize of the high calling of God in Christ Jesus" (Phil. 3:14). David is a man after God's own heart because he had something high and noble and lofty in his heart.

Moreover there are workmen with thee in abundance, hewers and workers of stone and timber, and all manner of cunning men for every manner of work [1 Chron. 22:15].

You see, he had arranged with Hiram to take charge of all the building.

> Of the gold, the silver, and the brass, and the iron, there
> is no number. Arise therefore, and be doing, and the
> Lord be with thee [1 Chron. 22:16].

Get busy, young man! Here is a goal that is worthwhile.

> David also commanded all the princes of Israel to help
> Solomon his son, saying,
>
> Is not the Lord your God with you? and hath he not
> given you rest on every side? for he hath given the inhab-
> itants of the land into mine hand; and the land is sub-
> dued before the Lord, and before his people.
>
> Now set your heart and your soul to seek the Lord your
> God; arise therefore, and build ye the sanctuary of the
> Lord God, to bring the ark of the covenant of the Lord,
> and the holy vessels of God, into the house that is to be
> built to the name of the Lord [1 Chron. 22:17-19].

David is commanding the leaders of Israel to become involved in this project also.

Now, my friend, whoever you are (and I am speaking to you as a Christian), you may have sunk down to a pretty low level in your living. It may be that all the church work you do is gossip, or all you do is find fault with the preacher. Maybe you are not guilty of these things, but instead of "standing on the promises, you are sitting on the premises"—you are doing nothing. I'd like to alert you, stick a pin in you, and say, wake up! Come alive and make a move toward Jesus Christ. Tell Him that you want to go along with Him, that you want a spiritual emphasis in your life. Do something definite; do something positive. Don't just sit there—do it right now. That is what David is saying to his boy Solomon. He really put a pin in him!

LEVITES ARE ORGANIZED TO SERVE AND SING

As we come to chapter 23, keep in mind that we are still in the section that is all about the temple. Again let me say that God considered this important, and here is the place He put the emphasis. David also considered it of utmost importance, and we see more of his zeal and enthusiasm for the worship of God in these arrangements he has made.

My friend, if you are a child of God, David is putting this challenge to you. Do you really put God first in your life? Is He a thrill to you? Do you rejoice in that relationship? Do you want to do something for God? Does He give direction and purpose to your life? Is it the desire of your heart to know Him and to serve Him?

Unfortunately, many of our churches feature activity without action. Like a merry-go-round, we get on and have a nice little ride, then we get off at the same place we got on. We are not going any place. David was on the move for God, and he is urging his son Solomon to get on the move and build this great temple.

> So when David was old and full of days, he made Solomon his son king over Israel [1 Chron. 23:1].

David now makes Solomon king in his stead.

Perhaps you are asking, "What did David die of?" Well, he was full of days—that was his problem. And it is the problem many of us have.

> And he gathered together all the princes of Israel, with the priests and the Levites.
>
> Now the Levites were numbered from the age of thirty years and upward: and their number by their polls, man by man, was thirty and eight thousand [1 Chron. 23:2-3].

When the Levites were numbered, as they came out of Egypt, there were about eight thousand of them. Now there are thirty-eight thousand. They have increased in numbers, as God said they would.

Not only did David gather the materials for the construction of the temple, but he also organized the Levites to serve in the temple.

> **Of which, twenty and four thousand were to set forward the work of the house of the LORD; and six thousand were officers and judges:**

> **Moreover four thousand were porters; and four thousand praised the LORD with the instruments which I made, said David, to praise therewith [1 Chron. 23:4–5].**

David put a great emphasis on music. Think of it—four thousand praised the Lord with music!

You will recall that the Levites served in the tabernacle. The family of Aaron served as the priests, and the three families of Levites had their duties.

> **And David divided them into courses among the sons of Levi, namely, Gershon, Kohath, and Merari [1 Chron. 23:6].**

The Gershonites, the Kohathites, and the Merarites all had definite assignments in caring for the tabernacle. On the wilderness march they were responsible for moving the tabernacle. They took it down and they put it up. The Gershonites carried the curtains and the coverings. The Kohathites carried the articles of furniture. The Merarites carried the boards and the bars and the pillars. As we saw in the Book of Numbers, it was quite an undertaking to take down the tabernacle in the morning and reassemble it in the evening and restore the service of it.

> **And also unto the Levites; they shall no more carry the tabernacle, nor any vessels of it for the service thereof [1 Chron. 23:26].**

The Levites' assignment to carry the tabernacle through the wilderness is over. Now they have a new ministry for the Lord.

Again, this is something that I wish we could learn. God has raised up may fine Christian organizations; then after they have served their purpose, there are folk who try to preserve them. Some of them are as dead as a dodo bird. They do not serve any good purpose. When God is through with a thing, He is through with it, my friend. It is time to get something new going. To the Levites, God is saying in effect, "We're not going to be trotting around in the wilderness any more. Now we will have a temple and your service is going to be different." Oh, my friend, let's keep step with God and do something that is alive and moving!

The Levites now have a new service. The staves are removed from the ark. It will not be moved again. It is to remain permanently in Jerusalem on the threshingfloor of Ornan. David has bought the place, and the temple will be erected there. In the temple there will be a great deal for the Levites to do; so David organizes them into shifts, selected by lot. They will serve for a period of time, then they will retire—have time off. This is the way David organized the service of the temple.

DIVISION OF THE SONS OF AARON

In chapter 24, David gives the divisions of the sons of Aaron into orders to serve in the temple.

> Now these are the divisions of the sons of Aaron. The sons of Aaron; Nadab, and Abihu, Eleazar, and Ithamar.

> But Nadab and Abihu died before their father, and had no children: therefore Eleazar and Ithamar executed the priest's office [1 Chron. 24:1–2].

Aaron's sons were priests, and this record takes us back to the time they were in the wilderness. The tenth chapter of Leviticus records the sin of Nadab and Abihu and their resulting death.

And David distributed them, both Zadok of the sons of Eleazar, and Ahimelech of the sons of Ithamar, according to their offices in their service [1 Chron. 24:3].

This is a very highly organized procedure that David is putting into force. David not only bought the property where the temple is to stand, he gathered the building materials, and now he organizes the priests to serve. This is my reason for saying that the temple was David's temple, not Solomon's temple.

Thus were they divided by lot, one sort with another; for the governors of the sanctuary, and governors of the house of God, were of the sons of Eleazar, and of the sons of Ithamar [1 Chron. 24:5].

There were twenty-four orders. These sons were organized into orders. One group would come and do their work under the direction of one of the sons, then another group under the direction of another son would come and replace them. I think it must have been quite interesting to watch. Not long ago I had the privilege of watching the changing of the guard at Buckingham Palace in London. What a ceremony, what a show that is! I have a suspicion that the kings of the past would be surprised to see how it is being done today, and I'm not sure they would be in favor of it. I think they really overdo the pageantry. However, I imagine that when the Levites changed shifts for temple service it was done with precision and order.

The families of the Levites had grown so in number that it would be impossible for all of them to serve at once. As we have seen, from the time of Moses to the time of David, the Levites had increased from about eight thousand to thirty-eight thousand. For this reason David divided them into orders.

In the next section, the sons of Kohath are divided, and following them, the sons of Merari were divided. David planned that each family would carry on the service of the temple.

SINGERS AND ORCHESTRA ARE ORGANIZED

In chapter 25, we find that David organized the singers in the same way.

> Moreover David and the captains of the host separated to the service of the sons of Asaph, and of Heman, and of Jeduthun, who should prophesy with harps, with psalteries, and with cymbals: and the number of the workmen according to their service was:
>
> Of the sons of Asaph; Zaccur, and Joseph, and Nethaniah, and Asarelah, the sons of Asaph under the hands of Asaph, which prophesied according to the order of the king [1 Chron. 25:1-2].

All of this was organized before the temple was built. You will find in the marvelous sixty-eighth Psalm, a song of David, these words: "Thy God hath commanded thy strength: strengthen, O God, that which thou has wrought for us. Because of thy temple at Jerusalem shall kings bring presents unto thee" (Ps. 68:28–29). David is anticipating the time the temple will stand in Jerusalem as a testimony to the world. Long before the temple was built, the singers were gathering in Jerusalem to worship God, and this is one of the songs they sang. You see, David had brought up the ark to Jerusalem, and it was kept in a tent. Also there was an altar there on the threshingfloor of Ornan where David, you recall, had offered sacrifices—burnt sacrifices and peace offerings—unto God.

> So the number of them, with their brethren that were instructed in the songs of the LORD, even all that were cunning, was two hundred fourscore and eight.
>
> And they cast lots, ward against ward as well the small as the great, the teacher as the scholar [1 Chron. 25:7-8].

They were divided by lot into twenty-four groups. This would mean that twice each month there would be a change in the service. Each of these would serve only two weeks out of the year. Then they would go back to the city from which they had come and there was service for them to perform in their hometowns. These priests and Levites served as instructors and in many ways throughout the land of Israel.

I believe all this organization was one of the greatest feats of David's reign. It is the thing which God noted and recorded here.

PORTERS AND GUARDS ARE ORGANIZED

Not only are the priests organized, but there are others. Who is going to sweep out the place? And who is going to guard it? In chapter 26 we see that David had all of this carefully planned.

> Concerning the divisions of the porters: Of the Korhites
> was Meshelemiah the son of Kore, of the sons of Asaph
> [1 Chron. 26:1].

They were divided in much the same way. And while all these people are serving, there will need to be someone on guard duty. There will be guards placed to watch the gates and they will be on duty twenty-four hours a day.

> And they cast lots, as well the small as the great, ac-
> cording to the house of their fathers, for every gate
> [1 Chron. 26:13].

Every gate was covered by guards.

TREASURERS APPOINTED

They will have to have a treasurer to keep track of the finances for the temple. He will have to make his report.

> And of the Levites, Ahijah was over the treasures of the
> house of God, and over the treasures of the dedicated
> things [1 Chron. 26:20].

The treasurers were responsible for the vast store of dedicated things which had been accumulating.

> **Which Shelomith and his brethren were over all the treasures of the dedicated things, which David the king, and the chief fathers, the captains over thousands and hundreds, and the captains of the host, had dedicated.**

> **Out of the spoils won in battles did they dedicate to maintain the house of the LORD.**

> **And all that Samuel the seer, and Saul the son of Kish, and Abner the son of Ner, and Joab the son of Zeruiah, had dedicated; and whosoever had dedicated any thing, it was under the hand of Shelomith, and of his brethren [1 Chron. 26:26–28].**

OFFICERS AND JUDGES APPOINTED

The Levites were to be the judges, you see. They also were to act in official capacities in many ways. It was God's original purpose that Israel be a theocracy with Him ruling, and with the tabernacle in the center of the community, and with the priesthood getting the decisions from God Himself. This changed because of the failure of the Levites. So God raised up judges, and the people demanded a king. This is the reason David is now on the throne. Although Israel is now a monarchy, David is putting great emphasis upon bringing it back under God's control.

CAPTAINS AND PRINCES APPOINTED

> **Now the children of Israel after their number, to wit, the chief fathers and captains of thousands and hundreds, and their officers that served the king in any matter of the courses, which came in and went out month by month throughout all the months of the year, of every course were twenty and four thousand [1 Chron. 27:1].**

Twelve captains were appointed, each man serving one month of the year over a course of twenty-four thousand.

> **Furthermore over the tribes of Israel: the ruler of the Reubenites was Eliezer the son of Zichri: of the Simeonites, Shephatiah the son of Maachah [1 Chron. 27:16].**

And so on—one man from each of the twelve tribes so that there were twelve princes of the tribes of Israel.

Now notice this verse:

> **But David took not the number of them from twenty years old and under: because the Lord had said he would increase Israel like to the stars of the heavens [1 Chron. 27:23].**

David took the census before because he didn't believe God; it was an act of unbelief. God told him, "Trust Me. I'll supply all the men you need for your army." Now David does not take a census. He rests upon God's promise.

Chapter 27 concludes with a list of officers which are in charge of King David's personal properties.

DAVID'S FINAL MESSAGE

In the last two chapters of 1 Chronicles, David calls together all the leaders in Israel. It is a great meeting, and it will be one of his last because he has come to the end of his life. He will have a message for Israel and a message for Solomon that the nation will hear. This is a wise move on David's part.

> **And David assembled all the princes of Israel, the princes of the tribes, and the captains of the companies that ministered to the king by course, and the captains over the thousands, and captains over the hundreds,**

> and the stewards over all the substance and possession
> of the king, and of his sons, with the officers, and with
> the mighty men, and with all the valiant men, unto Jeru-
> salem [1 Chron. 28:1].

These are the men who are responsible for the leadership of the nation.

> **Then David the king stood up upon his feet, and said,
> Hear me, my brethren, and my people: As for me, I had
> in mine heart to build an house of rest for the ark of the
> covenant of the LORD, and for the footstool of our God,
> and had made ready for the building [1 Chron. 28:2].**

Despite his age, he forces himself to stand as he delivers this important and final message to his people.

> **But God said unto me, Thou shalt not build an house for
> my name, because thou hast been a man of war, and
> hast shed blood [1 Chron. 28:3].**

David will not get away from this position of frank confession to the
people. He gives the reason God will not allow him to build the temple: he has been a bloody man.

> **And of all my sons, (for the LORD hath given me many
> sons,) he hath chosen Solomon my son to sit upon the
> throne of the kingdom of the LORD over Israel [1 Chron.
> 28:5].**

David makes it clear that God had chosen and commissioned Solomon. He turns over all the responsibility for Solomon to God. This
gives the impression that Solomon was not David's choice.

> **And he said unto me, Solomon thy son, he shall build
> my house and my courts: for I have chosen him to be my
> son, and I will be his father [1 Chron. 28:6].**

David's heart and soul were in the preparation for building the temple. God would not permit him to build it himself, and he acquiesced to the will of God. However, he made every preparation of material and workmen, and he encourages Solomon to build.

Now David gives the blueprint to Solomon.

> **Then David gave to Solomon his son the pattern of the porch, and of the houses thereof, and of the treasuries thereof, and of the upper chambers thereof, and of the inner parlours thereof, and of the place of the mercy seat.**
>
> **And the pattern of all that he had by the spirit, of the courts of the house of the LORD, and of all the chambers round about, of the treasuries of the house of God, and of the treasuries of the dedicated things:**
>
> **Also for the courses of the priests and the Levites, and for all the work of the service of the house of the LORD, and for all the vessels of service in the house of the LORD [1 Chron. 28:11-13].**

Just as Moses had been given the blueprint for the tabernacle, it was David (not Solomon) who had been given the blueprint for the temple.

Many models of the temple have been made, and they are very impressive. Obviously, they are not as the temple really looked. However, in the new section of Jerusalem there is a new, exclusive hotel called the Holyland Hotel. On the grounds of that hotel is a model of the city of Jerusalem. This is not a little cheap thing that has been thrown together, or something made by a person who doesn't really know what he is doing. But it was made after years of research by Jews in that land. They have made a model of the entire city. I was thrilled to see how it looked. The fact of the matter is, I took pictures of it myself. They say that they have it looking as it did in the days of Herod. Well, the days of Herod are the days of Christ. It is the way it looked in the days of our Lord and in New Testament times. And, my friend, it just doesn't look like the models we have had in the past. I believe it is probably nearer to how it really looked than any other model which has been made before.

The model is built in the spacious gardens in the rear of the hotel. The scale is 1:50 (2 centimeters equal 1 meter; 1/4 inch equals 1 foot). As you walk around it, it gives you a real conception of how Jerusalem looked (see reproductions on pages 120 and 153).

The model of the temple has a simplicity about it, and I believe that is how it actually was. Yet the details in Kings and Chronicles seem very complicated. It is not as simple as the tabernacle was, yet there is a simplicity about it. It was neither the architecture nor the size that was impressive, but the beauty and wealth that was bestowed upon it. Although the floor plan of Herod's temple was the same as God gave to David, it was not nearly as expensive as David's temple. Herod built the temple to gratify man, while David lavished the wealth of his kingdom upon it to glorify God.

David said to Solomon, "You don't need to stint. I have gathered enough material to make it magnificent." It was ornate, covered with gold and silver and precious stones.

It has always been my feeling that a church building should correspond to the neighborhood in which it is located. I do not like to see great cathedrals erected in poor communities and slum areas. In a rich neighborhood, you would want a building commensurate with the homes. However, today the emphasis should not be upon buildings because our bodies are the temple of God.

Of course David had no notion of making a temple for God to live in. God does not live in a box! Solomon in his prayer of dedication very frankly said, ". . . behold, the heaven and heaven of heavens cannot contain thee; how much less this house that I have builded?" (1 Kings 8:27). The whole created universe cannot contain God. How could a little house contain Him? The temple was to be a meeting place. God met with man there. And the temple was for the glory and honor of God. Today God does neither dwell nor meet you in a building. He dwells in individuals by the Holy Spirit.

David assigned the proportionate *weight* of gold or of silver that was to go into the articles of furniture and instruments of service.

> He gave of gold by weight for things of gold, for all in-
> struments of all manner of service; silver also for all in-
> struments of silver by weight, for all instruments of
> every kind of service:
>
> Even the weight for the candlesticks of gold, and for
> their lamps of gold, by weight for every candlestick, and
> for the lamps thereof: and for the candlesticks of silver
> by weight, both for the candlestick, and also for the
> lamps thereof, according to the use of every candlestick
> [1 Chron. 28:14–15].

The thought here is that there was to be no stinting. There was nothing parsimonious about the temple. It was a great expanse and expenditure of the wealth of the kingdom of David. Keep in mind that David did this in order to honor God.

> All this, said David, the Lord made me understand in
> writing by his hand upon me, even all the works of this
> pattern [1 Chron. 28:19].

This is a remarkable verse. The pattern of the temple was from God just as much as the pattern of the tabernacle was from God.

God gave the pattern, the blueprint; God selected the site—the threshingfloor of Ornan; God inspired and encouraged David but would not allow him to do the actual building.

> And David said to Solomon his son, Be strong and of
> good courage, and do it: fear not, nor be dismayed: for
> the Lord God, even my God, will be with thee; he will
> not fail thee, nor forsake thee, until thou hast finished
> all the work for the service of the house of the Lord
> [1 Chron. 28:20].

David is enthusiastic and excited about the temple, and he is doing all he can to stimulate Solomon. He wants Solomon to get busy on it.

> And, behold, the courses of the priests and the Levites, even they shall be with thee for all the service of the house of God: and there shall be with thee for all manner of workmanship every willing skilful man, for any manner of service: also the princes and all the people will be wholly at thy commandment [1 Chron. 28:21].

You see, David had everyone in the kingdom—the priests, the workmen, the princes, the Levites—all stimulated and stirred up to do this. All Solomon had to do was to carry out his orders and follow the plans David had set up for him.

DAVID EXHORTS THE PEOPLE

As we come to chapter 29, we find that the emphasis shifts from the temple to the kingdom, although he had in mind to his dying day that the center of the kingdom would be the temple.

This is David's last message to his people. You will recall that when old Jacob was dying he called in his sons. When Moses reached the end of his life, he had a message for all twelve tribes. Now David has a message for his people as he comes to the end of his life.

> Furthermore David the king said unto all the congregation, Solomon my son, whom alone God hath chosen, is yet young and tender, and the work is great: for the palace is not for man, but for the Lord God [1 Chron. 29:1].

When David says that Solomon is young and tender, he means that he is a sissy and inexperienced. Old David is a veteran. Although he is a gracious, generous man, he can be hard-boiled. Solomon is a novice.

> Now I have prepared with all my might for the house of my God the gold for things to be made of gold, and the silver for things of silver, and the brass for things of brass, the iron for things of iron, and wood for things of wood; onyx stones, and stones to be set, glistering

> stones, and of divers colours, and all manner of precious stones, and marble stones in abundance.

> Moreover, because I have set my affection to the house of my God, I have of mine own proper good, of gold and silver, which I have given to the house of my God, over and above all that I have prepared for the holy house [1 Chron. 29:2–3].

David says, "I have prepared with all my might for the house of my God." Oh, to have the heart of David, and put God first in our lives! These are gifts of his own individual property.

> The gold for things of gold, and the silver for things of silver, and for all manner of work to be made by the hands of artificers. And who then is willing to consecrate his service this day unto the LORD? [1 Chron. 29:5].

David has set the example. There was no stinting or holding back in his giving. Then he put out the challenge to his people.

> Then the chief of the fathers and princes of the tribes of Israel, and the captains of thousands and of hundreds, with the rulers of the king's work, offered willingly [1 Chron. 29:6].

Now there is a response on the part of the people.

> And gave for the service of the house of God of gold five thousand talents and ten thousand drams, and of silver ten thousand talents, and of brass eighteen thousand talents, and one hundred thousand talents of iron.

> And they with whom precious stones were found gave them to the treasure of the house of the LORD, by the hand of Jehiel the Gershonite [1 Chron. 29:7–8].

The people gave generously, and they gave with joy.

> **Then the people rejoiced, for that they offered willingly, because with perfect heart they offered willingly to the LORD: and David the king also rejoiced with great joy [1 Chron. 29:9].**

It was a great thrill to David to see his people give so willingly toward the enrichment of the temple.

My friend, I used to see a motto that read: "Give till it hurts." That motto may be all right for the world, but it is not God's motto. If it hurts you to give, don't give! God wants you to give when it brings joy to your heart and life. Give hilariously, Paul said. This is what the people are doing here, and it was a time of great rejoicing.

> **Wherefore David blessed the LORD before all the congregation: and David said, Blessed be thou, LORD God of Israel our father, for ever and ever [1 Chron. 29:10].**

Notice that David called God the father of the nation Israel. In the Old Testament He was not called the father of individuals. In fact, David never called Him Father. God called David His servant. That is very interesting. The Mosaic Law never made a son of God. Only faith in Jesus Christ can make us sons of God.

DAVID PRAYS

Now we have the great kingdom prayer of David.

> **Thine, O Lord, is the greatness, and the power, and the glory, and the victory, and the majesty: for all that is in the heaven and in the earth is thine; thine is the kingdom, O LORD, and thou art exalted as head above all [1 Chron. 29:11].**

Do these words sound familiar to you? You will recall that when the disciples asked the Lord Jesus to teach them to pray, He gave them a model prayer. He took them right back here to David's prayer. "Thy kingdom come" was in the heart of David. These are words of brevity and simplicity, and they gather up the aspiration and hopes of centuries. This is one of the greatest prayers in the Scriptures and certainly in the Old Testament. It is all-comprehensive, majestic and filled with adoration, praise and thanksgiving. It repudiates all human merit and declares human dependence upon God. It reveals self-humiliation, confession, and dedication of self. It admits that all belongs to God. David recognized that the kingdom is God's. The Lord Jesus laid hold of this to teach His disciples.

The Scriptural concept of the Kingdom is both an eternal kingdom and a temporal kingdom. It is a universal kingdom and a local kingdom. It is immediate, and it is mediated. Generally speaking, it is the reign of heaven over earth.

When God created Adam, He gave him dominion. Now what does He mean by "the kingdom"? It is the rule of God over the earth. It is a prayer for the recovery of the earth, to bring it back under the rule of God.

I hope you don't think that God is ruling the earth today. If He were, we would not have heartbreak, tears, disappointments, nor wars. This is the kingdom we should pray for. It will only come through divine protocol, and the divine aspects will be adhered to. Man will not be able to build this kingdom here on this earth; only the Lord Jesus Christ can establish the Kingdom. "Thine is the kingdom."

It is my personal feeling that the so-called Lord's Prayer is not for public praying. It is not just something to add to the ritual of a Sunday morning service. I believe it is good for private devotion. "Thine is the kingdom" ought to be the prayer of every believer. David was looking forward to the coming of the Kingdom here upon this earth. That will be a glorious day!

But who am I, and what is my people, that we should be able to offer so willingly after this sort? for all things

come of thee, and of thine own have we given thee
[1 Chron. 29:14].

The very interesting thing is that you can't give God anything because
it belongs to Him in the first place. But He can bless you when you
give, and He will bless you. The reason some of us are so poor and
narrow-minded and little is because we are not generous with God.
God can only bless us when we open our hearts to Him.

O LORD our God, all this store that we have prepared to
build thee an house for thine holy name cometh of thine
hand, and is all thine own [1 Chron. 29:16].

Oh, how we need to recognize this!

SOLOMON COMES TO THE THRONE

Now the people, having blessed God and having offered sacrifices to
Him, make Solomon king.

And did eat and drink before the LORD on that day with
great gladness. And they made Solomon the son of
David king the second time, and anointed him unto the
LORD to be the chief governor, and Zadok to be priest.

Then Solomon sat on the throne of the LORD as king instead of David his father, and prospered; and all Israel
obeyed him [1 Chron. 29:22-23].

The kingdom was united behind Solomon, and he exercised royal authority before David's death.

DAVID DIES

Thus David the son of Jesse reigned over all Israel.

And the time that he reigned over Israel was forty years;
seven years reigned he in Hebron, and thirty and three
years reigned he in Jerusalem.

And he died in a good old age, full of days, riches, and honour: and Solomon his son reigned in his stead [1 Chron. 29:26-28].

This is the record that God has given. He wants you to know how He feels about David. Maybe you don't like David; God does. I am glad that the Lord loved David and dealt with him as He did, because David is so human. This encourages me. Vernon McGee is very human also, and I have found that God will deal with him just as graciously and just as severely as He dealt with David. The Lord is good. The Lord is wonderful! You and I cannot build Him a temple, but we can offer the temples of our bodies to Him. He doesn't get very much when he gets me, but He does have me. Oh, what joy it is to be committed to Him!

(For Bibliography to 1 Chronicles, see Bibliography at the end of 2 Chronicles.)

2 CHRONICLES

2 CHRONICLES

The Book of
2 CHRONICLES

INTRODUCTION

We have seen at the conclusion of 1 Chronicles that David had as-
sembled all the material for the temple, had arranged for the man-
power, had given encouragement to the leaders of the nation Israel and
to the people, organized the service of the temple, provided all the
money, and told Solomon to get busy. Now in 2 Chronicles Solomon is
going to get busy.

We have seen that 1 Chronicles was actually all about David. It
began with those long genealogies. There was a lot of begetting from
Adam right on down to David. Why was the genealogy given? Because it led to David. Why David? Because David leads to Christ, and
the New Testament opens with: "The book of the generation of Jesus
Christ, the son of David ..." (Matt. 1:1). That is the reason it is given.

I will mention again that in the Books of Chronicles we are getting
God's viewpoint. In the Books of Samuel and the Books of Kings we
were given man's viewpoint. This does not mean that those books
were not inspired. They are inspired. But He gives first the human
viewpoint, then the divine viewpoint. And the emphasis is on David.
Where did David put the emphasis? He put it on the building of the
temple of God.

In 2 Chronicles we will find two major themes. The first is the
building of the temple. The second theme is revival. This book covers
chronologically the same period as Kings but gives certain notable
emphases.

The first nine chapters are given over to the reign of Solomon. Six
of those chapters are concerning the building of the temple. It is pretty

evident where God is putting the emphasis. The building of the temple was Solomon's greatest accomplishment. People always think of Solomon in regard to all the wives that he had. That is quite spectacular—no question about it—but it is not where God puts the emphasis. His having many wives wasn't in the will of God. That was contrary to the will of God, and that was a factor which brought about the division of the kingdom. Don't tell me he got by with it. He didn't. Sin always brings judgment. It doesn't matter who it is that commits the sin, it will bring judgment. The only way that anyone can get to heaven is to have a Savior, and that Savior is Jesus Christ.

So the first major theme of 2 Chronicles is Solomon's construction of the temple. That is important. God thought it was important and inspired the writer to devote six chapters to it.

From chapter 10 to the end of the book the kingdom is divided. We have seen from the Books of Kings that after the kingdom was divided there were many kings who ruled and that most of those kings were not very attractive. We have made the statement that there was not a single good king in Israel, the northern kingdom. So we find in Chronicles that there is no emphasis on the kingdom of Israel at all. The emphasis in this book is on the southern kingdom, Judah, and on David's line. That was a pretty bad lot, too. However, there were five of those kings who were outstanding: Asa, Jehoshaphat, Joash, Hezekiah, Josiah. These five kings were the means of bringing revival back to the nation. God puts the emphasis on revival, and we will spend a great deal of time talking about revival in this section.

Many years ago I belonged to a group of ministers who were praying for revival. I finally quit going because the attitude was that if we prayed hard enough, God would send revival.

May I say that God is sovereign. We are not going to make God do anything. God has a program and He is not about to change His program for you or for me. The important thing is for you and for me to get in step with God! I tell you, the will of God comes out of eternity, down through the centuries, and moves on through the centuries into eternity. God pity the little man who gets in front of that steam roller. It will go right over you, brother.

Someone will be sure to say he doesn't like that. May I remind you that we are the creatures. The creature does not try to get God to do something. It is God who is trying to get us to do something. That is the big problem. We tend to get things backwards. It is not God's duty to obey us. It is our duty to obey God. You may ask, "Well, doesn't God want to send revival?" Sure He does. And aren't we to meet His conditions? Yes, but I don't think they are meeting His conditions. It is interesting that the spiritual movement which has come about in our day did not come by these perspicuous theologians putting down conditions and the churches following them. The spiritual movement is not even in the church today. Most of the churches are as dead as dodo birds. The movement today is not among these brainy theologians. I get so tired and weary of reading their material today. Oh, they speak *ex cathedra*: they have all the answers! They have answers but no action—there's no spiritual movement.

Out of some of our seminaries today there is coming a great deal of material; these professors write with great authority. They have a lot of authority, but they haven't any action. (And I really don't think they have much authority.) May I say to you today, my friend, we need to learn to bow to the *will* of God and to come in very close to Him: cast ourselves upon Him. We're going to see that there are certain men— even kings—whom God used in a marvelous way, because they were willing to *take* orders and not *give* orders. I believe that the biggest hindrance to revival is the church leadership. They are the ones who are holding it back—and have been for years.

You may be saying, "Why, McGee, you sound like a revolutionary!" My friend, I have been a revolutionary ever since I entered the ministry, but nobody ever listened to me. I have said from the very beginning that we don't bring revival by listening to the theologians. We need to listen to the Word of God. And that is the reason I am trying to give out the Word of God. Now let me confess that I have had some ideas myself. But I am retired now, and I have discovered that the great ideas and the great programs that I had worked out were never used by God. I am beginning to suspect that revival could not come if God followed my plans either! It is ". . . Not by might, nor by power, but by my spirit, saith the LORD of hosts" (Zech. 4:6). It is not by brain nor by brawn, but by the Holy Spirit. It is hard to learn that, by the way.

The spotlight of this book is on the kings who followed in the line of David. Special prominence is given to the five kings in whose reigns were periods of revival, renewal, and reformation. The book concludes with the decree of Cyrus after the seventy years of captivity. No record is given of the period of the captivity. That was "time out" in God's program. Remember that this is the record from God's point of view.

OUTLINE

I. Solomon's Reign, Chapters 1—9

II. Division of the Kingdom and History of Judah, Chapters 10—36
Reformations Given Prominence:
A. Asa's, Chapters 14—16
B. Jehoshaphat's, Chapters 17—20
C. Joash's, Chapters 23—24
D. Hezekiah's, Chapters 29—32
E. Josiah's, Chapters 34—35

OUTLINE

CHAPTER 1

THEME: Solomon becomes king and prays for wisdom

And Solomon the son of David was strengthened in his kingdom, and the LORD his God was with him, and magnified him exceedingly [2 Chron. 1:1].

You will remember that I made the point that Solomon was not David's choice. He was God's choice. I really do not think that David wanted Solomon to be the next king. I think it is obvious that his choice would have been the boy who rebelled against him, Absalom. He loved Absalom. It broke David's heart when Absalom was slain. It crushed him. You remember that when he sent out his army he gave specific instructions to each of his captains that Absalom was not to be hurt. David was willing to sacrifice everything for that boy. He loved him. I think that Absalom had a lot of David's temperament. I believe in some ways he was very much like David, but he was not God's choice. God had chosen Solomon, and God is going to bless Solomon. God chooses the weak things of this world, and God is going to use Solomon. The strength of God is revealed in weakness. David is gone now. He had been a great man but Solomon is young and tender, a weakling. God will use Solomon and will allow Solomon to do the actual building of the temple.

"Solomon the son of David was strengthened in his kingdom"; the kingdom will come to its zenith under Solomon. David put the foundation under the kingdom. "And the LORD his God was with him, and magnified him exceedingly." How gracious God is!

We will see that Solomon will disobey God. He will come to the place where God will repudiate him and tell him that He will divide the kingdom. Solomon was responsible for that division. The reason God did not divide the kingdom during the reign of Solomon was for the sake of David, not for the sake of Solomon.

> Then Solomon spake unto all Israel, to the captains of
> thousands and of hundreds, and to the judges, and to
> every governor in all Israel, the chief of the fathers
> [2 Chron. 1:2].

You see, Solomon has a meeting of the leadership of Israel here.

> So Solomon, and all the congregation with him, went to
> the high place that was at Gibeon; for there was the tab-
> ernacle of the congregation of God, which Moses the
> servant of the LORD had made in the wilderness
> [2 Chron. 1:3].

The tabernacle was up there at Gibeon. We must remember that the ark
was brought by David to Jerusalem, and it is there in a tent. But they
couldn't come directly and immediately to God. This is tremendous!
The way to God was through that tabernacle because the brazen altar
was there, and that brazen altar speaks of the Cross of Christ. They had
to go there to approach God.

You and I must come before God in the same way. There is an idea
today that anybody, under any circumstances, can just rush into the
presence of God and that God has His listening-ear out. The Bible
teaches that the Lord does not always hear prayers. Listen to the words
of Peter: "For the eyes of the Lord are over the righteous, and his ears
are open unto their prayers: but the face of the Lord is against them
that do evil" (1 Pet. 3:12). God never said He would hear the prayers of
those who do evil. I believe that the only prayer the sinner can pray to
God is to go to Him and accept His mercy in Christ Jesus. If you wish
to approach God, you must approach Him through the Cross.

This is what Solomon does. He takes the leaders and they go to
Gibeon where the tabernacle and the brazen altar are. He is being
smart at the beginning of his reign.

> But the ark of God had David brought up from Kirjath-
> jearim to the place which David had prepared for it: for
> he had pitched a tent for it at Jerusalem.

> Moreover the brasen altar, that Bezaleel the son of Uri,
> the son of Hur, had made, he put before the tabernacle of
> the LORD: and Solomon and the congregation sought
> unto it [2 Chron. 1:4–5].

The way to God is through the brazen altar. They couldn't go to Him
through the ark. In other words, you and I don't come immediately to
God. The way of the Cross leads home. There is no other way.

> And Solomon went up thither to the brasen altar before
> the LORD, which was at the tabernacle of the congrega-
> tion, and offered a thousand burnt offerings upon it
> [2 Chron. 1:6].

They certainly are not stingy in their sacrifices. You will notice all the
way through this period that there was an abundance of sacrifices during Solomon's reign.

> In that night did God appear unto Solomon, and said
> unto him, Ask what I shall give thee.
>
> And Solomon said unto God, Thou hast shewed great
> mercy unto David my father, and hast made me to reign
> in his stead.
>
> Now, O LORD God, let thy promise unto David my father
> be established: for thou hast made me king over a peo-
> ple like the dust of the earth in multitude [2 Chron.
> 1:7–9].

God has made good a promise not only to David but to Abraham:
"Your offspring will be like the dust"—you can't number them.

> Give me now wisdom and knowledge, that I may go out
> and come in before this people: for who can judge this
> thy people, that is so great? [2 Chron. 1:10].

A model of the Temple reconstructed by Herod
(Holyland Hotel, Jerusalem; Photo by Ronald E. Pitkin).

People commend Solomon and say that he was so smart to ask for wisdom. God gave him credit for asking that. But where did he get the idea? If we turn back to chapter 22 of 1 Chronicles, we read, "And David said to Solomon, My son, as for me, it was in my mind to build an house unto the name of the LORD my God: but the word of the LORD came to me, saying, Thou hast shed blood abundantly, and hast made great wars: thou shalt not build an house unto my name, because thou hast shed much blood upon the earth in my sight . . . Now, my son, the LORD be with thee; and prosper thou, and build the house of the LORD thy God, as he hath said of thee. Only the LORD give thee wisdom and understanding, and give thee charge concerning Israel, that thou mayest keep the law of the LORD thy God" (1 Chron. 22:7–8 and 11–12). At least Solomon was listening to his father. When David had said, "The Lord give thee wisdom and understanding," he remembered that. So when the Lord asked, "What do you want, Solomon?" he said, "I need wisdom and understanding." God gives him credit for it, though.

> **And God said to Solomon, Because this was in thine heart, and thou hast not asked riches, wealth, or honour, nor the life of thine enemies, neither yet hast asked long life; but hast asked wisdom and knowledge for thyself, that thou mayest judge my people, over whom I have made thee king:**
>
> **Wisdom and knowledge is granted unto thee: and I will give thee riches, and wealth, and honour, such as none of the kings have had that have been before thee, neither shall there any after thee have the like [2 Chron. 1:11–12].**

God grants his request for wisdom and gives him other blessings besides. I want you to notice, though, that the request was for wisdom to rule the people. Solomon did not ask for spiritual discernment. We will see that Solomon lacked spiritual discernment in his own life. Although he was given divine wisdom to rule, he did not seem to have wisdom to order his personal life.

And Solomon gathered chariots and horsemen: and he had a thousand and four hundred chariots, and twelve thousand horsemen, which he placed in the chariot cities, and with the king at Jerusalem.

And the king made silver and gold at Jerusalem as plenteous as stones, and cedar trees made he as the sycomore trees that are in the vale for abundance [2 Chron. 1:14-15].

The sycamore tree grows over there today, but you don't see many cedar trees. He made cedar trees as abundant as the sycamore, and silver and gold like the stones. If you have ever been in that land or even seen pictures of it, you know that there are rocks and stones everywhere. There are more rocks in that land than any place I have ever been. Imagine Solomon making silver and gold as commonplace as those stones!

And Solomon had horses brought out of Egypt, and linen yarn: the king's merchants received the linen yarn at a price.

And they fetched up, and brought forth out of Egypt a chariot for six hundred shekels of silver, and an horse for an hundred and fifty: and so brought they out horses for all the kings of the Hittites, and for the kings of Syria, by their means [2 Chron. 1:16-17].

You will notice that he is already getting into an area which was forbidden to him. God had told them when the day should come that they would have a king ". . . he shall not multiply horses to himself, nor cause the people to return to Egypt, to the end that he should multiply horses: forasmuch as the LORD hath said unto you, Ye shall henceforth return no more that way. Neither shall he multiply wives to himself, that his heart turn not away: neither shall he greatly multiply to himself silver and gold" (Deut. 17:16–17). Solomon is amassing horses and he is becoming personally wealthy. We will find that he will also multiply wives to himself.

CHAPTERS 2—4

THEME: Construction of the temple

Solomon moves forward now according to the instructions that David his father had given him.

SOLOMON PREPARES TO BUILD

And Solomon determined to build an house for the name of the LORD, and an house for his kingdom.

And Solomon told out threescore and ten thousand men to bear burdens, and fourscore thousand to hew in the mountain, and three thousand and six hundred to oversee them [2 Chron. 2:1-2].

The blueprints are laid out, and Solomon begins the organization to build. Notice that building the temple is the part of Solomon's reign that God emphasizes.

And Solomon sent to Huram the king of Tyre, saying, As thou didst deal with David my father, and didst send him cedars to build him an house to dwell therein, even so deal with me [2 Chron. 2:3].

Hiram loved David, and David loved Hiram. On this basis Solomon appeals to him. I think Hiram had problems with Solomon, as we shall see. He had been very generous with David, but he finds Solomon a little difficult to deal with.

Behold, I build an house to the name of the LORD my God, to dedicate it to him, and to burn before him sweet incense, and for the continual shewbread, and for the

> burnt offerings morning and evening, on the sabbaths,
> and on the new moons, and on the solemn feasts of the
> LORD our God. This is an ordinance for ever to Israel
> [2 Chron. 2:4].

Notice that this is to be an ordinance *forever*. There have been criticisms of the restoration of temple sacrifices during the Millennium. Since the animal sacrifices pointed forward to the sacrifice of Christ on the Cross, why would animal sacrifices be resumed during the Millennium? Because God ordained it; that is answer enough. They will be meaningful, of course, and will be a reminder of the sacrifice of the Lord Jesus Christ.

> And the house which I build is great: for great is our
> God above all gods [2 Chron. 2:5].

In our day what makes a thing great? What makes a man great? What makes a nation great? What makes a church great? God, my friend. This is something else we are losing sight of.

> But who is able to build him an house, seeing the heaven
> and heaven of heavens cannot contain him? who am I
> then, that I should build him an house, save only to burn
> sacrifice before him? [2 Chron. 2:6].

It was by a sacrifice that they approached God. And the only way you and I can come to God is through the sacrifice of the Lord Jesus Christ. The important thing to note here is that Solomon had no misgivings as to who God was, or whether God would occupy and live in that house.

I once read an article about a theologian who made the statement that what Solomon was attempting to do was build a little house to put God in a box and that the people had the idea that God should be put in a box—that He could be held there. May I say to you that Solomon had no conception like that at all; neither did the people. They were much farther advanced than a great many people are today, even in our churches. Many people call the church "God's house." Well, God doesn't occupy a house. He never did. The temple was a place to make sacrifices. It was a place of *approach* to God. And it had to be worthy of Him. It was highly ornate, very beautiful. It was not very large compared to other buildings of that day. For instance, if you put the temple that Solomon built down beside the temple of Diana in Ephesus or the pyramids, it would be a pygmy. But it made up for its small size in its wealth—the tremendous amount of silver and gold that went into it.

> **Send me now therefore a man cunning to work in gold, and in silver, and in brass, and in iron, and in purple, and crimson, and blue, and that can skill to grave with the cunning men that are with me in Judah and in Jerusalem, whom David my father did provide [2 Chron. 2:7].**

You see, they had to get the skilled workmen from the outside, because the Israelites were an agricultural people, as God intended them to be. It is interesting to see that when Jewish people return to Israel in our day, they return to the soil. I have traveled from one end of Israel to the other end, and from the Dead Sea to the Mediterranean Sea, and some of the finest farms I have ever seen are there. I do not believe there is land anywhere any richer than the Valley of Esdraelon where Megiddo is located. It certainly is rich country. In Solomon's day the nation Israel did not have artificers or artisans, and they had to call upon Hiram for those.

> **Send me also cedar trees, fir trees, and algum trees, out of Lebanon: for I know that thy servants can skill to cut timber in Lebanon; and, behold, my servants shall be with thy servants [2 Chron. 2:8].**

In other words, Solomon's men would learn from them. These cedar trees are the famous cedars of Lebanon.

> **Even to prepare me timber in abundance: for the house which I am about to build shall be wonderful great [2 Chron. 2:9].**

It won't be large, but it will be great.

> And, behold, I will give to thy servants, the hewers that
> cut timber. twenty thousand measures of beaten wheat,
> and twenty thousand measures ot barley, and twenty
> thousand baths of wine, and twenty thousand baths of
> oil [2 Chron. 2:10].

Later on we shall see there was a misunderstanding relative to this payment that Solomon was to make.

> Then Huram the king of Tyre answered in writing,
> which he sent to Solomon, Because the LORD hath loved
> his people, he hath made thee king over them.

> Huram said moreover, Blessed be the LORD God of Is-
> rael, that made heaven and earth, who hath given to
> David the king a wise son, endued with prudence and
> understanding, that might build an house for the LORD,
> and an house for his kingdom.

> And now I have sent a cunning man, endued with un-
> derstanding, of Huram my father's [2 Chron. 2:11–13].

Then he goes on to describe this one whom he is sending.

> And Solomon numbered all the strangers that were in
> the land of Israel, after the numbering wherewith David
> his father had numbered them; and they were found an
> hundred and fifty thousand and six hundred.

> And he set threescore and ten thousand of them to be
> bearers of burdens, and fourscore thousand to be hewers
> in the mountain, and three thousand and six hundred
> overseers to set the people awork [2 Chron. 2:17–18].

These are to be the helpers, you see. These are the men who will do the common labor.

SOLOMON BEGINS CONSTRUCTION
OF THE TEMPLE

Then Solomon began to build the house of the LORD at Jerusalem in mount Moriah, where the LORD appeared unto David his father, in the place that David had prepared in the threshingfloor of Ornan the Jebusite [2 Chron. 3:1].

As we have seen, this threshing floor of Ornan is the site where centuries before Abraham had been told to offer Isaac. Then on that same ridge, right outside the city of Jerusalem, is located Golgotha, the place of the skull, where Jesus was crucified. David had bought this parcel of ground from Ornan. It is still the temple area today.

To those of us who are not in the construction business, the details of the blueprints and the building supplies are not particularly interesting. We will only cull out certain great truths which we do not find mentioned elsewhere.

Now these are the things wherein Solomon was instructed for the building of the house of God. The length by cubits after the first measure was threescore cubits, and the breadth twenty cubits [2 Chron. 3:3].

It is twice as large as the tabernacle was: 60 x 20 cubits. This translated into feet would be approximately 90 x 30 feet. These dimensions are for the temple proper; around it there are to be many other buildings. It was quite imposing when all the buildings were in place, but the temple proper was only twice as large as the tabernacle.

Now let me call your attention to certain things, some of which we have seen, and some we have not seen.

The wings of these cherubims spread themselves forth twenty cubits: and they stood on their feet, and their faces were inward [2 Chron. 3:13].

These are the cherubims that looked down on the mercy seat. You will recall that back in the tabernacle which Moses was instructed to build, God gave no measurement for the cherubim. They speak of Deity, and Deity cannot be measured. But here in the temple the measurement is given, and they are undoubtedly much larger than in the tabernacle. There is a note of deterioration here, as they are attempting to measure Deity, and that cannot be done.

Let me remind you that we are seeing the temple from God's viewpoint. What is it that God calls attention to which was not given from the human viewpoint in Kings? Well, it is the beauty of the veil.

> **And he made the veil of blue, and purple, and crimson, and fine linen, and wrought cherubims thereon [2 Chron. 3:14].**

The veil speaks of the humanity of Christ. God calls attention to that. When Christ was crucified, the veil of the temple was torn in two, since the veil represented the humanity of Christ. The rending of that veil signified that a "new and living way" was opened for all believers into the very presence of God with no other sacrifice than Christ's. Here in Chronicles God calls attention to the beauty of the veil. It is as if He said, ". . . This is my beloved Son, in whom I am well pleased" (Matt. 3:17).

Something else we should notice is the pillars.

> **Also he made before the house two pillars of thirty and five cubits high, and the chapiter that was on the top of each of them was five cubits [2 Chron. 3:15].**

This meant that these pillars went up very high (see model of the temple, pp. 120 and 153). Compared to the size of the building, they seem almost out of proportion. These pillars speak of strength and beauty.

Strength and beauty are two things which modern man thinks he has attained. We boast of our strength; yet we are powerless to maintain law and order. And as far as beauty is concerned, have you looked at modern art? My daughter majored in art, and she took me through a classroom to show me what they were doing. She would say, "Dad, isn't that beautiful?" Well, I didn't want to misrepresent how I felt—I couldn't say it was beautiful. I could say, "My, I haven't seen anything like that!" And believe me, I hadn't.

God is interested in strength and beauty, and those pillars of the temple were very impressive. In the next chapter He again mentions this matter of strength and beauty:

> **To wit, the two pillars, and the pommels, and the chapiters which were on the top of the two pillars, and the two wreaths to cover the two pommels of the chapiters which were on the top of the pillars [2 Chron. 4:12].**

God is calling particular attention to it.

> **And he made chains, as in the oracle, and put them on the heads of the pillars; and made an hundred pomegranates, and put them on the chains [2 Chron. 3:16].**

He mentions these chains. What do they represent? They speak of the unity of the nation. The chains picture the unity of the individuals that constitute the tribes, and the tribes in turn constitute the nation.

God is interested in absolute unity. This is something which God's people are losing sight of in our day. We are split and fragmented into thousands of different groups today. There are always new organizations coming into existence. I am not sure that all this is honoring to the Lord. You see, in the New Testament God has given a picture of unity that is even better than the chain. It is the body. He says His church is a body. In a body there can be many members, and some of the members are of honor and some of dishonor, but they are all in one body. That is the picture of the church.

Notice also the use of pomegranates—one hundred of them. Also we read:

> **And four hundred pomegranates on the two wreaths; two rows of pomegranates on each wreath, to cover the**

two pommels of the chapiters which were upon the pillars [2 Chron. 4:13].

Pomegranates speak of fruitfulness, and that is the emphasis here.

I didn't specifically mention the colors that are used here. Notice that the veil was of blue and purple and crimson and fine linen. Blue is the color of the heaven above. Purple is the color of royalty, and crimson speaks of redemption through the blood of Christ. White speaks of the holy walk. All these colors are important from God's point of view.

Chapter four gives details about the articles of furniture: the altar of brass, the huge laver, the ten smaller lavers, the candlesticks, the tables. Then there were pots and shovels and basins. The brazen altar was four times as large as the one in the tabernacle. There were additional lavers in the temple. There were other additions and changes.

The innovations and enlargements took away the simplicity of the tabernacle and the plain references to Christ. It is the tabernacle and not the temple which became the figure that was used in the Epistle to the Hebrews to depict the person and work of Christ.

CHAPTERS 5 AND 6

THEME: The completed temple

> Thus all the work that Solomon made for the house of the LORD was finished: and Solomon brought in all the things that David his father had dedicated; and the silver, and the gold, and all the instruments, put he among the treasures of the house of God.

> Then Solomon assembled the elders of Israel, and all the heads of the tribes, the chief of the fathers of the children of Israel, unto Jerusalem, to bring up the ark of the covenant of the LORD out of the city of David, which is Zion [2 Chron. 5:1–2].

After the temple was completed, the ark was brought into the temple. Zion is right up on the hill not very far from the temple area. I have walked it several times, both up and down, because it is not too far.

We don't know the exact spot where David was keeping the ark, but it was in the city of David which is Mount Zion. That is not a very large area and it is not far from the temple area.

> Also king Solomon, and all the congregation of Israel that were assembled unto him before the ark, sacrificed sheep and oxen, which could not be told nor numbered for multitude [2 Chron. 5:6].

The thought here is that there was no attempt to count them because they represent the sacrifice of Christ. And that is something which cannot be counted or measured.

And the priests brought in the ark of the covenant of the
LORD unto his place, to the oracle of the house, into the
most holy place, even under the wings of the cherubims:

For the cherubims spread forth their wings over the
place of the ark, and the cherubims covered the ark and
the staves thereof above.

And they drew out the staves of the ark, that the ends of
the staves were seen from the ark before the oracle; but
they were not seen without. And there it is unto this day
[2 Chron. 5:7–9].

"Unto this day" refers, of course, to the time of the writing of Chronicles. The staves were drawn out.

The ark is to move no more. You will remember that the ark was constructed in the wilderness at Mount Sinai, and then the children of Israel spent forty years wandering in the wilderness. The ark was always carried before them as they traveled. It was the ark that went first through the Jordan River when they entered the Promised Land. After they had arrived in the land, the ark was still moved from place to place. Remember that once it was even captured by the Philistines, and then it was sent back by them.

The ark had been brought to Jerusalem by David, and he had kept it at Mount Zion until the time when the temple should be completed. That time has now come, and the ark is placed into the most holy place, and the staves are removed. It is to move no more. The males of the children of Israel are to appear at the tabernacle at three feasts of the year: Passover, Pentecost, and the Feast of Tabernacles. This means that from now on they will come to Jerusalem on those feast days and appear at the temple where the ark rests.

You will remember that the ark speaks of the Lord Jesus Christ, of His person. Above the ark was the mercy seat which speaks of His work of redemption, His shedding of blood, the fact that He is now our propitiation. All of that is permanent. ". . . but now once in the end of the world [lit., the end of the age] hath he appeared to put away sin by the sacrifice of himself" (Heb. 9:26). It is permanent, it is basic, it is established. Let me use the figure of speech here: the staves have been pulled out. There will be no other way of salvation. Peter could say to his people, "Neither is there salvation in any other; for there is none other name under heaven given among men, whereby we must be saved" (Acts 4:12). My friend, the staves have been pulled out. The ark is not on the move any more.

Also the withdrawing of the staves indicates rest. The Lord Jesus gives rest to those who come to Him. Also there is to be a place of rest. Our Lord spoke of that place when He said to His own men in the Upper Room, ". . . I go to prepare a place for you. And if I go and prepare a place for you, I will come again, and receive you unto myself; that where I am, there ye may be also" (John 14:2–3). The place is prepared, and one of these days we will go to that place.

One of the characteristics of that place is its permanence, the fact that it is a place of eternity. "And God shall wipe away all tears from their eyes; and there shall be no more death, neither sorrow, nor crying, neither shall there be any more pain: for the former things are passed away" (Rev. 21:4). This is the city of God. It is permanent, and ". . . the Lord God Almighty and the Lamb are the temple of it" (Rev. 21:22). My friend, the staves are already pulled out. How wonderful that we are not going to be on the march. We don't have to go looking for God. As Paul said to the Romans, we don't have to go to heaven to bring Christ down, nor do we have to go down to hell to bring Him up. He is right there for us. This is permanent; it is eternal. It will not be changed. He drew out the staves.

> **There was nothing in the ark save the two tables which Moses put therein at Horeb, when the Lord made a covenant with the children of Israel, when they came out of Egypt [2 Chron. 5:10].**

Two things that had been placed in the ark by Moses are now missing: Aaron's rod and the pot of manna. The manna, you will recall from the account of Numbers 17, would disappear if the people didn't gather it. And if it was not eaten the same day, it would spoil. However a pot of manna was preserved in the ark as a memorial. Now it is gone. The manna was a symbol of Christ as the Bread of Life, who feeds those who are His own. Aaron's rod that budded (Exod. 16) is a symbol of Christ's resurrection. It has been actualized to us today by the historical fact that Jesus died (that's His humanity), was buried, then rose again the third day—that's not human; it reveals His deity. The priesthood of the Lord Jesus Christ rests upon His resurrection, just as Aaron's priesthood was confirmed by the budding of his rod, a type of resurrection.

> And it came to pass, when the priests were come out of the holy place: (for all the priests that were present were sanctified, and did not then wait by course) [2 Chron. 5:11].

You see, all the courses came up for this act of dedication. The singers were there, and the orchestra with cymbals and psalteries and harps, and 120 trumpet players!

> It came even to pass, as the trumpeters and singers were as one, to make one sound to be heard in praising and thanking the LORD; and when they lifted up their voice with the trumpets and cymbals and instruments of music, and praised the LORD, saying, For he is good; for his mercy endureth for ever: that then the house was filled with a cloud, even the house of the LORD [2 Chron. 5:13].

This was a great occasion!

> So that the priests could not stand to minister by reason of the cloud: for the glory of the LORD had filled the house of God [2 Chron. 5:14].

Now as we come to chapter 6 we have the message of Solomon for this occasion and his prayer of dedication.

SOLOMON'S MESSAGE

This is a tremendous message that Solomon gives.

> Then said Solomon, The LORD hath said that he would dwell in the thick darkness.

> But I have built an house of habitation for thee, and a place for thy dwelling for ever.

> And the king turned his face, and blessed the whole congregation of Israel: and all the congregation of Israel stood [2 Chron. 6:1-3].

Now Solomon addresses the people.

> And he said, Blessed be the LORD God of Israel, who hath with his hands fulfilled that which he spake with his mouth to my father David, saying [2 Chron. 6:4].

David, you see, is the one responsible for the temple.

> Since the day that I brought forth my people out of the land of Egypt I chose no city among all the tribes of Israel to build an house in, that my name might be there; neither chose I any man to be a ruler over my people Israel:

> But I have chosen Jerusalem, that my name might be there; and have chosen David to be over my people Israel [2 Chron. 6:5-6].

In God's sovereign will He chose Jerusalem to be the center and the capital of this earth. It will be that some day. He chose Jerusalem for the place the temple would stand. He chose David to be the king, and now one in David's line. This is the arbitrary, the absolute will of God in making this choice.

Now, my friend, our choices are often quite different from God's choices. For example, I would not have chosen Jerusalem. I think the most beautiful spot in that land is at Samaria where Ahab and Jezebel lived. Many folk build on a hillside so they have a view of the valley, but in Samaria you can look in every direction. On the west you see the Mediterranean Sea. On the east you see the Jordan Valley and the Sea of Galilee. On the south you see Jerusalem, and when you look to the north you see Mount Hermon. That's quite a view! I would choose that place for the capital. But God did not consult me or my wishes. God chose Jerusalem. This is the sovereign will of God. God says, "I have chosen Jerusalem."

My friend, God has His will for you and for me. I actually believe that for a child of God He has a certain place, a certain house for you to live in. His will for you involves everything in your life. The great problem for you and me is to get in the will of God. We can stand off and argue all we want to about the free will of man and God's sovereignty, but it is a fruitless waste of time. I'll tell you something that is very profitable: it is to get to the place—in fact, on the spot that God has marked "X"—which He has chosen for you and for me. When you and I get on that spot, we will be in the right place. God's will is the important thing.

God chose Jerusalem; God chose this man David.

> **Now it was in the heart of David my father to build an house for the name of the LORD God of Israel [2 Chron. 6:7].**

Solomon is saying that he has done what David wanted done; he is carrying out his wishes in building the temple.

> **The LORD therefore hath performed his word that he hath spoken: for I am risen up in the room of David my father, and am set on the throne of Israel, as the LORD promised, and have built the house for the name of the Lord God of Israel.**

> And in it have I put the ark, wherein is the covenant of
> the LORD, that he made with the children of Israel
> [2 Chron. 6:10-11].

This is all-important to see.

SOLOMON'S PRAYER

Now we have this wonderful prayer of dedication.

> And he stood before the altar of the LORD in the presence
> of all the congregation of Israel, and spread forth his
> hands:
>
> For Solomon had made a brasen scaffold, of five cubits
> long, and five cubits broad, and three cubits high, and
> had set it in the midst of the court: and upon it he stood,
> and kneeled down upon his knees before all the congre-
> gation of Israel, and spread forth his hands toward
> heaven [2 Chron. 6:12-13].

If you are wondering about the proper posture for prayer, Solomon
kneeled down. On your knees is a fitting posture for a creature in the
presence of his Creator.

Solomon begins with thanksgiving.

> And said, O LORD God of Israel, there is no God like thee
> in the heaven, nor in the earth; which keepest covenant,
> and shewest mercy unto thy servants, that walk before
> thee with all their hearts:
>
> Thou which hast kept with thy servant David my father
> that which thou hast promised him; and spakest with
> thy mouth, and hast fulfilled it with thine hand, as it is
> this day [2 Chron. 6:14-15].

He is thanking God because He is the Creator and because of His mercy and His faithfulness. In His grace He had moved into the heart of David, into the nation, and into the heart and life of Solomon.

In our day a great many Christians need an experience with God. It seems that they are satisfied to stand off and stiff-arm the Lord. They keep Him at a distance, yet they say, "Yes, I'm a Christian." My friend, let's have a close relationship with Him and real fellowship.

> **But will God in very deed dwell with men on the earth? behold, heaven and the heaven of heavens cannot contain thee; how much less this house which I have built! [2 Chron. 6:18].**

This is an important verse, to which I have referred before. Certainly neither Solomon nor the nation Israel had any notion of "boxing God in" when they built a temple for Him. Rather the temple was to be a meeting place between God and man.

> **That thine eyes may be upon this house day and night, upon the place whereof thou hast said that thou wouldest put thy name there; to hearken unto the prayer which thy servant prayeth toward this place [2 Chron. 6:20].**

You see, this temple was the place where man could meet God.

> **Hearken therefore unto the supplications of thy servant, and of thy people Israel, which they shall make toward this place: hear thou from thy dwelling place, even from heaven; and when thou hearest, forgive [2 Chron. 6:21].**

The temple was to become the very center of the life of the nation Israel.

> **And if thy people Israel be put to the worse before the enemy, because they have sinned against thee; and shall**

> **return and confess thy name, and pray and make supplication before thee in this house;**
>
> **Then hear thou from the heavens, and forgive the sin of thy people Israel, and bring them again unto the land which thou gavest to them and to their fathers [2 Chron. 6:24–25].**

When they had sinned, they were to come back to that temple.

> **When the heaven is shut up, and there is no rain, because they have sinned against thee; yet if they pray toward this place, and confess thy name, and turn from their sin, when thou dost afflict them [2 Chron. 6:26].**

When there is a drought in the land because of the sin of the people, what are they to do? Come back to God in prayer.

> **If there be dearth in the land, if there be pestilence, if there be blasting, or mildew, locusts, or caterpillars; if their enemies besiege them in the cities of their land; whatsoever sore or whatsoever sickness there be [2 Chron. 6:28].**

Whatever calamity might come to them, they were to return to the temple and pray to God.

> **Then hear thou from heaven thy dwelling place, and forgive, and render unto every man according unto all his ways, whose heart thou knowest; (for thou only knowest the hearts of the children of men:) [2 Chron. 6:30].**

God knows us, my friend. That is the reason we ought to be doing business with Him.

> Moreover concerning the stranger, which is not of thy people Israel, but is come from a far country for thy great name's sake, and thy mighty hand, and thy stretched out arm; if they come and pray in this house;

> Then hear thou from the heavens, even from thy dwelling place, and do according to all that the stranger calleth to thee for; that all people of the earth may know thy name, and fear thee, as doth thy people Israel, and may know that this house which I have built is called by thy name [2 Chron. 6:32–33].

You see, this was a great missionary project. The temple was not only for Israel—the whole world was to come there. If a stranger or foreigner would come from a far country—from the end of the earth—he could meet God at the temple.

> If they sin against thee, (for there is no man which sinneth not,) and thou be angry with them, and deliver them over before their enemies, and they carry them away captives unto a land far off or near [2 Chron. 6:36].

In the country to which they are taken captive, they are to turn in the direction of the temple and lift their voices to God. This is what Daniel did, you recall. Daniel opened his windows toward Jerusalem (the temple by that time had been destroyed), kneeled, and prayed to God three times a day (Dan. 6:10). And God heard his prayer.

> If they return to thee with all their heart and with all their soul in the land of their captivity, whither they have carried them captives, and pray toward their land, which thou gavest unto their fathers, and toward the city which thou hast chosen, and toward the house which I have built for thy name:

> Then hear thou from the heavens, even from thy dwelling place, their prayer and their supplications, and

> maintain their cause, and forgive thy people which have
> sinned against thee.
>
> Now, my God, let, I beseech thee, thine eyes be open,
> and let thine ears be attent unto the prayer that is made
> in this place [2 Chron. 6:38–40].

The temple was to be the meeting place.

> Now therefore arise, O LORD God, into thy resting place,
> thou, and the ark of thy strength: let thy priests, O LORD
> God, be clothed with salvation, and let thy saints rejoice
> in goodness.
>
> O LORD God, turn not away the face of thine anointed:
> remember the mercies of David thy servant [2 Chron.
> 6:41–42].

This is a glorious prayer. Notice that he makes it on the basis of the
mercy God extended to David.

You and I are to pray because Christ has made a mercy seat for us
by His shed blood. He made peace for us by the blood of His cross, and
God is prepared to extend mercy to us.

CHAPTER 7

THEME: God's acceptance of the temple

In the preceding chapter we have seen the dedication service of the temple. We have read Solomon's message and his great prayer of dedication. In this chapter we shall see God's response to it.

> **Now when Solomon had made an end of praying, the fire came down from heaven, and consumed the burnt offering and the sacrifices; and the glory of the Lord filled the house [2 Chron. 7:1].**

This is what happened, you recall, when Moses finished the construction of the tabernacle in the wilderness. When he set it up, the glory of the Lord filled it (Exod. 40:34–35). God accepts this temple that Solomon has built.

Notice that fire from heaven consumes the sacrifice. This means that the judgment of God has fallen upon sin. God does not accept the temple because it is beautiful—and it is that. He does not accept it because of the lavish expenditure of wealth. The basis of His acceptance is the fact that it is pointing to Christ. It is *His* sacrifice, actually, that makes this acceptable to God. The glory of the Lord filled the temple, as we have seen in the final verses of chapter 5, and now also fire from heaven consumes the burnt offering.

These people had the visible presence of God. In the New Testament, in Paul's Epistle to the Romans, he answers the question: who are Israelites? He gives eight fingerprints of identification, one of which is that they had the glory.

No other people have had the visible presence of God except the Israelites.

> **And the priests could not enter into the house of the Lord, because the glory of the Lord had filled the Lord's house.**

And when all the children of Israel saw how the fire
came down, and the glory of the LORD upon the house,
they bowed themselves with their faces to the ground
upon the pavement, and worshipped, and praised the
LORD, saying, for he is good; for his mercy endureth for
ever [2 Chron. 7:2–3].

And, my friend, this is an expression that I trust will get into your
vocabulary, and that you will say from time to time, "The LORD is
good; His mercy endureth forever." You recall that the psalmist said,
"The LORD is good. Let the redeemed of the LORD say so." If you and I
are not "say-so Christians," nobody else will be. Nobody in politics
will be saying how good God is; they will be telling us how great they
are and what their party is doing for the country. Candidly, none of the
politicians seem to be doing much good, by the way. But the Lord is
good. Let the redeemed of the Lord say so.

Then the king and all the people offered sacrifices before the LORD.

And king Solomon offered a sacrifice of twenty and two
thousand oxen, and an hundred and twenty thousand
sheep: so the king and all the people dedicated the
house of God [2 Chron. 7:4–5].

These verses have caused a great deal of criticism by the skeptics of
the Bible. They love to criticize on the basis of three issues: (1) They
say this offering and sacrifice was an extravagance; (2) they say it
would have been physically impossible to offer that many sacrifices
on the altar; and (3) they say there was no necessity for all this slaugh-
ter of animals. I'm sure the members of the Society for the Prevention
of Cruelty to Animals would protest this.

Now let us look at these three issues from a biblical perspective.
We need to look at things in the light of the Word of God. In the first
place, although the temple was the center for all this activity, I do not
think that every one of those animals was sacrificed on one altar. For

this special occasion they probably had erected altars all over that temple area. It was not a physical impossibility.

Now why was there all of this expenditure? Well, it was necessary in order for each area to have its own sacrifice. It was as when the people of Israel came out of the land of Egypt and a lamb was slain for each home. There must have been literally thousands of lambs that were slain that night. It was not a needless waste for two reasons. The primary meaning of it is that it symbolizes the sacrifice of the Lord Jesus Christ. And, my friend, it was Simon Peter who said that His blood was precious. "Forasmuch as ye know that ye were not redeemed with corruptible things, as silver and gold, from your vain conversation received by tradition from your fathers; but with the precious blood of Christ, as of a lamb without blemish and without spot" (1 Pet. 1:18–19). This is not a great expenditure because it is pointing to Christ. The second reason that it was not a "needless waste" was that the meat was used for food afterward. Although the "burnt offerings" were totally consumed by fire, other offerings, such as the peace offering, were eaten. This dedication of the temple was a time of great feasting and great celebrating.

Let's be fair with the Bible, my friend.

I have observed the people who are always talking about the great extravagance of money spent for the Lord. It is an amazing fact that even Christian people are guilty of this kind of criticism. I knew a dear lady who was very much interested in Bible classes; she had one in her home. We had a Bible teacher come to our church. The people liked him, and they gave him a generous offering. He stayed with us for about ten days and the church gave him $500.00 plus his expenses. This lady thought that was ridiculous; it was too great an expenditure. Also this lady was interested in music, and she was on the music committee of the town where she lived, and they brought a certain opera singer to town. He sang one night and they gave him $2,000.00. She thought that was wonderful. May I say to you, it is interesting that when something is being spent for the Lord it is just a waste, but when something is spent for the things of the world it is all right.

To anyone who thinks they were slaying too many animals for sacrifice, how many animals are slain in this country every day? There are thousands of animals slain every day in the packing houses of our country. No one raises a voice or does anything to protest that. After all, that is to satisfy us. But when something is done for the glory of God, there will always be people who will object. I don't know about you, but I'm on Solomon's side here. I think he did the right thing, because the sacrifices were pointing to the Lord Jesus Christ, and He shed His precious blood for me.

> And the priests waited on their offices: the Levites also with instruments of music of the LORD, which David the king had made to praise the LORD, because his mercy endureth for ever, when David praised by their minis-try; and the priests sounded trumpets before them, and all Israel stood [2 Chron. 7:6].

I wish I could get God's people to praise the Lord and to say that God is good and His mercy endures forever. Oh, how good God has been to me! Has He been good to you, friends? Well then, say so.

> Moreover Solomon hallowed the middle of the court that was before the house of the LORD: for there he offered burnt offerings, and the fat of the peace offerings, be-cause the brasen altar which Solomon had made was not able to receive the burnt offerings, and the meat of-ferings, and the fat.

> Also at the same time Solomon kept the feast seven days, and all Israel with him, a very great congregation, from the entering in of Hamath unto the river of Egypt [2 Chron. 7:7–8].

From the entering of Hamath to the river of Egypt means from the extreme north to the extreme south of the land.

GOD'S SECOND APPEARANCE TO SOLOMON

And the LORD appeared to Solomon by night, and said unto him, I have heard thy prayer, and have chosen this place to myself for an house of sacrifice.

If I shut up heaven that there be no rain, or if I command the locusts to devour the land, or if I send pestilence among my people;

If my people, which are called by my name, shall humble themselves, and pray, and seek my face, and turn from their wicked ways; then will I hear from heaven, and will forgive their sin, and will heal their land [2 Chron. 7:12–14].

I am going to spend time on this last verse because it has been so often used out of context without regard to its primary meaning. It has been quoted as a promise to us from God that if we do certain things, He will do certain things. This verse has been tailored to fit into any local situation. I don't believe I have ever participated in an evangelistic campaign without someone at some time getting up and quoting this verse of Scripture and saying that he was resting on these promises. I believe that a careful consideration of this verse, its location and content and context, will prevent us from taking it like a capsule and swallowing it without some attention to its real meaning. We do violence to it by wresting it from its place. Just because it seems to fit into our plans and says what we want to say, we ignore its primary purpose and rob it of its vitality. It becomes, actually, a meaningless verse as it is being used in our day.

Now I want to speak very plainly to you. I am a dispensationalist. I think it is the only system that deals with the entire Bible consistently. It gives a literal meaning to the Word of God and gives it a real meaning. I am a graduate of a denominational seminary in which most of the Scripture was absolutely ignored because they had no interpretation for it. The way we were taught the Bible was sort of like going to a corncrib and taking out enough to feed the chickens—and the rest you didn't worry about. That was because they had no interpretation for it. The problem was that no one wanted to come back for more because if you went into more sections of Scripture than just those few they taught, you might get into trouble. Although the dispensational interpretation has its problems, it solves more problems than any other interpretation that I have heard.

Let me give you examples of the position I take. I recognize that the Sermon on the Mount looks forward to the time of the Kingdom and it will be the law of the Kingdom. However, I also believe that it has a message for us today. I think the way the Lord's Prayer is used in a great many churches by an affluent society is absolutely meaningless. In the Great Tribulation that prayer will really mean something to people. Although I am a dispensationalist, I am not a hyper-dispensationalist. I don't exclude the Sermon on the Mount. I preach on it. It shows that man comes short of God's standards. I find the Lord's Prayer helpful. I pray it. I have written a little book on it entitled, *Let Us Pray*. There is an *interpretation* of Scripture—that is one thing. Then there is an *application* of Scripture, which is something else. Remember the old adage that "all Scripture is written *for* us, but not all Scripture is written *to* us." The interpretation of a verse of Scripture will teach what it means in its setting and context. It may not be written *to* us at all. We can think of many commands given in the Old Testament which are not commands given to us. However, the application of all of Scripture is *for* us. God has something to teach us throughout the entire Scripture.

Now let's go back to 2 Chronicles 7:14. The setting is at the dedication of David's temple which Solomon had built. It is God's Word to Solomon concerning that land in that day. At the dedication Solomon prayed this great prayer which we have seen. Now He remembers the prayers of His people, and He says to Solomon, "If my people, which are called by my name . . ." To whom is He talking? "My people, which are called by My name." That is Israel. God is talking to Solomon about Israel. Now, if these will humble themselves, if they will pray, if they will seek His face, if they will turn from their wicked ways, *then* God promises three things to Israel: He will hear their prayer, He will forgive them, He will heal their land. These were definite conditions that God put down for Israel, and their history demonstrates the accuracy and literalness of these specifics.

Now when you come to the New Testament, you find that John the Baptist says, ". . . Repent ye: for the kingdom of heaven is at hand" (Matt. 3:2). And the Lord Jesus Christ repeated that, calling upon the nation to meet these conditions—so that the promises of God could be fulfilled. It was a legitimate offer. In our day, the people of Israel have been scattered throughout the world. They cannot have peace in that land because they have not met those conditions. This is a *literal* interpretation.

Now there is an *application*. This verse has a message for me. I can't toss it aside just because God did not direct it to me. It contains a formula for this hour. *"My people"*—God has a people which we call the church or the body of Christ, those who have accepted the Savior, "Who gave himself for us, that he might redeem us from all iniquity, and purify unto himself a peculiar people, zealous of good works" (Titus 2:14). I guess one could say a lot of us are peculiar people, but this means a people for Himself. *"Shall humble themselves"*—the flesh is proud but we are admonished to be humble. "I therefore, the prisoner of the Lord, beseech you that ye walk worthy of the vocation wherewith ye are called, with all lowliness and meekness, with longsuffering, forbearing one another in love" (Eph. 4:1–2). We are told in Galatians 5:22–23 that longsuffering and meekness are fruits of the Spirit. Humbleness is commended for the believer today. *"And pray"*—certainly many, many times in the New Testament we are admonished to pray. The Lord Jesus told His disciples to watch and pray. The epistles contain numerous commands to pray. *"And seek My face"* is also a New Testament admonition: "If ye then be risen with Christ, seek those things which are above, where Christ sitteth on the right hand of God. Set your affection on things above, not on things on the earth" (Col. 3:1–2). *And turn from their wicked ways."* This also applies to us. God has a great deal to say about repentance for believers. "As many as I love, I rebuke and chasten: be zealous therefore, and repent" (Rev. 3:19). Repentance is for the child of God.

Now how about God's part? God had promised that He would

hear. "And whatsoever we ask, we receive of him, because we keep his commandments, and do those things that are pleasing in his sight" (1 John 3:22). He promised to *forgive:* "If we confess our sins, he is faithful and just to forgive us our sins, and to cleanse us from all unrighteousness" (1 John 1:9).

"And will heal their land." That does not apply to us. I can't find anywhere in the New Testament where the Lord has promised to heal a piece of real estate. If God has blessed you in a business way, that is extra—a blessing that He has not promised. Nowhere does God promise material blessing to us. We are blessed with all *spiritual* blessings in Christ Jesus. We were aliens, enemies of God, and now we have been made the blood of Christ, and He forgives us our sins. Heaven is our home, and the New Jerusalem is our goal. We have been delivered from hell. These are our blessings. Nowhere are we promised a land or healing in our land.

May I say to you that if you would wish to lift out verse 14 and apply the entire verse to your present situation, then you must take verse 15 along with it.

Now mine eyes shall be open, and mine ears attent unto the prayer that is made in this place [2 Chron. 7:15].

If you want to follow this particular injunction, then I suggest you board the next plane to Jerusalem and go to the temple site. You would find that the temple isn't even there—the Mosque of Omar is there now, but if you intend to follow this passage, you must go to Jerusalem because that is where "this place" is.

I don't know why folk will lift out of context one verse of Scripture and claim it for themselves. It was never intended that way. This promise was given to Israel at the dedication of the temple. Although it has application for us, it is better to go to the New Testament and find God's promises to us directly.

For now have I chosen and sanctified this house, that my name may be there for ever: and mine eyes and mine heart shall be there perpetually [2 Chron. 7:16].

I stayed for a week in a hotel overlooking the temple area. When I would get up in the morning, I would walk out to the window—actually a big glass door—and look at this temple area. I thought, *I am looking at a spot where God is also looking.* This is a spot that is very dear to Him.

> **And as for thee, if thou wilt walk before me, as David thy father walked, and do according to all that I have commanded thee, and shalt observe my statutes and my judgments;**
>
> **Then will I stablish the throne of thy kingdom, according as I have covenanted with David thy father, saying, There shall not fail thee a man to be ruler in Israel [2 Chron. 7:17–18].**

God has promised that in the Davidic line there would not be a time when there would not be a ruler. There is no ruler around on this earth today who can claim to be in David's line. But there is One sitting at God's right hand who is in David's line, and He has been told, ". . . Sit thou at my right hand, until I make thine enemies thy footstool" (Ps. 110:1; see also Heb. 10:12–13).

> **But if ye turn away, and forsake my statutes and my commandments, which I have set before you, and shall go and serve other gods, and worship them;**
>
> **Then will I pluck them up by the roots out of my land which I have given them; and this house, which I have sanctified for my name, will I cast out of my sight, and will make it to be a proverb and a byword among all nations [2 Chron. 7:19–20].**

It certainly has become a byword today. It is no longer a sacred spot—the Mosque of Omar stands there.

> **And this house, which is high, shall be an astonishment to every one that passeth by it; so that he shall say, Why**

hath the LORD done thus unto this land, and unto this house? [2 Chron. 7:21].

That place today is where the Mosque of Omar stands. I stood there with several folk overlooking the temple area and one of them raised the question stated in this verse. "Why, this is where God's house was supposed to be, and look at it today. There is heathenism and paganism here as much as there is anywhere on the earth. You'd think that since this is God's spot He would not permit this kind of thing to happen." Well, my friend, this is exactly what God said *would* happen.

> **And it shall be answered, Because they forsook the LORD God of their fathers, which brought them forth out of the land of Egypt, and laid hold on other gods, and worshipped them, and served them: therefore hath he brought all this evil upon them [2 Chron. 7:22].**

I was privileged to tell that individual that the Word of God says very clearly that this would happen because Israel had forsaken the Lord God. I could show him that God is true to His Word.

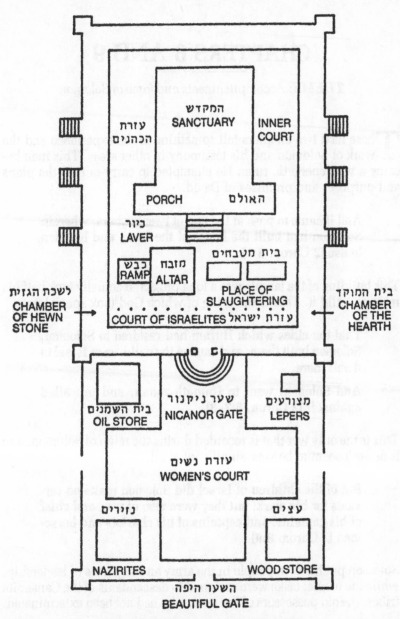

FLOORPLAN OF THE TEMPLE

CHAPTERS 8 AND 9

THEME: *Accomplishments and fame of Solomon*

These next two chapters tell something of the experience and the work of Solomon and his testimony in other areas. This man became a very energetic ruler. He attempted to carry out all the plans and purposes and promises of David.

> And it came to pass at the end of twenty years, wherein Solomon had built the house of the LORD, and his own house [2 Chron. 8:1].

This building of the temple was a long project. It actually took half his reign to build it. This is the thing of which God took special note.

> That the cities which Huram had restored to Solomon, Solomon built them, and caused the children of Israel to dwell there.

> And Solomon went to Hamath-zobah, and prevailed against it [2 Chron. 8:2–3].

This is the only war that is recorded during the reign of Solomon, and it doesn't seem to be very significant at all.

> But of the children of Israel did Solomon make no servants for his work; but they were men of war, and chief of his captains, and captains of his chariots and horsemen [2 Chron. 8:9].

Solomon put his own people in the army and in places of leadership, while the menial tasks were assigned to descendants of the Canaanite tribes, the old possessors of the land, who had not been exterminated.

And these were the chief of king Solomon's officers, even two hundred and fifty, that bare rule over the people [2 Chron. 8:10].

This is something that Solomon did which caused great difficulty later on. God notes it, but He does not commend it or bless it.

And Solomon brought up the daughter of Pharaoh out of the city of David unto the house that he had built for her: for he said, My wife shall not dwell in the house of David king of Israel, because the places are holy, where-unto the ark of the LORD hath come [2 Chron. 8:11].

This is an interesting decision which Solomon made in reference to his wife, the daughter of Pharaoh. He built her a palace away from the city of David.

I notice that an interpretation that one gets in Israel today is that Solomon married these different women from various other countries for political advantage. Your father-in-law is not apt to make war against you. So this was one of the ways in which Solomon brought peace to the land. A man would not come up to fight against a country in which his daughter was the queen. I do not know whether this reason for Solomon's many wives is true or not. I have a notion that it is partly accurate. Under any circumstance, it was against God's command.

The remainder of the chapter tells more about the temple and that Solomon celebrated the feasts and appointed the priests and Levites to their courses just as David had planned it.

As we come to chapter 9, we see that it is the final chapter that concerns Solomon. We have seen that Solomon's most important accomplishment was the construction of the temple. Now what else in Solomon's life does God consider important enough to record a second time? It is very interesting to see that Solomon did succeed in doing what God had intended Israel to do—that is, be a witness to the world. We are told here how it was accomplished.

The way Israel was to witness was different from the way the church is to witness in our day. Israel faced in; the church faces out. Israel was to go up to Jerusalem to the temple and invite the world to come with her to worship. But the church is to begin at Jerusalem and go to the ends of the earth. In other words, the church is to take the gospel to the world, and Israel was to invite the world to come and share in the revelation of God in the temple. Israel was to bear witness to the living and true God as a nation in a world of polytheism, of many gods. And the church is to bear witness to a resurrection, and the living Savior, as individuals to all the nations in a world of atheism. Now, Israel fulfilled her God-given purpose to a certain extent, which is evidenced by the number of Gentiles who came to Jerusalem to worship and to know God through the service of the temple there. The measuring rod for the success of the church is the number of tribes and nations to whom we carry the gospel today.

Now it is the inclination of all of us who are in the church to disparage the efforts of Israel and at the same time to magnify the success of the church. Constantly we hear on every hand of the failure of the nation Israel. And at the same time the exaggerated report is given of the success of the gospel in faraway places. I remember after World War II we heard about a revival in China and then a revival in Germany. I checked with those who were in both places and they said there was no revival there. It is interesting that we always hear of revivals in faraway places.

The fact of the matter is that we are in an awful apostasy today. The days are getting darker. There are many wonderful churches and pastors who are still faithful today, but they know the difficulty of the hour in which we are living. Although there are still a few preachers and teachers who are sheltered in institutions who see the present-day situation as though they were looking through rose-colored glasses, anyone who is working out in the world knows that we are in an apostasy today.

On the other hand, Israel succeeded in a far greater measure than we often realize. We tend to measure their success by their final failure—the final apostasy of the nation which led to their captivity. There *was* a period when they did not fail God. A witness went forth from Jerusalem to the nations of the world. They were drawn to Jerusalem like a magnet. The high water mark was during the reign of Solomon. The nation reached a pinnacle at that time. Afterward there was deterioration, and decline set in like dry rot.

The Scriptures give us two isolated examples of the influence on the Gentiles during the reign of David and Solomon. Undoubtedly there were many others that we do not know about. Hiram, the king of Tyre and friend of David, came to know God. He made lavish gifts for the temple. He furnished material and workmen for the temple. Do you remember what he wrote to Solomon? ". . . Blessed be the LORD God of Israel, that made heaven and earth, who hath given to David the king a wise son . . ." (2 Chron. 2:12). Hiram was a son of Japheth. The story of the queen of Sheba is given to us to record that Israel reached the ends of the then-known world with a witness for God. She is a representative of the son of Ham. It is her story that is given to us in this chapter.

May I remind you that in the New Testament, when we are told about the early church and its outreach into the world, we are also given just a few examples. There is the Ethiopian eunuch who is the son of Ham. There is Cornelius who is the son of Japheth. There is Saul of Tarsus who is the son of Shem.

VISIT OF THE QUEEN OF SHEBA

And when the queen of Sheba heard of the fame of Solomon, she came to prove Solomon with hard questions at Jerusalem, with a very great company, and camels that bare spices, and gold in abundance, and precious stones: and when she was come to Solomon, she communed with him of all that was in her heart.

And Solomon told her all her questions: and there was nothing hid from Solomon which he told her not [2 Chron. 9:1–2].

In other words, Solomon told her the secret of his kingdom. He told her that God had given him his wisdom. He told her that the temple

was their approach to God because God had said it was there He
would meet with His people.

> And when the queen of Sheba had seen the wisdom of
> Solomon, and the house that he had built,
>
> And the meat of his table, and the sitting of his servants,
> and the attendance of his ministers, and their apparel;
> his cupbearers also, and their apparel; and his ascent
> by which he went up into the house of the LORD; there
> was no more spirit in her [2 Chron. 9:3-4].

In 1 Kings 10:24 we are told, "And all the earth sought to Solomon, to
hear his wisdom, which God had put in his heart." We are given just
this one illustration of the queen of Sheba who came to see the wisdom of Solomon. You can see that the nation of Israel was successful
in witnessing to the world.

"His ascent by which he went up into the house of the Lord" was
the burnt offering which he made. That burnt offering speaks of
Christ. No nation on earth had anything that would compare to an
offering for sin. This was the thing which absolutely amazed her. This
was the offering that was pointing to Christ. David had said and written so much about Christ that I don't think Solomon left her without
an explanation of the One who was to come to take away sin.

> And she said to the king, It was a true report which I
> heard in mine own land of thine acts, and of thy wis-
> dom:
>
> Howbeit I believed not their words, until I came, and
> mine eyes had seen it: and, behold, the one half of the
> greatness of thy wisdom was not told me: for thou ex-
> ceedest the fame that I heard [2 Chron. 9:5-6].

This woman said, "When I heard about what God had done, I just
didn't believe it." But she had faith enough so that when she heard
about the greatness of Solomon, she made a long, arduous trip to see

for herself. Believe me, it was a long, arduous trip in that day. She couldn't go out to the airport and take a plane which would bring her there in a couple of hours. It was probably a couple of months across a hot, burning desert. She came all the way in order that she might know something of the wisdom of this man and learn about his approach to God. That was the thing that left no spirit in her. She couldn't believe it until she had seen it. Now listen to her:

> **Happy are thy men, and happy are these thy servants, which stand continually before thee, and hear thy wisdom.**
>
> **Blessed be the LORD thy God, which delighted in thee to set thee on his throne, to be king for the LORD thy God: because thy God loved Israel, to establish them for ever, therefore made he thee king over them, to do judgment and justice [2 Chron. 9:7–8].**

This woman is now praising God! When our Lord spoke of her, He said, "The queen of the south shall rise up in the judgment with this generation, and shall condemn it: for she came from the uttermost parts of the earth to hear the wisdom of Solomon . . ." (Matt. 12:42). There is a Sheba in southwestern Arabia and in Africa. Since the Lord Jesus said that she came from the uttermost parts of the earth, I assume she came from Africa. But her entourage reveals the wealth and luxury of the orient. The wise men never made a greater impression than did this woman. She came with great pomp and ceremony befitting an oriental monarch. It seems that the burnt offering was what impressed her the most. This was the most complete and perfect picture of Christ that was given in the Old Testament. How well did Israel succeed in giving a witness to the Gentiles? Well, this woman came to know the living and true God.

Our Lord, you recall, one day spoke to a woman at a well and said: "Woman, believe me, the hour cometh, when ye shall neither in this mountain, nor yet at Jerusalem, worship the Father" (John 4:21). In Jesus' day, that "hour" was coming. And that hour did come so that today we are to take the gospel to the ends of the earth. However, in Solomon's day, the world came to Jerusalem to hear the gospel.

SOLOMON'S SPLENDOR

And king Solomon passed all the kings of the earth in riches and wisdom.

And all the kings of the earth sought the presence of Solomon, to hear his wisdom, that God had put in his heart [2 Chron. 9:22–23].

Solomon was bearing a witness to the world in his day.

And Solomon had four thousand stalls for horses and chariots, and twelve thousand horsemen; whom he bestowed in the chariot cities, and with the king at Jerusalem [2 Chron. 9:25].

This reveals the defect in this man's character. The king had been forbidden by the Mosaic Law to multiply horses and wives. Solomon multiplied both. One of the most impressive things at Megiddo is the ruins of the stables that Solomon had there. And there are ruins of his stables in several other areas. He really multiplied horses!

And he reigned over all the kings from the river even unto the land of the Philistines, and to the border of Egypt.

And the king made silver in Jerusalem as stones, and cedar trees made he as the sycomore trees that are in the low plains in abundance.

And they brought unto Solomon horses out of Egypt, and out of all lands [2 Chron. 9:26–28].

Solomon was one of the great rulers of this world.

DEATH OF SOLOMON

Now the rest of the acts of Solomon, first and last, are they not written in the book of Nathan the prophet, and in the prophecy of Ahijah the Shilonite, and in the visions of Iddo the seer against Jeroboam the son of Nebat?

And Solomon reigned in Jerusalem over all Israel forty years.

And Solomon slept with his fathers, and he was buried in the city of David his father: and Rehoboam his son reigned in his stead [2 Chron. 9:29-31].

God had fulfilled His promise to Solomon. He had given him supernatural wisdom for which he had asked, and in addition He had given him riches and wealth and honor.

CHAPTERS 10—12

THEME: The division of the kingdom under Rehoboam

We have come now to the second and final division of the Book of 2 Chronicles. The first nine chapters were devoted to the reign of Solomon. Now Solomon is dead, and his son Rehoboam comes to the throne. The stupidity of Rehoboam leads to the division of the kingdom. The northern kingdom, composed of ten tribes, becomes known as Israel. The southern kingdom of two tribes takes the name of Judah. God puts the emphasis on the kingdom of Judah because this is the line of David which leads to Christ. In this section of the nation's history are five periods of revival. These are enlarged upon in Chronicles, as we are seeing them from God's viewpoint.

REHOBOAM COMES TO THE THRONE

And Rehoboam went to Shechem: for to Shechem were all Israel come to make him king.

And it came to pass, when Jeroboam the son of Nebat, who was in Egypt, whither he had fled from the presence of Solomon the king, heard it, that Jeroboam returned out of Egypt [2 Chron. 10:1–2].

The Book of 2 Chronicles does not tell us this, but back in Kings we are told that this man Jeroboam had attempted to lead a rebellion even before the death of Solomon. He was forced to flee for his life and had gone down into the land of Egypt. He stayed there until the death of Solomon. Now he has returned with the intent of raising up a rebellion in the kingdom. If Rehoboam had been wise in his judgment and had been a little more mild and modest, he could have prevented the splitting of the kingdom; but he did not.

Now Jeroboam is back in the land, and we read:

And they sent and called him. So Jeroboam and all Israel came and spake to Rehoboam, saying,

Thy father made our yoke grievous: now therefore ease
thou somewhat the grievous servitude of thy father, and
his heavy yoke that he put upon us, and we will serve
thee [2 Chron. 10:3–4].

Taxes were the cause of the dissension. Probably the single thing that
has caused more revolution and rebellion has been this matter of
taxes. It has been the downfall of many nations. It brought the Roman
Empire to its knees, and excessive taxation to support the royalty was
responsible for the French Revolution. Also it produced the American
Revolution. Taxation without representation brought about the Boston
Tea Party and the incidents which led to the revolution. If our taxes
keep going up as they are, we may have another tea party, because
high taxation will ultimately wreck any nation. Unfortunately, our
representatives in the state and national government don't seem to
think that it is a problem. Taxes were the problem in Rehoboam's time.
Solomon had carried on a tremendous building program. It was very
impressive. Not only had he built the temple, but we are told in Kings
that he built all sorts of palaces and buildings. Such a big building
program had to be paid for, and as a result there had been an enormous
increase in taxes. This gave Jeroboam a lever whereby he could make a
protest. He gathered with Israel and said to Rehoboam, "Now look
here, your father made our yoke grievous." Actually, Jeroboam was
very mild in his approach. He said to Rehoboam that if he would reduce the taxes, he would go along with him. If Rehoboam had done
that, there would not have been a rebellion.

And he said unto them, Come again unto me after three
days. And the people departed [2 Chron. 10:5].

What they had asked was really a fair thing. Rehoboam would have
had an opportunity to look at the indebtedness and decide what was
the wise thing to do. The wise thing would have been to reduce taxes.

> And king Rehoboam took counsel with the old men that had stood before Solomon his father while he yet lived, saying, What counsel give ye me to return answer to this people?
>
> And they spake unto him, saying, If thou be kind to this people, and please them, and speak good words to them, they will be thy servants for ever.
>
> But he forsook the counsel which the old men gave him, and took counsel with the young men that were brought up with him, that stood before him [2 Chron. 10:6–8].

Rehoboam definitely showed poor judgment. He should have followed the wisdom of the older men who had been counselors during the reign of Solomon. They knew the situation. Unfortunately, he turned to the young men.

> And the young men that were brought up with him spake unto him, saying, Thus shalt thou answer the people that spake unto thee, saying, Thy father made our yoke heavy, but make thou it somewhat lighter for us; thus shalt thou say unto them, My little finger shall be thicker than my father's loins.
>
> For whereas my father put a heavy yoke upon you, I will put more to your yoke: my father chastised you with whips, but I will chastise you with scorpions [2 Chron. 10:10–11].

The young men advised, "Don't ease up. We want this picnic to continue. All of us have public jobs, and those of us who are not eating out of the public trough would like very much to get in the trough. Don't reduce the taxes. Increase them!" This was probably the most foolish thing that young Rehoboam could have done.

The older men conceded that Solomon did overtax the people. They advised that it was time to stop the building program. It was time to put a lid on all the government spending. The time had come to reduce taxes.

By the way, have you ever heard of any government which has reduced taxes? Our politicians go into office saying they will reduce taxes. I think in my lifetime I have voted for half a dozen presidents and every one of them was going to reduce taxes. I have been voting for governors and for mayors, and they all promise to reduce the taxes. Yet our taxes continue to increase.

Rehoboam will follow this policy also.

> **So Jeroboam and all the people came to Rehoboam on the third day, as the king bade, saying, Come again to me on the third day.**

> **And the king answered them roughly; and king Rehoboam forsook the counsel of the old men,**

> **And answered them after the advice of the young men, saying, My father made your yoke heavy, but I will add thereto: my father chastised you with whips, but I will chastise you with scorpions [2 Chron. 10:12-14].**

Rehoboam delivers verbatim to the people the heartless and insensitive judgment of the young men.

> **So the king hearkened not unto the people: for the cause was of God, that the LORD might perform his word, which he spake by the hand of Ahijah the Shilonite to Jeroboam the son of Nebat [2 Chron. 10:15].**

The prophecy to which this refers is given in 1 Kings 11:9-39.

> **And when all Israel saw that the king would not hearken unto them, the people answered the king, saying, What portion have we in David? and we have none inheritance in the son of Jesse: every man to your tents, O**

> Israel, and now, David, see to thine own house. So all
> Israel went to their tents [2 Chron. 10:16].

Israel refers to the ten tribes. *Judah* refers to the two tribes of Judah and
Benjamin. However, the name *Israel* sometimes will refer to the southern kingdom also because God regards them as one people.

> But as for the children of Israel that dwelt in the cities of
> Judah, Rehoboam reigned over them.
>
> Then king Rehoboam sent Hadoram that was over the
> tribute; and the children of Israel stoned him with
> stones, that he died. But king Rehoboam made speed to
> get him up to his chariot, to flee to Jerusalem.
>
> And Israel rebelled against the house of David unto this
> day [2 Chron. 10:17–19].

King Rehoboam sent a tax gatherer to gather taxes and the people
stoned him to death. Rehoboam just hadn't realized how incensed
these people were. So Israel rebelled against the house of David.
"Unto this day" means up to the time when 2 Chronicles was written.

EARLY DAYS OF REHOBOAM'S REIGN

When Rehoboam goes back to Jerusalem, he finds that his kingdom
has really been cut down by quite a bit. Then he does another foolish
thing.

> And when Rehoboam was come to Jerusalem, he gath-
> ered of the house of Judah and Benjamin an hundred
> and fourscore thousand chosen men, which were war-
> riors, to fight against Israel, that he might bring the
> kingdom again to Rehoboam [2 Chron. 11:1].

First Rehoboam lost part of his kingdom by his own folly. Now he is
doing another foolish thing by attempting internal warfare. He wants
a civil war in Israel.

But the word of the LORD came to Shemiah the man of
God, saying,

Speak unto Rehoboam the son of Solomon, king of Judah, and to all Israel in Judah and Benjamin, saying,

Thus saith the LORD, Ye shall not go up, nor fight against
your brethren: return every man to his house: for this
thing is done of me. And they obeyed the words of the
LORD, and returned from going against Jeroboam
[2 Chron. 11:2–4].

God intervenes and prevents a civil war.

And he fortified the strong holds, and put captains in
them, and store of victual, and of oil and wine.

And in every several city he put shields and spears, and
made them exceeding strong, having Judah and Benjamin on his side [2 Chron. 11:11–12].

Now Rehoboam turns his attention to the building of fortifications to
protect himself from the northern kingdom. That which had been part
of the kingdom of David and Solomon is now lost to him and becomes
his enemy because of his very foolish decision to listen to the young
men rather than to the wise counselors of Solomon.

And the priests and the Levites that were in all Israel
resorted to him out of all their coasts [2 Chron. 11:13].

You remember that the Levites had been given certain cities throughout Israel but that they had no territory as a tribe such as the other
tribes had been given. Now the Levites leave all their cities in the
northern kingdom, and all the priests and Levites move south to Judah
and Jerusalem.

For the Levites left their suburbs and their possession,
and came to Judah and Jerusalem: for Jeroboam and his

> sons had cast them off from executing the priest's office
> unto the LORD:

> And he ordained him priests for the high places, and for
> the devils [demons], and for the calves which he had
> made [2 Chron. 11:14–15].

All the priests and Levites who lived up in the northern kingdom
moved south so that they could continue to serve at the temple. Then
Jeroboam institutes demon worship. The record in Kings gives us
more detail: "If this people go up to do sacrifice in the house of the
LORD at Jerusalem, then shall the heart of this people turn again unto
their lord, even unto Rehoboam king of Judah, and they shall kill me,
and go again to Rehoboam king of Judah. Whereupon the king took
counsel, and made two calves of gold, and said unto them, It is too
much for you to go up to Jerusalem: behold thy gods, O Israel, which
brought thee up out of the land of Egypt. And he set the one in Beth-
el, and the other put he in Dan" (1 Kings 12:27–29). The people worshiped the golden calves. Back of all this idolatry is Satan. This is
Satan worship.

I had the privilege of visiting the places of the seven churches of
Asia. You will recall that the Lord said to the church at Pergamos, "I
know thy works and where thou dwellest, even where Satan's seat
is . . ." (Rev. 2:13). That was a city given over to idolatry. Behind idolatry is Satan. Demonism manifests itself in many different ways.

> And after them out of all the tribes of Israel such as set
> their hearts to seek the LORD God of Israel came to Jeru-
> salem, to sacrifice unto the LORD God of their fathers.

> So they strengthened the kingdom of Judah, and made
> Rehoboam the son of Solomon strong, three years: for
> three years they walked in the way of David and Solo-
> mon [2 Chron. 11:16–17].

There were some folk in the ten northern tribes who were still faithful
to God, and they would come down to Jerusalem to worship.

Now we are told something of Rehoboam's personal life:

> And Rehoboam loved Maachah the daughter of Absalom
> above all his wives and his concubines: (for he took
> eighteen wives, and threescore concubines; and begat
> twenty and eight sons, and threescore daughters.)
>
> And Rehoboam made Abijah the son of Maachah the
> chief, to be ruler among his brethren: for he thought to
> make him king.
>
> And he dealt wisely, and dispersed of all his children
> throughout all the countries of Judah and Benjamin,
> unto every fenced city: and he gave them victual in
> abundance. And he desired many wives [2 Chron.
> 11:21-23].

Because the record of his many wives appears in the Bible, a great
many folk assume that God approves of polygamy. No. God records
this to let us know that He does not approve of it. This man Rehoboam
did wrong by not listening to the counselors of Solomon but listening
to the young men instead. He was wrong in trying to start a civil war.
He was wrong in having many wives. This is recorded because it is
history; it is what he did. It is one of the many things for which God
judged him.

REHOBOAM'S APOSTASY

In the life of Rehoboam one sin led to another. Now we see that he
leads his people in apostasy.

> And it came to pass, when Rehoboam had established
> the kingdom, and had strengthened himself, he forsook
> the law of the LORD, and all Israel with him [2 Chron.
> 12:1].

God did not approve of Rehoboam's conduct. People read the things
these men did in the Old Testament, and they say, "Look what they

did and they got by with it." That is often said about Abraham when he took Hagar and had the boy Ishmael. Friends, he didn't get by with it. Do you know who is the big problem in the Middle East today? The sons of Abraham—the Israelites and the Arabs. Who is the Arab? Well, I had an Arab guide take me down to the city of Jericho. I wanted someone who knew about the place, and this was a brilliant fellow who had worked with Sir Charles Marsdon and Miss Kathleen Kenyon in their excavations. He was very helpful to me. We were talking about the land, and I made the statement that God had given it to Abraham and to his offspring. This Arab smiled and looked me straight in the eye and said, "Dr. McGee, I am as much a son of Abraham as any Jew who is alive today." And he was right! He could trace his ancestry right back to Ishmael. He boasted of the fact that he was an Ismaelite, a son of Abraham. Did God approve when Abraham took Hagar? God records it as history. Then He lets you see the results. It certainly has never been a blessing. In fact, it has been a thorn in the flesh down through the centuries.

Now God records the apostasy of Jeroboam. Also He records the forsaking of the Law by Rehoboam and Israel. God condemns these things, but He records them as history.

INVASION OF EGYPT

Now God's judgment falls upon Rehoboam. For the first time He opens up that southern kingdom to the invasion of a major nation. You see, Rehoboam had forsaken the Word of God; he had led his people in apostasy. When he did this, God did something He had not done before. Previous to this, God had put a wall around His people, and the great nations of that day were not permitted to invade that territory.

> And it came to pass, that in the fifth year of king Rehoboam Shishak king of Egypt came up against Jerusalem, because they had transgressed against the LORD.

> With twelve hundred chariots, and threescore thousand horsemen: and the people were without number that

> came with him out of Egypt: the Lubims, the Sukkiims,
> and the Ethiopians [2 Chron. 12:2-3].

First, Shishak king of Egypt came up and carried away great booty. He lugged away a great deal of the gold and other wealth of that kingdom.

> So Shishak king of Egypt came up against Jerusalem,
> and took away the treasures of the house of the LORD,
> and the treasures of the king's house; he took all: he car-
> ried away also the shields of gold which Solomon had
> made.
>
> Instead of which king Rehoboam made shields of brass,
> and committed them to the hands of the chief of the
> guard, that kept the entrance of the king's house.
>
> And when the king entered into the house of the LORD,
> the guard came and fetched them, and brought them
> again into the guard chamber [2 Chron. 12:9-11].

These, you recall, are the great shields of gold that David brought and that Solomon placed in the temple. After these had been captured as booty, Rehoboam substitutes something inferior. No longer do they have shields of gold; now they have shields of brass. The judgment of God is upon them because of their sins.

This was a humbling experience for Rehoboam. He had been brought up in the affluence of the reign of Solomon and had experienced the blessing that had come. He had known nothing but wealth and luxury and expected it to go on forever. He begins to realize there may be an end to the glory of the kingdom of Solomon.

> And when he humbled himself, the wrath of the LORD
> turned from him, that he would not destroy him alto-
> gether; and also in Judah things went well [2 Chron.
> 12:12].

This reveals the amazing mercy of God. When this man humbles himself, God immediately withdraws judgment upon him and the people of Judah.

> So king Rehoboam strengthened himself in Jerusalem, and reigned: for Rehoboam was one and forty years old when he began to reign, and he reigned seventeen years in Jerusalem, the city which the LORD had chosen out of all the tribes of Israel, to put his name there. And his mother's name was Naamah an Ammonitess [2 Chron. 12:13].

It is interesting to learn who was Rehoboam's mother. You recall that David had been very friendly with the Ammonites—although they had made war against him. Now we find that Rehoboam, his grandson, was the son of an Ammonite woman. She undoubtedly had something to do with the character of this man. As we saw in the Book of Kings, God always mentions the mother's name. Why? Because she bears part of the responsibility for her son. If he turns out well, she shares in the credit. If he turns out to be a wicked, evil king, she must take part of the blame.

> And he did evil, because he prepared not his heart to seek the LORD.

> Now the acts of Rehoboam, first and last, are they not written in the book of Shemaiah the prophet, and of Iddo the seer concerning genealogies? And there were wars between Rehoboam and Jeroboam continually.

> And Rehoboam slept with his fathers, and was buried in the city of David: and Abijah his son reigned in his stead [2 Chron. 12:14–16].

CHAPTER 13

THEME: *Abijah reigns over Judah*

After Rehoboam's death, his son Abijah came to the throne. Although Abijah is not considered a good king, and the record in 1 Kings says that ". . . he walked in all the sins of his father . . . and his heart was not perfect with the LORD his God . . ." (1 Kings 15:3), yet here in Chronicles we read of an episode during which he honored the Lord.

> And Abijah set the battle in array with an army of valiant men of war, even four hundred thousand chosen men: Jeroboam also set the battle in array against him with eight hundred thousand chosen men, being mighty men of valour.
>
> And Abijah stood up upon mount Zemaraim, which is in mount Ephraim, and said, Hear me, thou Jeroboam, and all Israel;
>
> Ought ye not to know that the LORD God of Israel gave the kingdom over Israel to David for ever, even to him and to his sons by a covenant of salt?
>
> Yet Jeroboam the son of Nebat, the servant of Solomon the son of David, is risen up, and hath rebelled against his lord [2 Chron. 13:3–6].

As we have seen, there was a reason for that, a sufficient reason: the foolishness of Rehoboam.

> And there are gathered unto him vain men, the children of Belial, and have strengthened themselves against Rehoboam the son of Solomon, when Rehoboam was

> **young and tenderhearted, and could not withstand them
> [2 Chron. 13:7].**

He was not only young and tenderhearted, but he was very foolish.
    This is the plea on the part of Abijah to try to bring back the ten
tribes, but there is no use now because Jeroboam has made himself
king, and he is not about to make peace.

> **But Jeroboam caused an ambushment to come about be-
> hind them: so they were before Judah, and the ambush-
> ment was behind them.**

> **And when Judah looked back, behold, the battle was be-
> fore and behind: and they cried unto the LORD, and the
> priests sounded with the trumpets [2 Chron. 13:13-14].**

They cry unto God for help. Now notice God's gracious response.

> **Then the men of Judah gave a shout: and as the men of
> Judah shouted, it came to pass, that God smote Jero-
> boam and all Israel before Abijah and Judah.**

> **And the children of Israel fled before Judah: and God
> delivered them into their hand.**

> **And Abijah and his people slew them with a great
> slaughter: so there fell down slain of Israel five hundred
> thousand chosen men [2 Chron. 13:15-17].**

This is a great victory.

> **And Abijah pursued after Jeroboam, and took cities
> from him, Beth-el with the towns thereof, and Jeshanah
> with the towns thereof, and Ephrain with the towns
> thereof.**

> **Neither did Jeroboam recover strength again in the days
> of Abijah: and the LORD struck him, and he died
> [2 Chron. 13:19-20].**

CHRONOLOGICAL TABLE OF THE KINGS OF THE DIVIDED KINGDOM

	JUDAH				ISRAEL			
King	Reign	Char-acter	Prophet		King	Reign	Char-acter	Prophet
1. Rehoboam	931–913 B.C. [17 yrs.]	Bad	Shemaiah		1. Jeroboam I	931–910 B.C. (22 yrs.)	Bad	Ahijah
2. Abijah	913–911 [3 yrs.]	Bad						
3. Asa	911–870 [41 yrs.]	Good			2. Nadab	910–909 (2 yrs.)	Bad	
					3. Baasha	909–886 [24 yrs.]	Bad	
					4. Elah	886–885 (2 yrs.)	Bad	
					5. Zimri	885 (7 days)	Bad	
					6. Omri	885–874* (12 yrs.)	Bad	{Elijah
4. Jehoshaphat	870–848* [25 yrs.]	Good			7. Ahab	874–853 (22 yrs.)	Bad	{Micaiah
5. Jehoram	848–841* [8 yrs.]	Bad			8. Ahaziah	853–852 (2 yrs.)	Bad	Elisha
6. Ahaziah	841 [1 yr.]	Bad			9. Joram	852–841 (12 yrs.)	Bad	
7. Athaliah	841–835 [6 yrs.]	Bad			10. Jehu	841–814 (28 yrs.)	Bad	
8. Joash	835–796 [40 yrs.]	Good	Joel		11. Jehoahaz	814–798 (17 yrs.)	Bad	
9. Amaziah	796–767 [29 yrs.]	Good			12. Jehoash	798–782 (16 yrs.)	Bad	{Jonah
10. Azariah (or Uzziah)	767–740* [52 yrs.]	Good	Isaiah		13. Jeroboam II	782–753* (41 yrs.)	Bad	{Amos / {Hosea
					14. Zechariah	753–752 (6 mo.)	Bad	
					15. Shallum	752 (1 mo.)	Bad	
					16. Menahem	752–742 (10 yrs.)	Bad	
11. Jotham	740–732* [16 yrs.]	Good	Micah		17. Pekahiah	742–740 (2 yrs.)	Bad	
12. Ahaz	732–716 [16 yrs.]	Bad			18. Pekah	740–732* (20 yrs.)	Bad	
					19. Hoshea	732–721 (9 yrs.)	Bad	
					(Capture of Samaria and captivity of Israel)			
13. Hezekiah	716–687 [29 yrs.]	Good	Nahum					
14. Manasseh	687–642* [55 yrs.]	Bad	{Habakkuk					
15. Amon	642–640 [2 yrs.]	Bad	{Zephaniah					
16. Josiah	640–608 [31 yrs.]	Good	{Jeremiah					
17. Jehoahaz	608 [3 mo.]	Bad						
18. Jehoiakim	608–597 [11 yrs.]	Bad						
19. Jehoiachin	597 [3 mo.]	Bad						
20. Zedekiah	597–586 [11 yrs.]	Bad						
(Destruction of Jerusalem and captivity of Judah)								

*Co-regency

This is God's judgment upon Jeroboam for dividing the nation.

> But Abijah waxed mighty, and married fourteen wives,
> and begat twenty and two sons, and sixteen daughters.
>
> And the rest of the acts of Abijah, and his ways, and his
> sayings, are written in the story of the prophet Iddo
> [2 Chron. 13:21–22].

Abijah was no great king, but after him comes his son who will lead
the first revival.

CHAPTERS 14—16

THEME: Revival under Asa, king of Judah

During the reign of Asa we will come to the first revival. I believe that God has given us a lesson on revival in this book. The road to revival is a rocky, unpaved, uphill road. However, the road is well-marked, the road maps are clear, and there are certain bridges that must be crossed.

Asa is one of the five kings whom God used to bring revival to the southern kingdom. The northern kingdom never had a revival. They had nineteen kings, and all of them were bad. There's not one good one in the lot. Of the twenty kings over Judah, ten of them could be called good, and five of them were outstanding. These kings were Asa, Jehoshaphat, Joash, Hezekiah, and Josiah. During their reigns there was a period of reformation, which was incubated in a time of revival. There is a similarity among all the kings, but there are also some striking differences.

> So Abijah slept with his fathers, and they buried him in the city of David: and Asa his son reigned in his stead. In his days the land was quiet ten years [2 Chron. 14:1].

Asa is the first of the kings in whose reign there was a revival. Solomon was his great-grandfather, Rehoboam was his grandfather, and, of course, Abijah was his father.

> And Asa did that which was good and right in the eyes of the LORD his God:
>
> For he took away the altars of the strange gods, and the high places, and brake down the images, and cut down the groves:

And commanded Judah to seek the LORD God of their
fathers, and to do the law and the commandment
[2 Chron. 14:2-4].

Here is the character of the man. He is absolutely outstanding.

Also he took away out of all the cities of Judah the high
places and the images: and the kingdom was quiet before him.

And he built fenced cities in Judah: for the land had rest,
and he had no war in those years; because the LORD had
given him rest [2 Chron. 14:5-6].

He was also a man of peace. However, we find that Ethiopia made war
against him.

And there came out against them Zerah the Ethiopian
with an host of a thousand thousand, and three hundred
chariots; and came unto Mareshah.

Then Asa went out against him, and they set the battle
in array in the valley of Zephathah at Mareshah
[2 Chron. 14:9-10].

Not only was Asa a man of peace, he was also a man of prayer. We have
a glimpse into the private life of the king, and it is commendable.

And Asa cried unto the LORD his God, and said, LORD, it
is nothing with thee to help, whether with many, or with
them that have no power: help us, O LORD our God; for
we rest on thee, and in thy name we go against this multitude. O LORD, thou art our God; let not man prevail
against thee.

So the LORD smote the Ethiopians before Asa, and before
Judah: and the Ethiopians fled [2 Chron. 14:11-12].

This is real praying. It is not flowery, but direct and right to the point. He says exactly what he means. Asa was a great man of prayer. The revival that came to the nation came because he was this kind of a king.

> They smote also the tents of cattle, and carried away sheep and camels in abundance, and returned to Jerusalem [2 Chron. 14:15].

God gave Asa a great military victory.

ENCOURAGEMENT OF AZARIAH, THE PROPHET

On the road to revival there are three bridges which must be crossed. We come now to the first bridge, which is a knowledge of the Word of God.

> And the spirit of God came upon Azariah the son of Oded:
>
> And he went out to meet Asa, and said unto him, Hear ye me, Asa, and all Judah and Benjamin: The LORD is with you, while ye be with him; and if ye seek him, he will be found of you; but if ye forsake him, he will forsake you.
>
> Now for a long season Israel hath been without the true God, and without a teaching priest, and without law [2 Chron. 15:1-3].

The tragedy of the hour in our day is that there is not enough Bible teaching in the church. I say this very kindly, but we do not need more preachers. You can buy them like bananas, by the dozen. Bible teachers are few and far between; yet they are needed. And they were needed in Asa's day. They did not have a teaching priest. They had priests and Levites—they were knee-deep in priests and Levites—but they did not have a teaching priest. Consequently they were without the Law, without the Word of God.

> But when they in their trouble did turn unto the Lord
> God of Israel, and sought him, he was found of them
> [2 Chron. 15:4].

It's just that simple, and yet it is just that complicated.

My friend, if you mean business with God, God will means business with you. I hear people say, "Oh, I try to study. I try to pray. I try to do this but I don't get anywhere." My friend, who are you kidding? May I say to you that when you say that, you make God a liar. I have news for you—God is no liar. God says, "If you seek Me, I am there." If you mean business with God, God will mean business with you. Oh, search your heart, my friend. If you really want to know God's Word, then God is ready to meet you any time you are ready.

> And in those times there was no peace to him that went
> out, nor to him that came in, but great vexations were
> upon all the inhabitants of the countries.
>
> And nation was destroyed of nation, and city of city: for
> God did vex them with all adversity.
>
> Be ye strong therefore, and let not your hands be weak:
> for your work shall be rewarded [2 Chron. 15:5-7].

Asa is beginning to turn to God. This prophet encourages him in this, and he explains why they had had trouble and so many problems.

Now I strongly suspect that the prophet's message applies to us as well as to Judah. I'm not speaking ex cathedra but, in studying the Word of God and seeing how God dealt with these people here, I am wondering if the root of our national problems is not the same. We have all those smart boys in Washington, and they make stupid decisions. How can such smart boys make such stupid decisions? Why is it that we cannot have law and order? Why is it that we can't really have peace? Why is there such lawlessness today? Let me venture my opinion on the basis of the Word of God. It is because God has been left out. He is not in the government circles in Washington. They think they don't need God because they have the smart boys. My friend, in this hour in which we are living, our nation needs *God!*

> And when Asa heard these words, and the prophecy of Oded the prophet, he took courage, and put away the abominable idols out of all the land of Judah and Benjamin, and out of the cities which he had taken from mount Ephraim, and renewed the altar of the LORD, that was before the porch of the LORD.

> And he gathered all Judah and Benjamin, and the strangers with them out of Ephraim and Manasseh, and out of Simeon: for they fell to him out of Israel in abundance, when they saw that the LORD his God was with him [2 Chron. 15:8-9].

God always has a remnant that will turn to Him.

> So they gathered themselves together at Jerusalem in the third month, in the fifteenth year of the reign of Asa.

> And they offered unto the LORD the same time, of the spoil which they had brought, seven hundred oxen and seven thousand sheep.

> And they entered into a covenant to seek the LORD God of their fathers with all their heart and with all their soul [2 Chron. 15:10-12].

You will notice that these people are crossing the first bridge. They are not trying to detour around it. They have come to a knowledge of God's Word. They are turning to God and seeking Him with all their heart and soul. This characterized every one of the revivals. There was a return to the Word of God.

I am bold enough to state dogmatically that there has never been a revival without a return to the Word of God. There is no detour around the Bible. There is no substitute for it. The great spiritual movement in the days of John Wesley, my friend, was built around the Word of God. Wesley read the Bible in three languages every morning! Dwight L. Moody and the great spiritual awakening in his day led to the great Bible institute movement, one of the greatest movements in the study of the Word. It is dying out in our day. Why? Because they are getting away from the Word of God. We need more than just a superficial familiarity with the Word of God. We need more than an artificial vocabulary of the right words. Revival does not depend on an activity, nor on a service, nor on a method. It requires a real knowledge and love of the Word of God.

In our contemporary society there are movements and there are evangelists whom God is using, but I am disturbed because they are not making the study of the Word of God paramount. I find it difficult to get these movements, and even some of our schools, interested in studying the entire Word of God. My friend, we cannot have a real revival unless it is based on a thorough knowledge of the Bible. I hope revival will come. I believe this is the first bridge on the route. We'll have to cross over this bridge first.

Now at this great assembly which Asa had called in Jerusalem, they entered into a covenant with God to seek Him with all their hearts.

> **That whosoever would not seek the Lord God of Israel should be put to death, whether small or great, whether man or woman.**

> **And they sware unto the Lord with a loud voice, and with shouting, and with trumpets, and with cornets [2 Chron. 15:13–14].**

This was making it very harsh; yet there was a ready response from the hearts of the people. This man Asa brought about many reforms at this time.

> **And all Judah rejoiced at the oath: for they had sworn with all their heart, and sought him with their whole**

desire; and he was found of them: and the LORD gave them rest round about [2 Chron. 15:15].

My friend, if you seek the Lord with your whole heart, He will be found of you.

We have seen that the first bridge to revival is a knowledge of the Word of God. Now we come to the second bridge which is scriptural separation. The word *separation* is one of the most abused words in Christian circles. Asa here is practicing scriptural separation:

And also concerning Maachah the mother of Asa the king, he removed her from being queen, because she had made an idol in a grove: and Asa cut down her idol, and stamped it, and burnt it at the brook Kidron [2 Chron. 15:16].

This is indeed interesting—his own mother was engaged in idolatry! Notice that she wasn't just a friend of people who were idolaters, but she herself was an idolater. This is the reason Asa removed her from the place of influence.

But the high places were not taken away out of Israel: nevertheless the heart of Asa was perfect all his days [2 Chron. 15:17].

Asa could have removed these high places, but he did not. He went only part way with God—and yet God used him. How gracious God is!

I am weary of folk who consider themselves separated and roundly criticize everyone else in the ministry whose methods are different from theirs. My friend, that is not scriptural separation at all. Separation is not an attempt to straighten out every individual and try to force men whom God is using to conform to your pattern. That is the narrowest form of bigotry. I feel that some folk ought to get separated from themselves—that would really be separation! If you want revival, the place to begin is with yourself. I suggest that you get in a room by yourself, draw a circle right around you, and say, "Lord, begin a revival, and let it start inside this circle."

ASA'S LAPSE OF FAITH

In the six and thirtieth year of the reign of Asa Baasha king of Israel came up against Judah, and built Ramah, to the intent that he might let none go out or come in to Asa king of Judah [2 Chron. 16:1].

We have read in several verses that people from the northern kingdom would move to Judah because they saw that there was a revival going on under Asa. Baasha wanted to keep his people in his own kingdom and didn't want them to be moving south to Judah.

> **Then Asa brought out silver and gold out of the treasures of the house of the LORD and of the king's house, and sent to Ben-hadad king of Syria, that dwelt at Damascus, saying,**
>
> **There is a league between me and thee, as there was between my father and thy father: behold, I have sent thee silver and gold: go, break thy league with Baasha king of Israel, that he may depart from me [2 Chron. 16:2–3].**

Israel became a formidable enemy to Asa and Judah. So what does Asa do? He turns to a former ally that he had, King Ben-hadad of Syria. And what did that indicate? It indicated a lack of faith in God.

> **And Ben-hadad hearkened unto king Asa, and sent the captains of his armies against the cities of Israel; and they smote Ijon, and Dan, and Abel-maim, and all the store cities of Naphtali [2 Chron. 16:4].**

The king of Syria responded and sent in his troops.

> And it came to pass, when Baasha heard it, that he left off building of Ramah, and let his work cease.
>
> Then Asa the king took all Judah; and they carried away the stones of Ramah, and the timber thereof, wherewith Baasha was building; and he built therewith Geba and Mizpah [2 Chron. 16:5–6].

The maneuver was successful, but now the Lord has something to say to Asa.

> And at that time Hanani the seer came to Asa king of Judah, and said unto him, Because thou hast relied on the king of Syria, and not relied on the LORD thy God, therefore is the host of the king of Syria escaped out of thine hand.
>
> Were not the Ethiopians and the Lubims a huge host, with very many chariots and horsemen? yet, because thou didst rely on the LORD, he delivered them into thine hand.
>
> For the eyes of the LORD run to and fro throughout the whole earth, to shew himself strong in the behalf of them whose heart is perfect toward him. Herein thou hast done foolishly: therefore from henceforth thou shalt have wars [2 Chron. 16:7–9].

Why did God send a prophet to Asa to rebuke him? Why does God judge Asa? It is for his lack of faith.

The third bridge we must cross for revival is faith in God—not faith in methods, nor in man, nor in a church, nor in a system, nor in an organization. Revival requires faith in God.

When Baasha came against Asa in civil war, Asa turned to Ben-hadad of Syria, the ancient enemy. Hanani reminded him that he had every evidence that God would deliver him. God had delivered into his hand the army of the Ethiopians and the Lubims. Yet at this crisis point Asa demonstrated a lack of faith.

We need to clearly understand that although there is one act of faith which saves us—that is justification is by faith; the moment we put our trust in Jesus Christ, we are saved—life does not end when we are saved. My friend, we are to *live* by faith. Paul wrote to the Roman believers, "For I am not ashamed of the gospel of Christ: for it is the power of God unto salvation to every one that believeth; to the Jew first, and also to the Greek." Then he uses one of the strangest expressions imaginable: "For therein is the righteousness of God revealed from faith to faith: as it is written, The just shall live by faith" (Rom. 1:16–17). What does it mean that therein is the righteousness of God revealed from faith to faith? It means we are *saved* by faith, and we are to *live* by faith.

Hanani said to Asa, "For the eyes of the LORD run to and fro throughout the whole earth, to shew himself strong in the behalf of them whose heart is perfect toward him." This means that God is looking for a man or a woman who will believe in Him. By the way, would you like to be that person who believes God? I don't mean you are to become a fanatic, but you can believe God on the good solid testimony of His Word. Do you know that you cannot possibly please God unless you believe Him? "But without faith it is impossible to please him . . ." (Heb. 11:6). The writer to the Hebrews also tells us that we are compassed about with a great cloud of witnesses. Because of this, ". . . let us lay aside every weight, and the sin which doth so easily beset us. . . ." What is the sin? Unbelief. ". . . and let us run with patience the race that is set before us" (Heb. 12:1). Let's not only be saved by faith, my friend, let's live by faith. Many folk claim to be Christians, yet they live like agnostics.

> **Then Asa was wroth with the seer, and put him in a prison house; for he was in a rage with him because of this thing. And Asa oppressed some of the people the same time [2 Chron. 16:10].**

This is amazing! Asa will not accept the rebuke. Why? Because he didn't believe it. Neither did he have real faith and dependence on God.

Living without God means spiritual death for us. There could be no way in the world for us to be used of God.

Now we will see that God struck him with a disease.

And Asa in the thirty and ninth years of his reign was diseased in his feet, until his disease was exceeding great: yet in his disease he sought not to the LORD, but to the physicians [2 Chron. 16:12].

God struck him with a disease which was serious and then became critical. He turned to the physicians. There is nothing wrong in that. The point is that he didn't turn to God in all of this. It is just as important for a believer to go to God when he gets sick as it is to call the doctor. Not only do I believe that, but I am a walking proof that God is faithful. When it was discovered that I had cancer, I not only went to the doctor, I went to God in prayer. I didn't go to a so-called faith healer. I went to the Great Physician. When you get sick, there are two things you ought to do: you should call the doctor and you should call upon God. Probably the most practical writer in the New Testament said, "Is any sick among you? let him call for the elders of the church; and let them pray over him, anointing him with oil in the name of the Lord" (James 5:14). He said two things should be done. The first was prayer, turning to God, calling on the name of the Lord. The second was anointing the sick one with oil. Now that was not a ceremonial act, not a religious act; it was medicinal. He was saying they should call on the Lord and call the doctor. That is practical.

The difficulty with Asa was that he called the doctor, but he didn't call on the Lord. It is amazing and very sobering to see a man who had experienced revival but now is not walking with God and is not living by faith.

My friend, to live by faith is to have faith in God. It means we take our problems and our difficulties to the Lord and turn them over to Him. It is a faith that accepts whatever answer He gives us because He hears and answers our prayers in His own way. He may not answer in our way, but He will answer according to His will. You can be sure of one thing: if you turn things over to Him, you will be in His will. If you are in His will, that is the very best answer you can get—lots better than what you may have asked for.

> **And Asa slept with his fathers, and died in the one and fortieth year of his reign.**
>
> **And they buried him in his own sepulchres, which he had made for himself in the city of David, and laid him in the bed which was filled with sweet odours and divers kinds of spices prepared by the apothecaries' art: and they made a very great burning for him [2 Chron. 16:13-14].**

They burned a lot of candles for him.

During Asa's reign Judah experienced a touch of revival. He went only part way with God, and yet God used him.

CHAPTERS 17—20

THEME: Revival during Jehoshaphat's reign

This section records the second great revival period. It was much greater than the revival of Asa. Jehoshaphat, the son of Asa, was a man marvelously used of God. Remember that Chronicles gives God's viewpoint of the period of the kings and records what God considers important during the reigns of these men.

> **And Jehoshaphat his son reigned in his stead, and strengthened himself against Israel [2 Chron. 17:1].**

That is, he strengthened the kingdom of Judah against Israel, the northern kingdom.

> **And he placed forces in all the fenced cities of Judah, and set garrisons in the land of Judah, and in the cities of Ephraim, which Asa his father had taken [2 Chron. 17:2].**

You recall in the previous chapter we are told of war between Judah and Israel. Jehoshaphat is taking precautions to protect his kingdom.

> **And the LORD was with Jehoshaphat, because he walked in the first ways of his father David, and sought not unto Baalim [2 Chron. 17:3].**

Notice that it says he walked in the "first ways" of his father—not in the way David walked in his old age, but when he was a young king, trusted the Lord.

> **But sought to the LORD God of his father, and walked in his commandments, and not after the doings of Israel.**

> Therefore the LORD stablished the kingdom in his hand;
> and all Judah brought to Jehoshaphat presents; and he
> had riches and honour in abundance [2 Chron. 17:4–5].

In the Old Testament a sign of God's approval was material prosperity.

TEACHING THE WORD

> And his heart was lifted up in the ways of the LORD:
> moreover he took away the high places and groves out of
> Judah.
>
> Also in the third year of his reign he sent to his princes,
> even to Ben-hail, and to Obadiah, and to Zechariah,
> and to Nethaneel, and Michaiah, to teach in the cities of
> Judah.
>
> And with them he sent Levites, even Shemaiah, and
> Nethaniah, and Zebadiah, and Asahel, and Shemira-
> moth, and Jehonathan, and Adonijah, and Tobijah, and
> Tobadonijah, Levites; and with them Elishama and Je-
> horam, priests.
>
> And they taught in Judah, and had the book of the law of
> the LORD with them, and went about throughout all the
> cities of Judah, and taught the people [2 Chron. 17:6–9].

Do you realize what Jehoshaphat did? He started a "Thru the Bible" program! Because I sign my name J. Vernon McGee, people ask me what the "J" stands for, and I generally give them some facetious answer. So I'll give you one: it stands for *Jehoshaphat* because he was the first one to start a "Thru the Bible" program. He sent out the Levites. Since they didn't have mechanical means of communication, they had to go out personally. Jehoshaphat sent them out by the hundreds and maybe even by the thousands. They spread throughout the entire kingdom teaching the Word of God. My friend, that is the way of revival.

Until the church gets back to the Word of God, there will be no real revival. All movements in or out of the church will come to naught unless they are anchored in the Word of God. There are wonderful things that are happening today. Some are inside the church; some are outside the organized church. If they are rooted in the Word of God, revival will be the result.

Now notice the reaction to the teaching of the Word of God.

> **And the fear of the LORD fell upon all the kingdoms of the lands that were round about Judah, so that they made no war against Jehoshaphat.**
>
> **Also some of the Philistines brought Jehoshaphat presents, and tribute silver; and the Arabians brought him flocks, seven thousand and seven hundred rams, and seven thousand and seven hundred he goats.**
>
> **And Jehoshaphat waxed great exceedingly; and he built in Judah castles, and cities of store [2 Chron. 17:10–12].**

Jehoshaphat had to build great storage places to house all the gifts that were brought to him. You see, this man was marvelously used of God. When revival came to Judah, it had its effect upon all the nations around them. The revival spread. Even the Philistines, who were the inveterate enemies of David, became friendly and sent gifts and silver for tribute to him. It even penetrated among the Arabian people. The Arabs sent flocks of animals to him.

You will also notice that there was no war against him. Spiritual revival is a cure for war. If a nation wishes to have peace, it must turn to God. That is God's method and always has been. If a nation is constantly at war, it is because that nation has turned away from God.

> **And he had much business in the cities of Judah: and the men of war, mighty men of valour, were in Jerusalem [2 Chron. 17:13].**

This was a time of peace, but Jehoshaphat kept an army for protection.

The captains are listed in the next few verses. He is a great ruler. He has provided ample protection in case there should be an attack by the enemy, but God has given him peace.

> **These waited on the king, beside those whom the king put in the fenced cities throughout all Judah [2 Chron. 17:19].**

Jehoshaphat is a great man by all measurements. But now we see him doing something that is almost unbelievable.

JEHOSHAPHAT'S ALLIANCE WITH AHAB

> **Now Jehoshaphat had riches and honour in abundance, and joined affinity with Ahab [2 Chron. 18:1].**

Jehoshaphat teamed up with Ahab. He had fellowship with Ahab. I cannot think of two men more unlike than these two men.

> **And after certain years he went down to Ahab to Samaria. And Ahab killed sheep and oxen for him in abundance, and for the people that he had with him, and persuaded him to go up with him to Ramoth-gilead [2 Chron. 18:2].**

This seems unbelievable. It is one of the strangest partnerships on record in the pages of Scripture, or anywhere else. It is almost like saying that you could have day and night at the same time or that you can have light and darkness at the same time. How these two ever came together is a mystery. They have nothing in common spiritually. Jehoshaphat is one of the most godly kings personally, and he has been used to bring revival to his nation. He loves God, and he loves the Word of God. He is what we would call a spiritually minded man. On the other hand, Ahab is as godless as they come. He hates God. He has given himself over to idolatry and immorality. How can these two be buddy-buddy? How can they enjoy each other's company? What is it that they have in common? Well, let's do a little investigation here.

They had a threefold alliance and partnership. It is all based on material reasons, physical reasons. They had nothing in common spiritually.

1. There was a matrimonial alliance between the two. Jehoram, the son of Jehoshaphat, married Athaliah, the daughter of Ahab and Jezebel. This Athaliah was a bloody woman who walked in the ways of her parents. We have already seen that in the Books of Kings. I suppose these two men thought they could cement relations between Judah and Israel and bring about an undivided kingdom. They tried to do this by intermarrying. What they did was wrong.

This is also a significant spot in our contemporary culture. I may sound like an antiquated preacher to a lot of folk, but I must speak out on a subject which is clearly taught in the Word of God. Here in Southern California we lead the world in divorce rates. Although I am not an authority in this field, there is one area on which I can speak loud and clear: a believer and an unbeliever—a Christian and a non-Christian—should not get married under any circumstances. Here the son of Jehoshaphat, hot out of a revival, marries that cold-blooded daughter of Ahab and Jezebel. That brought tragedy. In fact, it almost exterminated the line of David.

There is more tragedy, more heartache and heartbreak, more broken lives, more maladjusted children over this one problem of broken homes than anything else I know about. It will not work for a professing Christian to marry one who is not a Christian. If two non-Christian people get married and one is converted after they have married, that is a different situation. The apostle Paul writes specifically about that situation. However, God has much to say against a Christian deliberately walking into the trap of marrying a non-Christian—and it is a trap.

2. Jehoshaphat and Ahab had a market alliance. We are told that Jehoshaphat joined himself with Ahaziah, the son of Ahab, when he became king of Israel, and they sent ships to Tarshish. This is recorded in 1 Kings 22 and also in 2 Chronicles 20. The ships were sent

for commerce in grain and gold. There was a shipwreck, and the cargo was lost. God could not bless this alliance.

3. Jehoshaphat and Ahab had a military alliance. Ahab was having problems with Syria; so he asked Jehoshaphat to enter into an alliance with him and go with him up to Ramoth-gilead. He gave a big feast for Jehoshaphat with sheep and oxen in abundance. And so he persuaded Jehoshaphat. Notice that Jehoshaphat is now sitting ". . . in the seat of the scornful" (Ps. 1:1). What the armies of the northern kingdom could not accomplish against the southern kingdom of Judah, Ahab accomplished by involving Jehoshaphat in a war with Syria. It reminds one of Chamberlain at Munich with Hitler and Mussolini. It reminds one of Yalta with Roosevelt and Churchill. It reminds one of Marshall in London. I'm sure there are alliances being made today, alliances which should never be made at all and which God cannot bless.

> **And Ahab king of Israel said unto Jehoshaphat king of Judah, Wilt thou go with me to Ramoth-gilead? And he answered him, I am as thou art, and my people as thy people; and we will be with thee in the war [2 Chron. 18:3].**

Jehoshaphat is in the family of Ahab now by this intermarrying of their children. So he is willing to make an alliance and says, "We are one. We are together." Now remember, God had given Jehoshaphat peace. Ahab is asking him to go to war. Jehoshaphat agrees. And yet he is disturbed. He has a mind for God, and this situation gives him a certain amount of anxiety.

> **And Jehoshaphat said unto the king of Israel, Inquire, I pray thee, at the word of the LORD to-day [2 Chron. 18:4].**

Jehoshaphat says, "Let's find out what God has to say about this venture." So Ahab brings in his whole army of prophets.

> Therefore the king of Israel gathered together of
> prophets four hundred men, and said unto them, Shall
> we go to Ramoth-gilead to battle, or shall I forbear? And
> they said, Go up; for God will deliver it into the king's
> hand [2 Chron. 18:5].

Who are these prophets? They are prophets of Baal!

Now Jehoshaphat has discernment enough to know there is something wrong here.

> But Jehoshaphat said, Is there not here a prophet of the
> LORD besides, that we might inquire of him?

> And the king of Israel said unto Jehoshaphat, There is
> yet one man, by whom we may inquire of the LORD: but I
> hate him; for he never prophesied good unto me, but
> always evil: the same is Micaiah the son of Imla. And
> Jehoshaphat said, Let not the king say so [2 Chron.
> 18:6-7].

Jehoshaphat says, "You don't really mean that you hate him because he gives you the Word of God!" So Ahab agreed to send for him.

There are a lot of folk in our day also who hate a man who gives out the Word of God. In the church which I served for many years was a sign on the pulpit which I saw every time I stood there to speak. It read: "Sir, we would see Jesus." I like that. But I always felt there ought to be another verse of Scripture on the congregation's side of the pulpit: "Am I therefore become your enemy, because I tell you the truth?" (Gal. 4:16).

Micaiah is one of the great men of the Bible, as we have seen in 1 Kings 22. He was a man of God who gave out the Word of God. He told Ahab the truth at the peril of his own life. This man is now called on the scene.

> And the king of Israel and Jehoshaphat king of Judah sat
> either of them on his throne, clothed in their robes, and

> they sat in a void place at the entering in of the gate of
> Samaria; and all the prophets prophesied before them
> [2 Chron. 18:9].

You can imagine those four hundred prophets running around saying
to Ahab, "Go up against the king of Syria." One of them was especially dramatic. Zedekiah ran around with iron horns, pushing at
everyone with them, saying, "This is the way you are going to do it!"
What a scene—two kings on their thrones and all those prophets running around crying, "Go up and fight. You'll win!"

> And the messenger that went to call Micaiah spake to
> him, saying, Behold, the words of the prophets declare
> good to the king with one assent; let thy word therefore,
> I pray thee, be like one of theirs, and speak thou good
> [2 Chron. 18:12].

The messenger tries to tip off Micaiah as to the situation he will face
and advises him to get in step with the rest of them. He says all the
prophets agree that they should go up to war so the smart thing for
Micaiah to do is to agree with them. Maybe he even brought along a
copy of *How to Win Friends and Influence People.* He told him to be
sure to say the right thing to get on the good side of the king.

> And Micaiah said, As the LORD liveth, even what my
> God saith, that will I speak [2 Chron. 18:13].

Micaiah is not intimidated. He is going to say what God has for him to
say. You can be sure of that.

> And when he was come to the king, the king said unto
> him, Micaiah, shall we go to Ramoth-gilead to battle, or
> shall I forbear? And he said, Go ye up, and prosper, and
> they shall be delivered into your hand [2 Chron. 18:14].

Micaiah does have a sense of humor. I enjoy that. I often say—and I say it reverently—that God has a sense of humor in the Bible. This is one instance of that.

Remember the scene. The two kings are sitting on their thrones. Four hundred men are running around saying, "Go up, go up." Now with biting sarcasm Micaiah joins the parade, and says, "Go up, go up."

> **And the king said to him, How many times shall I adjure thee that thou say nothing but the truth to me in the name of the LORD [2 Chron. 18:15].**

Ahab says to him, "Stop kidding me. You can't fool me. I know you don't agree with them." You see, Ahab wanted the Word of God, but he didn't want it. He knew the difference between truth and falsehood, but he didn't want to obey the truth. There are a lot of folk like that today.

Now Micaiah becomes serious. Here is God's message: Not only will they lose the battle, but Ahab will be slain.

> **Then he said, I did see all Israel scattered upon the mountains, as sheep that have no shepherd: and the LORD said, These have no master; let them return therefore every man to his house in peace.**
>
> **And the king of Israel said to Jehoshaphat, Did I not tell thee that he would not prophesy good unto me, but evil? [2 Chron. 18:16–17].**

The king of Israel says to Jehoshaphat, "I told you so—I told you he would predict nothing but evil unto me!"

Now Micaiah really lets him have it. He is serious now, and he is sarcastic. Oh, with what biting irony he gives this parable to Ahab!

> Again he said, Therefore hear the word of the Lord; I
> saw the Lord sitting upon his throne, and all the host of
> heaven standing on his right hand and on his left.
>
> And the Lord said, Who shall entice Ahab king of Is-
> rael, that he may go up and fall at Ramoth-gilead? And
> one spake saying after this manner, and another saying
> after that manner [2 Chron. 18:18–19].

This is ridiculous! Can you imagine God calling a board of directors'
meeting to find out what He should do? The Lord doesn't ask for advice, my friend. Oh, what biting sarcasm this is! There were all kinds
of suggestions. Now there comes out a wee little spirit and says he has
a good idea.

> Then there came out a spirit, and stood before the Lord,
> and said, I will entice him. And the Lord said unto him,
> Wherewith?
>
> And he said, I will go out, and be a lying spirit in the
> mouth of all his prophets. And the Lord said, Thou shalt
> entice him, and thou shalt also prevail: go out, and do
> even so [2 Chron. 18:20–21].

Micaiah's ridiculous parable is a subtle way of saying that all these
prophets of Baal are a pack of liars!

> Now therefore, behold, the Lord hath put a lying spirit
> in the mouth of these thy prophets, and the Lord hath
> spoken evil against thee [2 Chron. 18:22].

In other words, these prophets have not been telling you the truth.
God is going to judge you.

Now Ahab is not about to pay any attention to what Micaiah says.
He gives orders to put him in prison and keep him there.

> Then the king of Israel said, Take ye Micaiah, and carry
> him back to Amon the governor of the city, and to Joash
> the king's son;

> And say, Thus saith the king, Put this fellow in the prison, and feed him with bread of affliction and with water of affliction, until I return in peace [2 Chron. 18:25-26].

Old Micaiah has the parting shot. Listen to him:

> And Micaiah said, If thou certainly return in peace, then hath not the LORD spoken by me. And he said, Hearken, all ye people [2 Chron. 18:27].

I love this! Before Micaiah was taken off, he said, "Look, if you come back, the Lord hasn't spoken by me. But you are not coming back." So he turns to the people, "He won't be here, but you will be here. Remember what I said!" This is tremendous!

> **So the king of Israel and Jehoshaphat the king of Judah went up to Ramoth-gilead.**
>
> **And the king of Israel said unto Jehoshaphat, I will disguise myself, and will go to the battle; but put thou on thy robes. So the king of Israel disguised himself; and they went to the battle [2 Chron. 18:28-29].**

Ahab proved he was a deceiver all the way through. You see, the only man in the battle who was wearing royal robes was Jehoshaphat, which made him a marked man. Clever old Ahab had disguised himself. You might say that Ahab set Jehoshaphat up as a clay pigeon to be slain in the battle. It was not Jehoshaphat's fight at all, but he almost got killed!

> **Now the king of Syria had commanded the captains of the chariots that were with him, saying, Fight ye not with small or great, save only with the king of Israel.**
>
> **And it came to pass, when the captains of the chariots saw Jehoshaphat, that they said, It is the king of Israel.**

> Therefore they compassed about him to fight: but Je-
> hoshaphat cried out, and the LORD helped him; and God
> moved them to depart from him [2 Chron. 18:30–31].

The only reason he came out alive is because God intervened on his behalf.

Old Ahab is feeling very satisfied with himself. Because of his cleverness he expects to come through the battle unscathed. But notice what happens.

> And a certain man drew a bow at a venture, and smote
> the king of Israel between the joints of the harness:
> therefore he said to his chariot man, Turn thine hand,
> that thou mayest carry me out of the host; for I am
> wounded [2 Chron. 18:33].

On the Syrian side there was a soldier who ended up with one arrow left in his quiver. "He drew his bow at a venture"—he wasn't aiming at anything. But that arrow had old Ahab's name on it, and it got him. What happened? He died, just as Micaiah said he would.

Jehoshaphat went back home a sadder and wiser man.

JEHOSHAPHAT REBUKED FOR HIS ALLIANCE

As Jehoshaphat returns home, he is met by a prophet with a message from God.

> And Jehoshaphat the king of Judah returned to his
> house in peace to Jerusalem.

> And Jehu the son of Hanani the seer went out to meet
> him, and said to king Jehoshaphat, Shouldest thou help
> the ungodly, and love them that hate the LORD? therefore
> is wrath upon thee from before the LORD [2 Chron.
> 19:1–2].

"Shouldest thou help the ungodly?" is a very good question. It is something our generation, which has gone lovey-dovey on everything, should think about. My friend, God never asks you to love one who is an enemy of God. It is one thing to love a sinner. It is another thing to love his sin. We need to distinguish between the two. We are to hate the sinner's sin. If the sinner will not change, but persists and insists on sticking with his sin, there is no alternative, my beloved. There are people who are actually God's enemies, they are enemies of the Word of God, and they are inveterate enemies of Christianity. Years ago a very pious fellow said to me, "I pray for Joe Stalin." Well, I didn't, and I make no apology for it. Stalin was brought up in a school in which he was given some Bible teaching. He had an opportunity to know God. Yet he turned into an avowed enemy of God. I do not believe God expected us to pray for him. I don't feel that this lovey-dovey hypocrisy is honoring to God. I have had folk tell me how much they love me. Several have been very extravagant in their statements, and they were the ones I found out who were not even my friends. God cannot honor this hypocritical position of running around mouthing that we love everybody when really there are only a very few people whom we do love. We are to love God's people; this is His command. And we are to love the sinner in the sense that we should try to bring him to Christ. However, this does not mean that we are to compromise with sin!

There is another tremendous lesson here that I don't want us to miss. God did not send Jehu to Jehoshaphat *before* he went up to join himself with Ahab and Jezebel. At that time He did not send him to give him a little message on separation. Jehoshaphat was a man of God. He made his mistakes. God allowed him to go through this experience with Ahab because God was going to teach him a lesson from this.

We have a great many people today who have made themselves to be like God's spiritual policemen. They like to tell everybody else how they should be separated and with whom they should associate and with whom they should not associate. God makes it very clear that we are not to judge others in questionable matters. Remember that people are not coming before us in judgment anyway. "Who art thou that judgest another man's servant? to his own master he standeth or falleth. Yea, he shall be holden up: for God is able to make him stand" (Rom. 14:4). We fall into the error of criticizing others because they are not as separated as we think they should be. You see, God is able to make him stand. If he has a personal faith in Jesus Christ, God will hold him. I would like to put it like this. I must give an account some day for my life to the Lord Jesus Christ. He is my Master. You are not. In the same way, I am not your master. The Lord Jesus Christ is your Master. You will give your account to Him. The fact that I will some day give an account to the Lord Jesus Christ keeps me plenty busy. I don't have time to sit in judgment on you, and I trust that you do not have the time to sit in judgment on me. It is not our business; it is *His* business. God will rebuke me if I do the wrong thing. That's what he did for Jehoshaphat. He taught him through this experience and Jehoshaphat learned his lesson.

> **Nevertheless there are good things found in thee, in that thou hast taken away the groves out of the land, and hast prepared thine heart to seek God [2 Chron. 19:3].**

Jehoshaphat was a remarkable man, but the marriage of his son into the family of Ahab brought judgment from God upon him and his nation, as we shall see.

> **And Jehoshaphat dwelt at Jerusalem: and he went out again through the people from Beer-sheba to mount Ephraim, and brought them back unto the LORD God of their fathers [2 Chron. 19:4].**

Now we will see some of the reforms that Jehoshaphat engaged in here. He was a wonderful man.

> **And he set judges in the land throughout all the fenced cities of Judah, city by city,**

And said to the judges, Take heed what ye do: for ye judge not for man, but for the LORD, who is with you in the judgment.

Wherefore now let the fear of the LORD be upon you; take heed and do it: for there is no iniquity with the LORD our God, nor respect of persons, nor taking of gifts [2 Chron. 19:5-7].

In my judgment, this is the entire difficulty with our legal system today. When a godless man sits on the judge's bench, he does not feel a responsibility to God. He is a dangerous judge, regardless of who he is. He is a dangerous judge because he is subject to all these vices. To begin with, he is apt to make a wrong judgment. Also he is apt to show respect of persons, and may be led to take a bribe.

Moreover in Jerusalem did Jehoshaphat set of the Levites, and of the priests, and of the chief of the fathers of Israel, for the judgment of the LORD, and for controversies, when they returned to Jerusalem.

And he charged them, saying, Thus shall ye do in the fear of the LORD, faithfully, and with a perfect heart [2 Chron. 19:8-9].

You see how Jehoshaphat organized everything in his kingdom around God.

INVASION BY ENEMY NATIONS

It came to pass after this also, that the children of Moab, and the children of Ammon, and with them other beside the Ammonites, came against Jehoshaphat to battle.

Then there came some that told Jehoshaphat, saying, There cometh a great multitude against thee from be-

> yond the sea on this side Syria; and, behold, they be in
> Hazazon-tamar, which is En-gedi.
>
> And Jehoshaphat feared, and set himself to seek the
> LORD, and proclaimed a fast throughout all Judah
> [2 Chron. 20:1-3].

You see, now this man has a normal reaction: he is afraid. He goes to
God in prayer and sends word out to his people to join him in fasting
and prayer.

> And Judah gathered themselves together, to ask help of
> the LORD: even out of all the cities of Judah they came to
> seek the LORD.
>
> And Jehoshaphat stood in the congregation of Judah and
> Jerusalem, in the house of the LORD, before the new court
> [2 Chron. 20:4-5].

JEHOSHAPHAT'S PRAYER

> And said, O LORD God of our fathers, art not thou God in
> heaven? and rulest not thou over all the kingdoms of the
> heathen? and in thine hand is there not power and
> might, so that none is able to withstand thee?
>
> Art not thou our God, who didst drive out the inhabit-
> ants of this land before thy people Israel, and gavest it to
> the seed of Abraham thy friend for ever? [2 Chron.
> 20:6-7].

Jehoshaphat is doing something that his father, Asa, did not do. Asa
did not rest upon the experiences of the past, which would have given
him faith. Jehoshaphat, knowing what God has promised in the past
and what God has done in the past, now rests upon the promises of
God. He goes over this entire situation in his prayer to God and then
he concludes his prayer:

> O our God, wilt thou not judge them? for we have no
> might against this great company that cometh against
> us; neither know we what to do: but our eyes are upon
> thee.
>
> And all Judah stood before the LORD, with their little
> ones, their wives, and their children [2 Chron.
> 20:12-13].

What a scene! What a king! He casts himself entirely upon God in a helpless situation. What a wonderful thing it is.

GOD'S ANSWER

> Then upon Jahaziel the son of Zechariah, the son of Be-
> naiah, the son of Jeiel, the son of Mattaniah, a Levite of
> the sons of Asaph, came the spirit of the LORD in the
> midst of the congregation [2 Chron. 20:14].

Notice how often genealogies are used in the Scripture to identify the prophets or some of the other men who are brought across the pages of the Bible. It is very important. I wonder if you know who your great-great-great-grandfather was. I haven't any idea who mine was. But these folk kept accurate genealogies.

Listen to the word of Jahaziel. He is God's spokesman now.

> And he said, Hearken ye, all Judah, and ye inhabitants
> of Jerusalem, and thou king Jehoshaphat, Thus saith the
> LORD unto you, Be not afraid nor dismayed by reason of
> this great multitude; for the battle is not yours, but God's
> [2 Chron. 20:15].

I need to remind myself of this. It is easy for me to forget that the ministry God has given me is the Lord's. I go at it like it is mine; I begin to carry the burden and face the problems and worry about the difficulties. Every now and then I have to remind myself that this is God's work. And since it is His (I say this reverently), He will have to work out the problems. The secret of prayer is to go to God in faith. As the hymn has it, "Take your burden to the Lord, and leave it there." The trouble with me is that I don't leave it there. I spread my problems out before the Lord, then I sack them up, put them right back on my back, and go on carrying them.

Oh, how wonderful God is! He says, "Don't be afraid, Jehoshaphat. The battle is not yours—you couldn't fight it; it is Mine." I find myself—and I'm sure you do also—in situations from which I cannot extricate myself. God says, "Turn it over to Me. I'll take care of it." Oh, that you and I might learn to turn it over to Him as Jehoshaphat did!

> **And they rose early in the morning, and went forth into the wilderness of Tekoa: and as they went forth, Jehoshaphat stood and said, Hear me, O Judah, and ye inhabitants of Jerusalem; Believe in the LORD your God, so shall ye be established; believe his prophets, so shall ye prosper [2 Chron. 20:20].**

Now they are going out to meet the advancing enemy. Jehoshaphat encourages his troops to put their trust in the Lord.

God is saying to you and me, "Believe in Me. Rest in Me and believe My Word." Don't listen to what Mr. Ph.D. has to say; listen to what God has to say. "Believe in the LORD your God, so shall ye be established; believe his prophets, so shall ye prosper."

> **And when he had consulted with the people, he appointed singers unto the LORD, and that should praise the beauty of holiness, as they went out before the army, and to say Praise the LORD; for his mercy endureth for ever [2 Chron. 20:21].**

This is an unusual way to organize an army! He didn't get out his atom bomb; he just organized a choir to go ahead and praise the Lord—for His mercy endureth forever.

This whole chapter is thrilling to read. Now notice what happened. The Lord gave them the victory. God won the battle for them.

> **And on the fourth day they assembled themselves in the valley of Berachah; for there they blessed the LORD: therefore the name of the same place was called, The valley of Berachah, unto this day [2 Chron. 20:26].**

Berachah is a name which has been taken by several churches in this country. It is a good name for a church, by the way. It means "the place to bless the Lord" or "the place to praise the Lord." Every church ought to be a Berachah church.

> **Then they returned, every man of Judah and Jerusalem, and Jehoshaphat in the forefront of them, to go again to Jerusalem with joy; for the LORD had made them to rejoice over their enemies.**
>
> **And they came to Jerusalem with psalteries and harps and trumpets unto the house of the LORD.**
>
> **And the fear of God was on all the kingdoms of those countries, when they heard that the LORD fought against the enemies of Israel.**
>
> **So the realm of Jehoshaphat was quiet: for his God gave him rest round about [2 Chron. 20:27-30].**

It is God who gives rest and peace. Our nation hasn't learned that. We think if we make this kind of an alignment, this kind of treaty, we won't have to fight in war. Well, we have fought two world wars in order to bring peace in the world and all we have is war. Do you know why? Because God hasn't given us peace. Our world is not trusting the Prince of Peace. This is the reason.

The chapter ends with the market alliance Jehoshaphat had with the son of Ahab, to which we have already referred. God could not bless this alliance with the ungodly son of Ahab.

Although Jehoshaphat was a great king, he was not perfect. God says that he ". . . departed not from it, doing that which was right in the sight of the LORD" (see v. 32).

> **Howbeit the high places were not taken away: for as yet the people had not prepared their hearts unto the God of their fathers [2 Chron. 20:33].**

Idolatry was the ultimate downfall of the nation.

CHAPTERS 21 AND 22

W e come now to a section of the Word of God that in many senses
is complicated. Sin is the reason for its complication because
sin is always complicated. Let me illustrate this. If I say to you that I
am holding in my hand a stick that is absolutely straight, you will
know exactly how it looks because it can be straight in only one way.
But suppose I say that I am holding a stick that is crooked. You would
have no idea how it looks because a thing can be crooked in a million
different ways. In just such a way, sin allures a great many folk because it is devious. It is enticing because it seems to be unusual and
strange and it is complicated. We will see this in the life of Jehoram,
who comes to the throne after the death of Jehoshaphat.

JEHORAM'S EVIL REIGN

**Now Jehoshaphat slept with his fathers, and was buried
with his fathers in the city of David. And Jehoram his
son reigned in his stead [2 Chron. 21:1].**

Jehoram happened to be the son who had married into the family of
Ahab and Jezebel, and he learned to do evil from them. I think he was
a very apt pupil, by the way.

**And he had brethren the sons of Jehoshaphat, Azariah,
and Jehiel, and Zechariah, and Azariah, and Michael,
and Shephatiah: all these were the sons of Jehoshaphat
king of Israel.**

**And their father gave them great gifts of silver, and of
gold, and of precious things, with fenced cities in Judah:
but the kingdom gave he to Jehoram: because he was the
firstborn.**

> Now when Jehoram was risen up to the kingdom of his
> father, he strengthened himself, and slew all his breth-
> ren with the sword, and divers also of the princes of Is-
> rael [2 Chron. 21:2–4].

He eliminated all the competition by the most dastardly means imaginable. He slew all his brothers and others of the royal family. Why did
he do this?

> And he walked in the way of the kings of Israel, like as
> did the house of Ahab: for he had the daughter of Ahab
> to wife: and he wrought that which was evil in the eyes
> of the LORD [2 Chron. 21:6].

God does not bless mixed marriages, my friend.

> Howbeit the LORD would not destroy the house of David,
> because of the covenant that he had made with David,
> and as he promised to give a light to him and to his sons
> for ever [2 Chron. 21:7].

This man was so wicked that God would have been justified in exter-
minating the line. But, you see, God is faithful to His promises. He
would not destroy the line of David because He had made a covenant
with David.

Now we find that judgment immediately begins to come upon
him.

> In his days the Edomites revolted from under the domin-
> ion of Judah, and made themselves a king.

> Then Jehoram went forth with his princes, and all his
> chariots with him: and he rose up by night, and smote
> the Edomites which compassed him in, and the cap-
> tains of the chariots.

> So the Edomites revolted from under the hand of Judah
> unto this day. The same time also did Libnah revolt from

under his hand; because he had forsaken the LORD God of his fathers [2 Chron. 21:8–10].

God makes it very clear why this judgment came upon Jehoram. The Word says that this judgment was from the hand of God. He can't have peace because he has forsaken the Lord God of his fathers.

I get just a little impatient with people who say the Bible doesn't teach God's judgment on sin. What they really mean is that they don't believe the Bible. If they would say that, I would not find fault with them. What they believe is their business. But when they try to tell me that the Bible doesn't teach God's judgment, when it is as clear as it possibly can be, I object. God says He judges sin, and a great many of us can testify to the fact in our own lives.

> **Moreover he made high places in the mountains of Judah, and caused the inhabitants of Jerusalem to commit fornication, and compelled Judah thereto [2 Chron. 21:11].**

He actually pushed the people back into the idolatry from which his father, Jehoshaphat, had delivered them.

THE MESSAGE OF ELIJAH

Now God calls in an old friend whom you may have forgotten about. This is the man whom God always called in to deliver the difficult message. He was a troubleshooter, and he is the right man for the job. The man is Elijah.

> **And there came a writing to him from Elijah the prophet, saying, Thus saith the LORD God of David thy father, Because thou hast not walked in the ways of Jehoshaphat thy father, nor in the ways of Asa king of Judah [2 Chron. 21:12].**

There are many people who speak of Elijah as one of the prophets who did not write. He is called one of the nonwriting prophets. Of course, this means that there is no book in the Bible named for him or written by him. Although he didn't write a book, he did write a message. And when this man Elijah wrote a message, it singed the paper! He began by citing the reason for this harsh message: "Because thou hast not walked in the ways of Jehoshaphat thy father, nor in the ways of Asa king of Judah . . ." Now let's read the message.

> **But hast walked in the ways of the kings of Israel, and hast made Judah and the inhabitants of Jerusalem to go a-whoring, like to the whoredoms of the house of Ahab, and also hast slain thy brethren of thy father's house, which were better than thyself:**
>
> **Behold, with a great plague will the LORD smite thy people, and thy children, and thy wives, and all thy goods:**
>
> **And thou shalt have great sickness by disease of thy bowels, until thy bowels fall out by reason of the sickness day by day [2 Chron. 21:13–15].**

Elijah would be the prophet who could deliver a message like this. It is a harsh message but one that God wanted delivered to this man Jehoram.

The contents of the message are not unusual. This is the kind of message you would expect Elijah to deliver. However, the circumstances are extraordinary. It raises three questions: who? when? where? Let's first consider the "who?"—who is Elijah? This message is directed to Jehoram, the son of Jehoshaphat. The record in Kings tells us that Elijah was translated in the eighteenth year of Jehoshaphat. He was not on earth during the reign of Jehoram, and the assumption is that he could not write this prophecy. Some Bible students conclude that this is another Elijah, that he is not Elijah the Tishbite. That reminds me of the argument as to whether or not Shakespeare wrote the works of Shakespeare. As you know, some believe the author was Francis Bacon or someone else. I like Mark Twain's comment. He said, "Shakespeare did not write Shakespeare, but it was written by another man by the same name!" I consider that a conclusive answer in Elijah's case also. If this had not been Elijah the Tishbite, God would have made that clear. There is no impossible barrier, unless you reject the supernatural. If you do that, you will reject not only this but a great deal of the Bible. Our old friend, Elijah the prophet, is the one who wrote the message.

Now the second question is "when?"—when did Elijah write it? Did he write it after his translation? Grotius maintains that the postmark was Paradise. Well, we can dismiss that as pure speculation. There is a very simple explanation: he wrote it *before* his translation. You may say, "But that's supernatural." Exactly. That is the point I am trying to make. Prophecy is supernatural. A prediction projects into the future; that's what makes it prophecy. We have many incidents of this. Isaiah spoke of Cyrus of Persia two centuries before he was even born. Daniel wrote of Alexander the Great. Elisha predicted the reign of Hazael over Syria. Micah named the town of Bethlehem as being the place where the Messiah would be born. Only God can prophesy with such accuracy.

The final question is "where?"—where did Elijah write this prophecy? Elijah was a prophet to the northern kingdom. This is the only reference to Elijah in Chronicles, because Chronicles is giving God's viewpoint. Didn't God take delight in Elijah? Of course He did. Then why isn't Elijah mentioned in this book in more detail? It is not that God omitted Elijah and his work; God omits the whole history of the northern kingdom. Elijah was the prophet to the northern kingdom, and this is the only time Elijah spoke to a king in the south. He never spoke to Jehoshaphat for the simple reason that Jehoshaphat was a good king and did not need one of the scorching messages from Elijah. Now when Jehoram, his son, comes to the throne, there is a message waiting for him. Elijah had written it before he was translated. Elijah not only left his mantle with Elisha, he left this message for Jehoram. He said, "You'll be seeing him; I won't."

This would suggest that when Elijah was translated, his message was not finished. It makes me believe that this man Elijah is one of the two witnesses mentioned in Revelation, chapter 11. He is going to deliver a harsh message again in a day when men have turned from God. I think this makes for a very intriguing passage of Scripture, with an unusual message delivered at this time.

What we find here is that when Jehoram came to the throne, he found a message on the front steps of the palace. It was thrown there by God's paperboy.

JUDGMENT FALLS ON JEHORAM

Now we'll see the accuracy of Elijah's prediction.

> Moreover the LORD stirred up against Jehoram the spirit of the Philistines, and of the Arabians, that were near the Ethiopians:
>
> And they came up into Judah, and brake into it, and carried away all the substance that was found in the king's house, and his sons also, and his wives; so that there was never a son left him, save Jehoahaz, the youngest of his sons [2 Chron. 21:16–17].

All of these had been at peace with both Asa and Jehoshaphat. Now their spirit is stirred up. War is coming. Why? War is the result of sin. We sometimes think of war as being made out on the battlefield. War takes place right at home, friends. It begins in the sinfulness of the human heart.

> And after all this the LORD smote him in his bowels with an incurable disease.
>
> And it came to pass, that in process of time, after the end of two years, his bowels fell out by reason of his sickness: so he died of sore diseases. And his people made no burning for him, like the burning of his fathers.
>
> Thirty and two years old was he when he began to reign, and he reigned in Jerusalem eight years, and de-

> parted without being desired. Howbeit they buried him
> in the city of David, but not in the sepulchres of the
> kings [2 Chron. 21:18–20].

It was good riddance of bad rubbish when he died. The place in which
they buried him and the lack of respect at his burial show how this
man was hated. We will see in the next chapters that his wife was one
of the most hated women who ever reigned.

AHAZIAH'S WICKED REIGN

> And the inhabitants of Jerusalem made Ahaziah his
> youngest son king in his stead: for the band of men that
> came with the Arabians to the camp had slain all the
> eldest. So Ahaziah the son of Jehoram king of Judah
> reigned [2 Chron. 22:1].

The names get confusing because sometimes different names are
used for the same person. Ahaziah is the Jehoahaz of 2 Chronicles
21:17. He is the only son left. All the other sons of Jehoram were
killed.

> Forty and two years old was Ahaziah when he began to
> reign, and he reigned one year in Jerusalem. His
> mother's name also was Athaliah the daughter of Omri.
>
> He also walked in the ways of the house of Ahab: for his
> mother was his counsellor to do wickedly.
>
> Wherefore he did evil in the sight of the Lord like the
> house of Ahab: for they were his counsellors after the
> death of his father to his destruction [2 Chron. 22:2–4].

Athaliah is really the queen on the throne. She is the power behind
the throne. She is the daughter of Ahab and Jezebel, and the grand-
daughter of Omri. She never really gave up her position. Remember
that she turned her husband, Jehoram, away from God. Now her son,

Ahaziah, listens to her and aligns himself with the northern kingdom and with the house of Ahab—which was to his destruction. Justice with a vengeance will be wrought upon him.

> He walked also after their counsel, and went with Jehoram the son of Ahab king of Israel to war against Hazael king of Syria at Ramoth-gilead: and the Syrians smote Joram [2 Chron. 22:5].

This gets confusing, too, because there was a Jehoram in both the northern and the southern kingdoms. It looks as though we have the same man back again, but Jehoram, king of Judah, is dead. His son, Ahaziah, is the king, and now he aligns himself with Jehoram, king of Israel. Jehoram was wounded in this battle with the Syrians.

> And he returned to be healed in Jezreel because of the wounds which were given him at Ramah, when he fought with Hazael king of Syria. And Azariah the son of Jehoram king of Judah went down to see Jehoram the son of Ahab at Jezreel, because he was sick [2 Chron. 22:6].

Azariah, king of Judah, went to visit Jehoram, king of Israel, who was recovering at Jezreel, and he probably took him a basket of fruit or something.

> And the destruction of Ahaziah was of God by coming to Joram: for when he was come, he went out with Jehoram against Jehu the son of Nimshi, whom the LORD had anointed to cut off the house of Ahab [2 Chron. 22:7].

The interesting thing is that Jehu didn't know that Ahaziah, this king from the southern kingdom, was up there. Notice what happened.

> And it came to pass, that, when Jehu was executing judgment upon the house of Ahab, and found the

princes of Judah, and the sons of the brethren of Ahaziah, that ministered to Ahaziah, he slew them [2 Chron. 22:8].

These "sons of the brethren of Ahaziah" were not the brothers of Ahaziah, since they had been slain by Arabian marauders (2 Chron. 21:17), but these were the sons of these brothers, and therefore Ahaziah's nephews. The "princes of Judah" were probably distant relatives who held important offices in the court. Jehu slew them all. Now he goes after Ahaziah, who had escaped, and he is found and slain.

And he sought Ahaziah: and they caught him, (for he was hid in Samaria,) and brought him to Jehu: and when they had slain him, they buried him: Because, said they, he is the son of Jehoshaphat, who sought the LORD with all his heart. So the house of Ahaziah had no power to keep still the kingdom [2 Chron. 22:9].

This is a bloody period. God records it to let us know that He judges sin. He wants us to know that man doesn't get by with sin. How complicated it is! I said before that the way of sin is crooked and complicated.

ATHALIAH'S BRUTAL REIGN

But when Athaliah the mother of Ahaziah saw that her son was dead, she arose and destroyed all the seed royal of the house of Judah [2 Chron. 22:10].

I'll be very frank with you. It takes a bloody person and a mean one to kill her own grandchildren! If you are a grandparent, you share my feeling about grandchildren. I know why they call them grandchildren—they are grand. The fact of the matter is, I think grandchildren are more wonderful than children. If I had known how wonderful they were, I'd have had my grandchildren before I had my children!

I do not understand how this bloody queen could slay her grand-children, but that is what she did. She slew all but one—because she couldn't find him.

> **But Jehoshabeath, the daughter of the king, took Joash the son of Ahaziah, and stole him from among the king's sons that were slain, and put him and his nurse in a bedchamber. So Jehoshabeath, the daughter of king Je-horam, the wife of Jehoiada the priest, (for she was the sister of Ahaziah,) hid him from Athaliah, so that she slew him not.**
>
> **And he was with them hid in the house of God six years: and Athaliah reigned over the land [2 Chron. 22:11-12].**

If this had not taken place, the line of David would have been cut off. And God's promise to David concerning the coming of the Messiah would never have taken place. This is how close it was.

You can see that Satan has made attempts again and again to try to destroy the line that would lead to Christ. You will recall how Satan tried to destroy the line that would lead to Christ when all the male babies were to be slain down in the land of Egypt. He tried to have all the Jews exterminated at the time of Haman. After Jesus was born, he worked through old Herod and tried to kill Jesus by killing all the baby boys around Bethlehem. Here is another instance when Satan had the line of David reduced so there was only one survivor.

This little fellow, Joash, was one year old when he was hidden. He was kept hidden away in the temple for six years. During that time the bloody queen ruled the land.

CHAPTERS 23 AND 24

THEME: Revival during Joash's reign

During the reign of Joash, the third period of revival came to the southern kingdom of Judah. Of course it was not much of a revival, and most of the credit for a return to God belongs to the priest Jehoiada.

JOASH IS MADE KING

And in the seventh year Jehoiada strengthened himself, and took the captains of hundreds, Azariah the son of Jeroham, and Ishmael the son of Jehohanan, and Azariah the son of Obed, and Maaseiah the son of Adaiah, and Elishaphat the son of Zichri, into covenant with him [2 Chron. 23:1].

The leadership of Judah was dissatisfied with the bloody queen Athaliah. So now Jehoiada, the priest, calls them to a meeting, a very private meeting, to let them know that there is a son of David who is still alive. They all pledge themselves to make this little fellow of the line of David their king.

They gathered Levites and the chiefs of Israel and laid careful plans to crown little Joash who was in the line of David. A third part of the group would act as porters at the doors of the temple on the sabbath. A third part would be at the king's house. A third part would be at the gate of the foundation. They would not permit anyone inside the temple except the priests and the Levites. The Levites around the little king would all be armed with weapons. Jehoiada gave out spears and bucklers and shields which were kept in the temple. All of these arrangements were carried out.

> Then they brought out the king's son, and put upon him
> the crown, and gave him the testimony, and made him
> king. And Jehoiada and his sons anointed him, and
> said, God save the king [2 Chron. 23:11].

This was an exciting and thrilling coup, and little seven-year-old
Joash, who is in the line of David, is now on the throne of Judah.

EXECUTION OF ATHALIAH

Athaliah thought that she had killed off all her offspring. Why had
she done such a brutal act? She had a thirst for power. She wanted to
be queen.

There are certain men and certain women in this world who will
do anything for power. Every group or class of people has them. There
are preachers who will do that, deacons will do it, politicians and
dictators will do that. There are many members of the human family
who will stoop to almost anything in order to have power. They are,
like this queen, craving for power.

> Now when Athaliah heard the noise of the people run-
> ning and praising the king, she came to the people into
> the house of the Lord [2 Chron. 23:12].

I tell you, this woman Athaliah was taken by surprise.

> And she looked, and, behold, the king stood at his pillar
> at the entering in, and the princes and the trumpets by
> the king: and all the people of the land rejoiced, and
> sounded with trumpets, also the singers with instru-
> ments of music, and such as taught to sing praise. Then
> Athaliah rent her clothes, and said, Treason, Treason
> [2 Chron. 23:13].

From her standpoint it was high treason!

Then Jehoiada the priest brought out the captains of hundreds that were set over the host, and said unto them, Have her forth of the ranges: and whoso followeth her, let him be slain with the sword. For the priest said, Slay her not in the house of the LORD.

So they laid hands on her; and when she was come to the entering of the horse gate by the king's house, they slew her there [2 Chron. 23:14-15].

REVIVAL THROUGH JEHOIADA

Joash is still a little fellow, only seven years old; so Jehoiada is his regent. Jehoiada is actually the one who will make the decisions until this boy comes of age. Jehoiada is God's priest, and he leads the nation back to the worship of God.

And Jehoiada made a covenant between him, and between all the people, and between the king, that they should be the LORD's people [2 Chron. 23:16].

Jehoiada broke down the altars of Baal and killed the priests of Baal. He revived worship of Jehovah by setting up the order of priests and Levites for the burnt offerings. Singing was restored as it had been ordained by David. Porters watched the gates so nothing unclean entered the temple.

And all the people of the land rejoiced: and the city was quiet, after that they had slain Athaliah with the sword [2 Chron. 23:21].

There is repetition over and over of the same theme. Sin always brings complications, trouble, heartbreak, and the judgment of God. Revival restores peace and quiet to the land.

REIGN OF JOASH

Joash was seven years old when he began to reign, and he reigned forty years in Jerusalem. His mother's name also was Zibiah of Beer-sheba [2 Chron. 24:1].

Jehoiada, the priest, is the one who really guided and led this little fellow during the early part of his reign. However, his mother's name is given to us, and she must have been a good mother. She apparently agreed with the return to the Lord which was taking place. Her home was in Beer-sheba. When I was down there not long ago, I thought of the mother of Joash. Beer-sheba is also the town of Abraham.

And Joash did that which was right in the sight of the LORD all the days of Jehoiada the priest.

And Jehoiada took for him two wives; and he begat sons and daughters [2 Chron. 24:2–3].

Joash did what was right under the coaching of Jehoiada; then we have the strange statement that he took two wives for him. Of course this didn't happen when he was seven years old—remember that he reigned forty years. Is the implication that it was all right to have two wives? No. It was wrong. It is not recorded because God approved of it; it is recorded because that is what he did. Considering the background of that day, two wives was really a small number. This was extremely mild, especially for a king in that period.

And it came to pass after this, that Joash was minded to repair the house of the LORD [2 Chron. 24:4].

As Joash grew up, Jehoiada grew old—he was one hundred thirty years old when he died. Apparently he lost his control over the other priests, and the temple was not restored. Although it is questionable to say that Joash led in the revival—there wasn't much of a revival under him—it *was* revival. And he was the one who planned and insisted on repairing the temple of God.

> And he gathered together the priests and the Levites, and said to them, Go out unto the cities of Judah, and gather of all Israel money to repair the house of your God from year to year, and see that ye hasten the matter. Howbeit the Levites hastened it not.
>
> And the king called for Jehoiada the chief, and said unto him, Why hast thou not required of the Levites to bring in out of Judah and out of Jerusalem the collection, according to the commandment of Moses the servant of the LORD, and of the congregation of Israel, for the tabernacle of witness? [2 Chron. 24:5–6].

Apparently Jehoiada has grown old, and the priests are indifferent. They have fallen down on their job.

> For the sons of Athaliah, that wicked woman, had broken up the house of God: and also all the dedicated things of the house of the LORD did they bestow upon Baalim [2 Chron. 24:7].

This tells us what had actually happened to the temple and who was responsible. God's temple was in a terribly disreputable condition. So Joash takes the matter in his own hands.

> And at the king's commandment they made a chest, and set it without at the gate of the house of the LORD.
>
> And they made a proclamation through Judah and Jerusalem, to bring in to the LORD the collection that Moses the servant of God laid upon Israel in the wilderness.

And all the princes and all the people rejoiced, and
brought in, and cast into the chest, until they had made
an end [2 Chron. 24:8–10].

"Until they had made an end" means that they got all they needed.

Now it came to pass, that at what time the chest was
brought unto the king's office by the hand of the Levites,
and when they saw that there was much money, the
king's scribe and the high priest's officer came and
emptied the chest, and took it, and carried it to his place
again. Thus they did day by day, and gathered money in
abundance [2 Chron. 24:11].

Joash couldn't trust the Levites going out and collecting the money, so
he puts this chest there in the temple, and people put their contribu-
tions there.

By the way, many organizations since then have used this method.
They put out what they call a "chest of Joash" and ask folk to put their
offerings in it.

And the king and Jehoiada gave it to such as did the
work of the service of the house of the LORD, and hired
masons and carpenters to repair the house of the LORD,
and also such as wrought iron and brass to mend the
house of the LORD.

So the workmen wrought and the work was perfected by
them, and they set the house of God in his state, and
strengthened it [2 Chron. 24:12–13].

As a result, the repair work of the temple was completed.

And when they had finished it, they brought the rest of
the money before the king and Jehoiada, whereof were
made vessels for the house of the LORD, even vessels to

minister, and to offer withal, and spoons, and vessels of
gold and silver. And they offered burnt offerings in the
house of the LORD continually all the days of Jehoiada
[2 Chron. 24:14].

There were sufficient funds to remake the vessels and implements to
carry on the regular services in the temple.

But Jehoiada waxed old, and was full of days when he
died; an hundred and thirty years old was he when he
died [2 Chron. 24:15].

This gives the explanation of why the priests were negligent in carrying out the order of the king. Jehoiada was probably senile. He had
experienced bringing up this boy, and I suppose he had liberties that
no one else would have had with the king.

And they buried him in the city of David among the
kings, because he had done good in Israel, both toward
God, and toward his house [2 Chron. 24:16].

Jehoiada actually received royal honors in his death.

APOSTASY AFTER JEHOIADA

Now after the death of Jehoiada, a new era begins.

Now after the death of Jehoiada came the princes of Judah, and made obeisance to the king. Then the king
hearkened unto them.

And they left the house of the LORD God of their fathers,
and served groves and idols: and wrath came upon Judah and Jerusalem for this their trespass [2 Chron.
24:17-18].

You see, as long as Jehoiada lived, the princes did not dare go into idolatry. Jehoiada maintained a very strong influence. Joash is a young king and probably very lenient. These princes pledge allegiance to him, but they go out and worship idols again.

> Yet he sent prophets to them, to bring them again unto the LORD; and they testified against them: but they would not give ear [2 Chron. 24:19].

In His mercy, God sends prophets to warn them, but they will not listen. So God sends a message by a man who is the son of Jehoiada.

> And the spirit of God came upon Zechariah the son of Jehoiada the priest, which stood above the people, and said unto them, Thus saith God, Why transgress ye the commandments of the LORD, that ye cannot prosper? because ye have forsaken the LORD, he hath also forsaken you [2 Chron. 24:20].

Now notice the shocking thing that happens.

> And they conspired against him, and stoned him with stones at the commandment of the king in the court of the house of the LORD [2 Chron. 24:21].

My thought is that Joash has been given wrong information about this man. He was the son of Jehoiada! You would think that Joash would never have done a thing like this, but it reveals the evil influence of the princes and the despicable deeds that they were engaged in. They put him to death.

> Thus Joash the king remembered not the kindness which Jehoiada his father had done to him, but slew his son. And when he died, he said, The LORD look upon it, and require it [2 Chron. 24:22].

In other words, this dying man calls upon God to take vengeance upon the king for this.

JUDGMENT UPON JOASH

And it came to pass at the end of the year, that the host of Syria came up against him: and they came to Judah and Jerusalem, and destroyed all the princes of the people from among the people, and sent all the spoil of them unto the king of Damascus.

For the army of the Syrians came with a small company of men, and the LORD delivered a very great host into their hand, because they had forsaken the LORD God of their fathers. So they executed judgment against Joash [2 Chron. 24:23-24].

God judges them by defeat in battle. Although Joash had been a good king, he had ordered this heartless murder. God must judge him because he is the king and because of his influence upon the whole nation.

And when they were departed from him, (for they left him in great diseases,) his own servants conspired against him for the blood of the sons of Jehoiada the priest, and slew him on his bed, and he died: and they buried him in the city of David, but they buried him not in the sepulchres of the kings [2 Chron. 24:25].

Jehoiada the priest had been buried with honor; now Joash the king is buried with dishonor.

Now concerning his sons, and the greatness of the burdens laid upon him, and the repairing of the house of God, behold, they are written in the story of the book of

**the kings. And Amaziah his son reigned in his stead
[2 Chron. 24:27].**

So we see that Joash at the beginning led a revival under the influence
of Jehoiada; but, after Jehoiada's death, he apparently lapsed into a
state of apostasy.

CHAPTERS 25—28

THEME: The reigns of Amaziah, Uzziah, Jotham, and Ahaz

AMAZIAH'S REIGN

Amaziah was twenty and five years old when he began to reign, and he reigned twenty and nine years in Jerusalem. And his mother's name was Jehoaddan of Jerusalem.

And he did that which was right in the sight of the LORD, but not with a perfect heart [2 Chron. 25:1–2].

I guess you could say he was a moderately good king.

Now it came to pass, when the kingdom was established to him, that he slew his servants that had killed the king his father [2 Chron. 25:3].

He executed the men who had murdered his father.

But he slew not their children, but did as it is written in the law in the book of Moses, where the LORD commanded, saying, The fathers shall not die for the children, neither shall the children die for the fathers, but every man shall die for his own sin [2 Chron. 25:4].

He obeyed the Mosaic Law in this respect.

This is an important principle. You will never be judged because of the sins of your mother or the sins of your father. You stand judged on the basis of your *own* sins. On the other hand you may have a very goodly mother or father, but you will never go to heaven because of godly parents. You will go to heaven because of the faith that you must exercise in Christ. This is a tremendous principle that is put down here.

> Moreover Amaziah gathered Judah together, and made them captains over thousands and captains over hundreds, according to the houses of their fathers, throughout all Judah and Benjamin: and he numbered them from twenty years old and above, and found them three hundred thousand choice men, able to go forth to war, that could handle spear and shield [2 Chron. 25:5].

He is getting ready for war. Also he hires an enemy—mercenary soldiers from Israel.

> But there came a man of God to him, saying, O king, let not the army of Israel go with thee; for the LORD is not with Israel, to wit, with all the children of Ephraim.
>
> But if thou wilt go, do it, be strong for the battle: God shall make thee fall before the enemy: for God hath power to help, and to cast down [2 Chron. 25:7-8].

He warns Amaziah to trust God. After all, he has the example of Jehoshaphat and Asa in the past. He should know that God would not want him to hire men of Israel.

> And Amaziah said to the man of God, But what shall we do for the hundred talents which I have given to the army of Israel? And the man of God answered, The LORD is able to give thee much more than this.
>
> Then Amaziah separated them, to wit, the army that was come to him out of Ephraim, to go home again: wherefore their anger was greatly kindled against Judah, and they returned home in great anger.

> And Amaziah strengthened himself, and led forth his
> people, and went to the valley of salt, and smote of the
> children of Seir ten thousand [2 Chron. 25:9–11].

Amaziah obeyed what the man of God had told him. He separated the
army of Israel from his own army and sent them back to Israel. Then
God gave him a victory over the children of Seir. The battle was fought
down by the Dead Sea.

> Now it came to pass, after that Amaziah was come from
> the slaughter of the Edomites, that he brought the gods
> of the children of Seir, and set them up to be his gods,
> and bowed down himself before them, and burned in-
> cense unto them [2 Chron. 25:14].

It is amazing that this man would do a thing like this, but it reveals the
iniquity that is in the human heart.

> Wherefore the anger of the LORD was kindled against
> Amaziah, and he sent unto him a prophet, which said
> unto him, Why hast thou sought after the gods of the
> people, which could not deliver their own people out of
> thine hand?
>
> And it came to pass, as he talked with him, that the king
> said unto him, Art thou made of the king's counsel? for-
> bear; why shouldest thou be smitten? Then the prophet
> forbare, and said, I know that God hath determined to
> destroy thee, because thou hast done this, and hast not
> hearkened unto my counsel [2 Chron. 25:15–16].

Now civil war breaks out again.

> Then Amaziah king of Judah took advice, and sent to
> Joash, the son of Jehoahaz, the son of Jehu, king of Is-

> rael, saying, Come let us see one another in the face
> [2 Chron. 25:17].

Amaziah said, "Let's see each other eyeball to eyeball." He was challenging Israel to go to war. Joash replies to Amaziah with a little parable.

> And Joash king of Israel sent to Amaziah king of Judah,
> saying, The thistle that was in Lebanon sent to the cedar
> that was in Lebanon, saying, Give thy daughter to my
> son to wife: and there passed by a wild beast that was in
> Lebanon, and trode down the thistle.

> Thou sayest, Lo, thou hast smitten the Edomites; and
> thine heart lifteth thee up to boast: abide now at home;
> why shouldest thou meddle to thine hurt, that thou
> shouldest fall, even thou and Judah with thee? [2 Chron.
> 25:18-19].

In other words, the parable was an insulting way of saying, "If you stay home and mind your own business, you won't get hurt."

> But Amaziah would not hear; for it came of God, that he
> might deliver them into the hand of their enemies, be-
> cause they sought after the gods of Edom [2 Chron.
> 25:20].

Amaziah would not listen. Now God judges him.

> And Joash the king of Israel took Amaziah king of Ju-
> dah, the son of Joash, the son of Jehoahaz, at Beth-
> shemesh, and brought him to Jerusalem, and brake
> down the wall of Jerusalem for the gate of Ephraim to
> the corner gate, four hundred cubits.

> And he took all the gold and the silver, and all the ves-
> sels that were found in the house of God with Obed-

edom, and the treasures of the king's house, the hostages also, and returned to Samaria [2 Chron. 25:23-24].

Of course it was an easy victory for Israel. It was a fulfillment of the prophet's warning, "I know that God hath determined to destroy thee, because thou hast done this, and hast not hearkened unto my counsel."

Now after the time that Amaziah did turn away from following the LORD they made a conspiracy against him in Jerusalem; and he fled to Lachish: but they sent to Lachish after him, and slew him there.

And they brought him upon horses, and buried him with his fathers in the city of Judah [2 Chron. 25:27-28].

UZZIAH'S REIGN

Now the son of Amaziah, Uzziah, came to the throne when he was only a teenager.

Then all the people of Judah took Uzziah, who was sixteen years old, and made him king in the room of his father Amaziah.

He built Eloth, and restored it to Judah, after that the king slept with his fathers.

Sixteen years old was Uzziah when he began to reign, and he reigned fifty and two years in Jerusalem. His mother's name also was Jecoliah of Jerusalem [2 Chron. 26:1-3].

Uzziah was a good king but not an outstanding one. There was no revival during his reign. It was during this period, by the way, that Isaiah began his ministry. He was commissioned at the death of Uz-

ziah, as Isaiah tells us in Isaiah 6:1. As we have seen, the northern
kingdom did not have a good king, not one. In the southern kingdom
there were a few good kings. Five of them could be considered excep-
tional because during their reign there was revival and reformation.
Uzziah's reign did not produce revival, but he was a good king. The
denominational seminary from which I graduated was quite liberal,
but it did have a Bible course, although it was very fragmentary. One
of the questions that had been asked from time immemorial was to
name the kings of Israel and Judah and briefly describe the reign of
each. Some ingenious freshman of days gone by had discovered that if
you would write after each one of them, "A bad king," you couldn't
make less than ninety-five percent—and what freshman wants to
make more than that? So what we all did was memorize the kings and
write after each one of them, "A bad king." Now when we wrote, "Bad
king" after Uzziah's name, we were wrong; Uzziah was not excep-
tional, but he was a good king.

**And he did that which was right in the sight of the LORD,
according to all that his father Amaziah did.**

**And he sought God in the days of Zechariah, who had
understanding in the visions of God: and as long as he
sought the LORD, God made him to prosper [2 Chron.
26:4–5].**

UZZIAH'S SUCCESSES

**And he went forth and warred against the Philistines,
and brake down the wall of Gath, and the wall of Jab-
neh, and the wall of Ashdod, and built cities about
Ashdod, and among the Philistines [2 Chron. 26:6].**

Gath was one of the strongholds of the Philistines.

I visited Ashdod some time ago. It is experiencing a tremendous
business boom today because they have made a harbor there. In the
old days the ancient ships could come to Caesarea but not to Ashdod.
Now there is a wonderful man-made harbor there, and I suppose it

receives more of the goods that are being shipped in and out of Israel than any other port. It is the place where the oil pipe lines come from the Red Sea. The oil is piped, put into the tankers, and carried from there. There is building going on everywhere. Now this entire area is what Uzziah took. All of this was Philistine country. But that wasn't all:

> And the Ammonites gave gifts to Uzziah: and his name spread abroad even to the entering in of Egypt; for he strengthened himself exceedingly.
>
> Moreover Uzziah built towers in Jerusalem at the corner gate, and at the valley gate, and at the turning of the wall, and fortified them.
>
> Also he built towers in the desert, and digged many wells: for he had much cattle, both in the low country, and in the plains: husbandmen also, and vine dressers in the mountains, and in Carmel: for he loved husbandry [2 Chron. 26:8–10].

We are told that he "loved husbandry"—he was a farmer at heart, a farmer and a rancher. Down in that area from Ashdod and Ashkelon and Gath, all the way down to Beer-sheba, is great pasture land. It is today a great place for raising cattle and sheep, which is what Uzziah did. Then on up toward Carmel is the Valley of Esdraelon, and that is great fruit country, especially vineyards. We are told that King Uzziah loved that sort of thing.

> Moreover Uzziah had an host of fighting men, that went out to war by bands, according to the number of their account by the hand of Jeiel the scribe and Maaseiah the ruler, under the hand of Hananiah, one of the king's captains.
>
> The whole number of the chief of the fathers of the mighty men of valour were two thousand and six hundred.

> And under their hand was an army, three hundred
> thousand and seven thousand and five hundred, that
> made war with mighty power, to help the king against
> the enemy [2 Chron. 26:11-13].

The southern kingdom of Judah was strong militarily at this time.

> And Uzziah prepared for them throughout all the host
> shields, and spears, and helmets and habergeons, and
> bows, and slings to cast stones.
>
> And he made in Jerusalem engines, invented by cunning
> men, to be on the towers and upon the bulwarks, to
> shoot arrows and great stones withal. And his name
> spread far abroad; for he was marvellously helped, till
> he was strong [2 Chron. 26:14-15].

In ancient warfare they had certain kinds of machines that would hurl
rocks. Also they could fix bows that would shoot arrows without being pulled by human power. And they were able to build bows of tremendous size that would shoot arrows a great distance. It is
interesting to note that this man Uzziah was responsible for this new
method of warfare.

Now Uzziah—as we have seen with all the kings, even the good
ones—has a chink in his armor. Each has a weakness; each has his
Achilles' heel. That is man even today. Regardless of what man he is,
there is a weak spot in him.

UZZIAH'S WEAKNESS

Sometimes success is the worst thing that can happen to any of us,
because we become lifted up with pride. Pride was Uzziah's downfall.

> But when he was strong, his heart was lifted up to his
> destruction: for he transgressed against the LORD his

> God, and went into the temple of the LORD to burn in-
> cense upon the altar of incense [2 Chron. 26:16].

He went into the temple of the Lord to burn incense upon the altar of
incense. Wasn't that all right? No, it was all wrong for him. Why?

> And Azariah the priest went in after him, and with him
> fourscore priests of the LORD, that were valiant men:
>
> And they withstood Uzziah the king, and said unto him,
> It appertaineth not unto thee, Uzziah, to burn incense
> unto the LORD, but to the priests the sons of Aaron, that
> are consecrated to burn incense: go out of the sanctu-
> ary; for thou hast trespassed; neither shall it be for thine
> honour from the LORD God [2 Chron. 26:17-18].

The priests could actually resist the king in this matter. The king was
usurping the priest's office; he was doing what was strictly forbidden
for anyone to do except the sons of Aaron. Only the priests of the line
of Aaron could enter into the holy place—the golden lampstand and
the altar of incense were there.

> Then Uzziah was wroth, and had a censer in his hand to
> burn incense: and while he was wroth with the priests,
> the leprosy even rose up in his forehead before the
> priests in the house of the LORD, from beside the incense
> altar [2 Chron. 26:19].

This was instant judgment from God upon Uzziah.

> And Azariah the chief priest, and all the priests, looked
> upon him, and, behold, he was leprous in his forehead,
> and they thrust him out from thence; yea, himself
> hasted also to go out, because the LORD had smitten him.
>
> And Uzziah the king was a leper unto the day of his
> death, and dwelt in a several house, being a leper; for he

> was cut off from the house of the LORD: and Jotham his
> son was over the king's house, judging the people of the
> land [2 Chron. 26:20–21].

The son of Uzziah had to take over the affairs of state, because Uzziah
was in quarantine for the rest of his life.

> Now the rest of the acts of Uzziah, first and last, did
> Isaiah the prophet, the son of Amoz, write [2 Chron.
> 26:22].

In the prophecy of Isaiah, we read that Isaiah began his ministry at the
death of Uzziah (Isa. 6:1).

> So Uzziah slept with his fathers, and they buried him
> with his fathers in the field of the burial which belonged
> to the kings; for they said, He is a leper: and Jotham his
> son reigned in his stead [2 Chron. 26:23].

Uzziah's funeral could almost be called a happy funeral. Death for a
Christian should not be a dread. Paul could say to the Thessalonian
believers, "But I would not have you to be ignorant, brethren, concerning them which are asleep, that ye sorrow not, even as others
which have no hope" (1 Thess. 4:13). Also to the Corinthian Christians he said, "O death, where is thy sting? O grave, where is thy
victory?" (1 Cor. 15:55). Funerals are not always as sad as they seem.
The funeral of Uzziah was not sad. Why not? He was a leper. Uzziah
had been a good king, but God records his sin also. He had intruded
into the priest's office. That was the spot on the apple. His sin was the
sin of presumption. There are still people today who sin by presumption. They attempt to approach God by man's way and not by God's
way. God has told us that we must come to him in His way. The Lord
Jesus Christ said, ". . . I am the way, the truth, and the life: no man
cometh unto the Father, but by me" (John 14:6). Uzziah had tried to
come to God in his own way, and he had become a leper. This was a
terrible disease. It was an awful disease physically, it was an awful

disease psychologically, and it was an awful disease in every way. It entailed a great deal of suffering. Death for Uzziah was a sweet release. Uzziah was God's man in spite of his sin, and God judged him for his sin. Remember that Paul wrote to the believers, "For if we would judge ourselves, we should not be judged" (1 Cor. 11:31). Uzziah was judged of God down here, but he went to Paradise as God's man.

There are multitudes of believers who are helpless and hopeless in a frail and feeble body. One of these days there will be a sweet release for them. What a wonderful and joyful thing it is to go into the presence of Christ! There is nothing to sorrow about in a case like that. I imagine Jotham was dry-eyed at the funeral of his father. I'm sure he loved his father, and he understood that his father was a saved man.

JOTHAM'S REIGN

Jotham is another king whom we would classify as a good king. Judah has had three good kings in a row—that was unusual.

> Jotham was twenty and five years old when he began to reign, and he reigned sixteen years in Jerusalem. His mother's name also was Jerushah, the daughter of Zadok.

> And he did that which was right in the sight of the LORD, according to all that his father Uzziah did: howbeit he entered not into the temple of the LORD. And the people did yet corruptly [2 Chron. 27:1-2].

Something very strange and interesting is said about this man: "he entered not into the temple of the LORD." There is a background for this. When his father went into the temple, he was a made a leper. But, of course, he went the wrong way—he intruded into the holy place. This boy Jotham did what was right in the sight of the Lord, but he stayed away from the temple. You can't help but feel sympathetic toward him, but he set a very bad example for the nation. As a result "the people did yet corruptly." They did not turn to God. Here is a man with a tremendous opportunity to lead his people back to God, but he had this hang-up—perhaps a root of bitterness. His father was made a leper in the temple, and he didn't want to go into that temple.

There are a great many people today who do just that sort of thing. They are kept away from God's house by prejudice. I have seen a number of folk who had dropped out of God's service because of prejudice, or an unfortunate incident which had happened years before or had involved a loved one. When I was a young man, I got acquainted with the son of a great Baptist preacher from Texas. He was really living it up in Pasadena when I met him. We used to play handball and volleyball together back in those days. When I tried to talk with him, he said, "Now listen, don't talk to me about religion. I know as much about it as you do." Then he told me how a group of deacons of the church had mistreated his father. He said, "I will never again darken the door of a church." I think he was wrong and I told him that. But very candidly, there was a background for it. That is the way it was with Jotham. There was an understandable background for his action.

> He built the high gate of the house of the LORD, and on the wall of Ophel he built much.
>
> Moreover he built cities in the mountains of Judah, and in the forests he built castles and towers [2 Chron. 27:3-4].

In that day the land was wooded. Today the hills are bare, for the most part. However trees are being planted now so that more of the land is becoming wooded again. Back in those days it was a land flowing with milk and honey. Jotham built castles among the hills. He was a great builder. I guess he is the man who started building subdivisions.

> He fought also with the king of the Ammonites, and prevailed against them. And the children of Ammon gave him the same year an hundred talents of silver, and ten thousand measures of wheat, and ten thousand of bar-

> ley. So much did the children of Ammon pay unto him,
> both the second year, and the third.
>
> So Jotham became mighty, because he prepared his
> ways before the LORD his God [2 Chron. 27:5-6].

He kept his nation strong militarily as his father had done.

> He was five and twenty years old when he began to
> reign, and reigned sixteen years in Jerusalem.
>
> And Jotham slept with his fathers, and they buried him
> in the city of David: and Ahaz his son reigned in his
> stead [2 Chron. 27:8-9].

Only one brief chapter is devoted to the reign of Jotham. Here is a
young man who could have been a great king, but a prejudice prevented him from being a great king and doing great things for God.

AHAZ' REIGN

We knew that sooner or later Judah would get a bad king, and here he
is. At this time the northern kingdom of Israel was on the verge of
going into captivity, and the southern kingdom of Judah was brought
very low by the sins of Ahaz, as we shall see.

> Ahaz was twenty years old when he began to reign, and
> he reigned sixteen years in Jerusalem: but he did not
> that which was right in the sight of the LORD, like David
> his father:
>
> For he walked in the ways of the kings of Israel, and
> made also molten images for Baalim [2 Chron. 28:1-2].

Ahaz was a bad king. He walked in the ways of the kings of Israel, and
that meant evil ways. David was the human standard by which these
kings were measured, and this man fell far short of that human stan-

dard. As a result we now begin to see the sad future of the southern kingdom. The northern kingdom will go into captivity to the Assyrians. God will give many warnings to the southern kingdom, but they, likewise, will follow into captivity—not to Assyria, but later on to Babylon.

> **Moreover he burnt incense in the valley of the son of Hinnom, and burnt his children in the fire, after the abominations of the heathen whom the LORD had cast out before the children of Israel [2 Chron. 28:3].**

This means he offered his children on a red-hot altar. Actually, it was an idol that was heated red-hot for human sacrifices.

> **He sacrificed also and burnt incense in the high places, and on the hills, and under every green tree [2 Chron. 28:4].**

Ahaz went completely into idolatry and plunged the southern kingdom into idolatry.

INVASION BY SYRIA AND ISRAEL

> **Wherefore the LORD his God delivered him into the hand of the king of Syria; and they smote him, and carried away a great multitude of them captives, and brought them to Damascus. And he was also delivered into the hand of the king of Israel, who smote him with a great slaughter [2 Chron. 28:5].**

As it were, God opens up the doors of His nation, His people, and permits the enemy to come in. Syria comes down, and for the first time the wall is breached into the southern kingdom. There are many who are taken captive. The sad part is that the northern kingdom had joined with Syria in making this attack, and so we find that many who were taken captive actually became captives of Israel, the northern kingdom. Israel took men of Judah into captivity.

> For Pekah the son of Remaliah slew in Judah an hundred and twenty thousand in one day, which were all valiant men; because they had forsaken the LORD God of their fathers [2 Chron. 28:6].

God makes the reason crystal-clear.

> And Zichri, a mighty man of Ephraim, slew Maaseiah the king's son, and Azrikam the governor of the house, and Elkanah that was next to the king.

> And the children of Israel carried away captive of their brethren two hundred thousand, women, sons, and daughters, and took also away much spoil from them, and brought the spoil to Samaria [2 Chron. 28:7-8].

This is the very sad plight of the southern kingdom. God permitted this to happen because Ahaz and the people had plunged into idolatry with abandon.

Now God sends a prophet to Israel to speak to them because of their extreme cruelty to their brethren.

> But a prophet of the LORD was there, whose name was Oded: and he went out before the host that came to Samaria, and said unto them, Behold, because the LORD God of your fathers was wroth with Judah, he hath delivered them into your hand, and ye have slain them in a rage that reacheth up unto heaven.

> And now ye purpose to keep under the children of Judah and Jerusalem for bondmen and bondwomen unto you: but are there not with you, even with you, sins against the LORD your God? [2 Chron. 28:9-10].

God had expressly forbidden taking their brethren into slavery (Lev. 25:39–40).

> Now hear me therefore, and deliver the captives again, which ye have taken captive of your brethren: for the fierce wrath of the LORD is upon you.

> Then certain of the heads of the children of Ephraim, Azariah the son of Johanan, Berechiah the son of Meshillemoth, and Jehizkiah the son of Shallum, and Amasa the son of Hadlai, stood up against them that came from the war [2 Chron. 28:11–12].

A group of leaders in the northern kingdom took their stand against enslaving their brethren from the southern kingdom.

> And said unto them, Ye shall not bring in the captives hither: for whereas we have offended against the LORD already, ye intend to add more to our sins and to our trespass: for our trespass is great, and there is fierce wrath against Israel.

> So the armed men left the captives and the spoil before the princes and all the congregation.

> And the men which were expressed by name rose up, and took the captives, and with the spoil clothed all that were naked among them, and arrayed them, and shod them, and gave them to eat and to drink, and anointed them, and carried all the feeble of them upon asses, and brought them to Jericho, the city of palm trees, to their brethren: then they returned to Samaria [2 Chron. 28:13–15].

They were able to secure their release and return them to their homes.

The southern kingdom of Judah was in a really sad plight at this time. If it had not been for the fact that God intervened, they would have been almost eliminated as a nation. It did weaken them a great deal and laid them open to further invasion.

INVASION BY EDOM AND PHILISTIA

At that time did king Ahaz send unto the kings of Assyria to help him.

For again the Edomites had come and smitten Judah, and carried away captives.

The Philistines also had invaded the cities of the low country, and of the south of Judah, and had taken Beth-shemesh, and Ajalon, and Gederoth, and Shocho with the villages thereof, and Timnah with the villages thereof, Gimzo also and the villages thereof: and they dwelt there [2 Chron. 28:16-18].

When God removed His protection, it was like opening the flood gates and letting the enemy come in. This was, of course, the result of the nation's sin. Wars are the direct result of sin. In the New Testament James asks the question, "From whence come wars and fightings among you?" The answer is, "come they not hence, even of your lusts that war in your members? Ye lust, and have not: ye kill, and desire to have . . ." (James 4:1-2). As long as there is sin in the heart of man, he cannot have peace. He can't have any kind of peace—peace with God, peace in his own heart, or peace with his fellowman. There must be a settling of the sin question in order to have peace. The experience of Judah illustrates this. Because of sin on the part of the people they will not have peace.

Ahaz made another big mistake. Instead of turning to God, he turned to Assyria for help.

And Tilgath-pilneser king of Assyria came unto him, and distressed him, but strengthened him not.

For Ahaz took away a portion out of the house of the LORD, and out of the house of the king, and of the

> princes, and gave it unto the king of Assyria: but he
> helped him not [2 Chron. 28:20–21].

Ahaz put his trust in the king of Assyria. He sent him a generous gift
from the wealth of the temple and of the palace. The king of Assyria
accepted it, but he never did send any help to Ahaz. He didn't need to.
He was a powerful king, and poor Ahaz was a very weak king. Ahaz
had turned from God and trusted in Assyria, and Assyria let him
down. Assyria did not make good on their treaty. You cannot expect
nations to be true to their treaties. Why not? Very simply, as long as
men are sinners, men will be liars, which means you cannot trust
them. The Bible tells us we are not to put our trust in man. We are to
put our trust in God.

> And in the time of his distress did he trespass yet more
> against the LORD: this is that king Ahaz.
>
> For he sacrificed unto the gods of Damascus, which
> smote him: and he said, Because the gods of the kings of
> Syria help them, therefore will I sacrifice to them, that
> they may help me. But they were the ruin of him, and of
> all Israel [2 Chron. 28:22–23].

Ahaz then cut up the vessels of the house of God, he shut up the doors
of the temple, and he made heathen altars in every corner of Jerusalem.

> And Ahaz slept with his fathers, and they buried him in
> the city, even in Jerusalem: but they brought him not into
> the sepulchres of the kings of Israel: and Hezekiah his
> son reigned in his stead [2 Chron. 28:27].

So ends this very sad and sordid and sorry reign of Ahaz.

CHAPTERS 29—32

THEME: Revival during Hezekiah's reign

We come now to the reign of Hezekiah and one of the periods of revival in the nation of Judah. You would think that after the reign of Ahaz there would be no hope for the nation. They were depleted of their resources, they had been defeated in war, they had been betrayed by Assyria, and you would think there would be no help for them from any quarter. However, Hezekiah came to the kingdom for such a time as this, because he is God's man.

> **Hezekiah began to reign when he was five and twenty years old, and he reigned nine and twenty years in Jerusalem. And his mother's name was Abijah, the daughter of Zechariah [2 Chron. 29:1].**

Both the mother and the grandfather are mentioned here, but there is no mention of his father, old Ahaz. Apparently Hezekiah had a godly mother and a godly grandfather, and they influenced this young man.

> **And he did that which was right in the sight of the LORD, according to all that David his father had done [2 Chron. 29:2].**

The Book of 2 Kings has a more succinct account of the revival under Hezekiah. "He removed the high places, and brake the images, and cut down the groves, and brake in pieces the brasen serpent that Moses had made: for unto those days the children of Israel did burn incense to it: and he called it Nehushtan. He trusted in the LORD God of Israel; so that after him was none like him among all the kings of Judah, nor any that were before him. For he clave to the LORD, and departed not from following him, but kept his commandments, which the LORD commanded Moses. And the LORD was with him; and he prospered whithersoever he went forth . . ." (2 Kings 18:4-7).

When you come down all the list of the twenty-one kings of Judah who followed David, there is none greater than Hezekiah. He is the outstanding one, a man who turned to God. I believe he led in one of the greatest revivals, and there were some great ones.

I mentioned that his revival is recorded in 2 Kings. Here in 2 Chronicles, which is written from God's point of view, four lengthy chapters are devoted to Hezekiah. Evidently God took great delight in Hezekiah. Also Isaiah the prophet has in the center of his book several chapters which are historical and not prophetic. They have to do with—yes, you guessed it—Hezekiah. Three times in the Word of God we are told about this man and the great return to God which he led.

In Chronicles we are told the positive things which he did to restore worship. In Kings we are told the negative things he had to do. He had to remove the high places and break the images and had to break in pieces the brazen serpent that Moses had made because the people were burning incense to it. He had to get rid of that stumbling block. He contemptuously called it "Nehushtan"—it was just a piece of brass. There had been one time when the people had looked at the serpent in faith, trusting the promise of God, then the brazen serpent had been the basis of physical salvation for those who were bitten by the poisonous snakes. Now it had become an object of worship. It had become an idol. It was a stumbling block to the people.

There are those today who worship the symbol of the cross. They feel that there is some merit in having a cross in their possession. My friend, there would be no merit in it at all. You can make an idol of anything—you can worship the spigot because it gives you water, you could worship the window because it brings you light, or you could worship the automobile because it transports you. A great many people today worship the television screen; they sit before it for hours each day. May I say to you, there is no merit in objects. The merit is in God, of course; this is written from God's viewpoint.

Now in Chronicles we are given the positive side of Hezekiah's reforms.

> He in the first year of his reign, in the first month,
> opened the doors of the house of the LORD, and repaired
> them [2 Chron. 29:3].

Remember that Ahaz had nailed shut the doors of the temple. Nobody was using it. As soon as Hezekiah began to reign, he opened the doors of the temple. They were open for the first time in a long time. Now Hezekiah tells them to clean everything.

> And he brought in the priests and the Levites, and gath-
> ered them together into the east street.
>
> And said unto them, Hear me, ye Levites, sanctify now
> yourselves, and sanctify the house of the LORD God of
> your fathers, and carry forth the filthiness out of the
> holy place [2 Chron. 29:4–5].

Hezekiah says, "Sanctify now yourselves." There had to be a return to holy living, to honesty, and to integrity. There had to be a setting-apart for God. That was something that was needed. I think we need the same thing today. We have too much of this homogenized Christianity today—mixing good and bad together.

> For our fathers have trespassed, and done that which
> was evil in the eyes of the LORD our God, and have for-
> saken him, and have turned away their faces from the
> habitation of the LORD, and turned their backs.
>
> Also they have shut up the doors of the porch, and put
> out the lamps, and have not burned incense nor offered
> burnt offerings in the holy place unto the God of Israel
> [2 Chron. 29:6–7].

He places the blame where it belongs. They have brought disaster upon themselves because of their sins.

> Wherefore the wrath of the LORD was upon Judah and
> Jerusalem, and he hath delivered them to trouble, to as-
> tonishment, and to hissing, as ye see with your eyes.
>
> For, lo, our fathers have fallen by the sword, and our
> sons and our daughters and our wives are in captivity
> for this [2 Chron. 29:8–9].

Now he tells them what is upon his heart.

> Now it is in mine heart to make a covenant with the LORD
> God of Israel, that his fierce wrath may turn away from
> us [2 Chron. 29:10].

TEMPLE WORSHIP RESTORED

> Then Hezekiah the king rose early, and gathered the
> rulers of the city, and went up to the house of the LORD.
>
> And they brought seven bullocks, and seven rams, and
> seven lambs, and seven he goats, for a sin offering for
> the kingdom, and for the sanctuary, and for Judah. And
> he commanded the priests the sons of Aaron to offer
> them on the altar of the LORD [2 Chron. 29:20–21].

Hezekiah set a good example. He took a public stand for God. I believe this is one of the things that is needed today. God's people need
to take a public stand for God. We need to stand for God in our place of
work and in our social gatherings.

The priests made an atonement for all Israel with the burnt offerings and sin offering. Music was again brought into the worship in the
temple. There was singing and instrumental music as David had organized it. The whole congregation sang praises to God and worshiped
Him.

> And Hezekiah rejoiced, and all the people, that God
> had prepared the people: for the thing was done sud-
> denly [2 Chron. 29:36].

FEAST OF PASSOVER RESTORED

And Hezekiah sent to all Israel and Judah, and wrote letters also to Ephraim and Manasseh, that they should come to the house of the LORD at Jerusalem, to keep the passover unto the LORD God of Israel [2 Chron. 30:1].

Here is another wonderful thing this man did. Remember that his father had carried on warfare against the northern kingdom, and many of those from Judah had been taken captive. You might think that Hezekiah would have come to the throne with a spirit of vengeance in his heart and with a spirit of getting even. But notice that after he had opened up the temple of God, restoring the worship of God and giving his own public testimony, he sends an invitation to the northern kingdom to come and worship God. What a wonderful, marvelous spirit this is!

For the king had taken counsel, and his princes, and all the congregation in Jerusalem, to keep the passover in the second month [2 Chron. 30:2].

Authority for observing the Passover in the second month, instead of the first, is given in Numbers 9:10–11.

Although the invitation, which Hezekiah sent into the northern kingdom, was rejected and ridiculed by some, many responded and came to keep the Passover with their brethren.

Then they killed the passover on the fourteenth day of the second month: and the priests and the Levites were ashamed, and sanctified themselves, and brought in the burnt offerings into the house of the LORD.

And they stood in their place after their manner, according to the law of Moses the man of God: the priests sprinkled the blood, which they received of the hand of the Levites.

> For there were many in the congregation that were not
> sanctified: therefore the Levites had the charge of the
> killing of the passovers for every one that was not clean,
> to sanctify them unto the LORD [2 Chron. 30:15-17].

The people had come from all over Israel, and some of them were not
sanctified.

> For the multitude of the people, even many of Ephraim,
> and Manasseh, Issachar, and Zebulun, had not
> cleansed themselves, yet did they eat the passover other-
> wise than it was written. But Hezekiah prayed for them,
> saying, The good LORD pardon every one

> That prepareth his heart to seek God, the LORD God of
> his fathers, though he be not cleansed according to the
> purification of the sanctuary.

> And the LORD hearkened to Hezekiah, and healed the
> people [2 Chron. 30:18-20].

This, I think, is one of the loveliest things Hezekiah did. When he sent
invitations to the people of Israel in the north, many came down out of
the different tribes to Jerusalem to worship. But, you see, these people
have been without the Word of God all their lives. They had been living in the northern kingdom, in the place of idolatry, and yet they had
a hunger and a desire to serve God and to obey Him. When they came
down for the feast, they were supposed to have been cleansed, to have
prepared their hearts for the Passover, and they hadn't done that. They
went ahead and ate the Passover without knowing that they should
have been cleansed. When it was told to Hezekiah, he prayed for
them: "The good Lord pardon every one." Isn't that a lovely thing
which he did for them? It was ignorance on their part. Their hearts
had been seeking the Lord, but they didn't understand that they had to
be purified. The Lord listened to the prayer of Hezekiah and healed
the people. This reveals that the form and the ceremony are not the

important things. God is interested in the condition of the hearts of the people. What a wonderful, glorious lesson this is here.

> And the children of Israel that were present at Jerusalem kept the feast of unleavened bread seven days with great gladness: and the Levites and the priests praised the Lord day by day, singing with loud instruments unto the LORD [2 Chron. 30:21].

They were having such a wonderful time, that they decided to extend the feast for another week.

> And the whole assembly took counsel to keep other seven days: and they kept other seven days with gladness [2 Chron. 30:23].

This was a joyous return to the Lord and to His Word.

> So there was great joy in Jerusalem: for since the time of Solomon the son of David king of Israel there was not the like in Jerusalem.

> Then the priests the Levites arose and blessed the people: and their voice was heard, and their prayer came up to his holy dwelling place, even unto heaven [2 Chron. 30:26–27].

Now I want you to notice this man Hezekiah. His father, old Ahaz, had made idolatry the state religion in Judah. Now Hezekiah begins to rid the land of idols.

> Now when all this was finished, all Israel that were present went out to the cities of Judah, and brake the images in pieces, and cut down the groves, and threw down the high places and the altars out of all Judah and Benjamin, in Ephraim also and Manasseh, until they

had utterly destroyed them all. Then all the children of
Israel returned, every man to his possession, into their
own cities [2 Chron. 31:1].

After this, there was a great period of reformation that took place. Hezekiah was the man who led in all of this.

> And thus did Hezekiah throughout all Judah, and
> wrought that which was good and right and truth before
> the LORD his God.

> And in every work that he began in the service of the
> house of God, and in the law, and in the command-
> ments, to seek his God, he did it with all his heart, and
> prospered [2 Chron. 31:20-21].

Now let's look a little more closely at the life of Hezekiah. What kind of man was he?

First of all, he was a man of faith. When I say *faith*, I mean more than what is generally thought of as faith.

A member of a certain "ism" told me that there were four things one had to do to be saved. So I asked him, "What do you think you have to do to be saved?" I won't mention all four things, but one of them was faith. I told him, "I don't agree with you on any of the four." He was a little shocked. He said, "Well, certainly you believe in faith, because I know you preach on that." I said, "But I don't mean *faith* in the same way that you mean *faith*. You are saying that if one believes hard enough he will be saved."

The modern conception of faith reminds me of the county fairs I used to go to when I was a boy. At each fair there was a gadget to test a man's strength. There was weight on a pair of scales that looked like a giant thermometer. A man would come along and hit the thing with a sledge hammer, which would knock the weight up. A fellow would come along with his girl friend, and they would challenge him to try out his strength. He would take off his coat, spit on his hands, and swing that hammer with all his might to see if he could ring the bell up at the top. He would make the supreme effort. He would really try hard.

That's the way some folk think faith is. They say, "If I could only believe hard enough." My friend, faith is not a psychological response to anything. Faith is not in the feelings; it is an accomplished fact. Faith is that which is wrought in the soul by the Holy Spirit. It is a conviction that is born in the spirit of man.

After Peter made his great confession of faith in Jesus Christ, the Lord Jesus said, ". . . Blessed art thou, Simon Bar-jona: for flesh and blood hath not revealed it unto thee, but my Father which is in heaven" (Matt. 16:17). Faith is not self-meritorious. "For by grace are ye saved through faith . . ." (Eph. 2:8). Faith is only the instrument. Christ is the Savior and He is the object of faith.

Spurgeon said, "It is not thy hold on Christ that saves thee. It is Christ. It is not thy joy in Christ that saves thee. It is Christ. It is not even thy faith, though that be the instrument; it is Christ's blood and merit." There is no merit in faith. It is not a matter of believing enough. You could believe the wrong thing. There are many people who die as martyrs for fanatic beliefs. They can have ever so much faith, but it is in the wrong thing or the wrong person.

True faith "brings nothing so that it may take all." Faith says, "Lord, I believe; help Thou mine unbelief." Faith trusts God.

Now in the remainder of chapter 31, we see Hezekiah's further reforms. Also there will be reformation in your life when the Lord Jesus saves you, my friend. He is going to change your life.

Remember that when the man sick of the palsy was brought to Christ, Jesus told him his sins were forgiven. The crowd of scribes and Pharisees began to murmur, and call this a case of blasphemy. Jesus said, ". . . What reason ye in your hearts? Whether is easier, to say, Thy sins be forgiven thee; or to say, Rise up and walk?" They had no answer for Jesus. Obviously, it is just as easy to do the one as to do the other. It is also just as difficult to do the one as to do the other. Only God can do either one of them. Only God can forgive sin. Only God can make a person get up and walk. "But that ye may know that the

Son of man hath power upon earth to forgive sins, (he said unto the sick of the palsy,) I say unto thee, Arise, and take up thy couch, and go into thine house" (Luke 5:22–24).

My friend, if Christ has forgiven your sin, you have taken up your bed and you have walked. You have walked away from your old life. You have walked away from your old sin. You have been changed. If you have not walked away, you are still paralyzed with sin.

Hezekiah is a man of real faith in God, and it changed his life. And now he is changing the kingdom.

Hezekiah is not only a man of faith, he is a man of prayer. In chapter 32 it looks as if the Lord allowed Judah to pass from the sunlight of God's blessing to the darkness of disaster. Sennacherib came down from Assyria again, and he was ready to make an attack upon the city of Jerusalem. He began by terrifying the inhabitants.

> **After these things, and the establishment thereof, Sennacherib king of Assyria came, and entered into Judah, and encamped against the fenced cities, and thought to win them for himself [2 Chron. 32:1].**

Hezekiah took steps to strengthen and fortify the city, but his confidence was in God. He encouraged his people to trust in Him.

> **Be strong and courageous, be not afraid nor dismayed for the king of Assyria, nor for all the multitude that is with him: for there be more with us than with him:**

> **With him is an arm of flesh; but with us is the Lord our God to help us, and to fight our battles. And the people rested themselves upon the words of Hezekiah king of Judah [2 Chron. 32:7–8].**

After this Sennacherib sent representatives to intimidate the people and break down their morale and shake their confidence in God.

> **Who was there among all the gods of those nations that my fathers utterly destroyed, that could deliver his peo-**

ple out of mine hand, that your God should be able to deliver you out of mine hand?

Now therefore let not Hezekiah deceive you, nor persuade you on this manner, neither yet believe him: for no god of any nation or kingdom was able to deliver his people out of mine hand, and out of the hand of my fathers: how much less shall your God deliver you out of mine hand? [2 Chron. 32:14–15].

Also Sennacherib sent letters to demoralize them.

He wrote also letters to rail on the LORD God of Israel, and to speak against him, saying, As the gods of the nations of other lands have not delivered their people out of mine hand, so shall not the God of Hezekiah deliver his people out of mine hand [2 Chron. 32:17].

The record in 2 Kings gives this in more detail. When Hezekiah received the letter, he went up into the house of the Lord, and spread the letter before Him. His wonderful prayer is recorded in 2 Kings 19:14–19. Hezekiah was a real man of prayer.

And for this cause Hezekiah the king, and the prophet Isaiah the son of Amoz, prayed and cried to heaven [2 Chron. 32:20].

Hezekiah depended upon the Lord for help, and He delivered the city in a miraculous way.

And the LORD sent an angel, which cut off all the mighty men of valour, and the leaders and captains in the camp of the king of Assyria. So he returned with shame of face to his own land. And when he was come into the house of his god, they that came forth of his own bowels slew him there with the sword.

Thus the LORD saved Hezekiah and the inhabitants of Jerusalem from the hand of Sennacherib the king of Assyria, and from the hand of all other, and guided them on every side [2 Chron. 32:21-22].

THE ILLNESS OF HEZEKIAH

In those days Hezekiah was sick to the death, and prayed unto the LORD: and he spake unto him, and he gave him a sign [2 Chron. 32:24].

In 2 Kings 20, the record tells us that Hezekiah turned his face to the wall and prayed and wept before the Lord.

I think I understand how he felt. It rocked me when the doctor told me I had cancer. I could not believe it. When I had to accept the fact, I was not given any assurance at all that I would live. When I was taken to the hospital, I had no idea what the outcome of my illness would be. The nurse had to help me get into bed because I was so weak. I was not physically weak, I was frightened—I am a coward! She asked, "Are you sick?" "No," I said, "I am scared to death!" She was a Christian nurse, and she smiled at that. I asked her to leave me alone for a while, and I turned my face to the wall, just as Hezekiah had done, and I cried out to God. I told Him that I did not want to die.

When we are sick, I believe we should go to God in prayer and ask others to pray for us. I believe in faith healing (but not in faith *healers*); I know God can heal. Well, an acquaintance wrote me a letter in which she said, "I am not going to pray that you get well because I know that you are ready to go and be with the Lord. I am praying that He will take you home." I got an answer back to her in a hurry. I wrote, "Now look here. You let the Lord handle this. Don't try and tell Him how I feel. I don't want to die. I want to live. I want to live as long as I can!"

Now Hezekiah was in that same position. Only God could help him. When he turned his face to the wall, he reminded the Lord that he had walked before Him in truth and with a perfect heart and he had done that which was good in His sight.

They put a poultice of figs on his "boil"—it could have been cancer. Whatever it was, God healed him and gave him fifteen more years.

> **But Hezekiah rendered not again according to the benefit done unto him; for his heart was lifted up: therefore there was wrath upon him, and upon Judah and Jerusalem.**
>
> **Notwithstanding Hezekiah humbled himself for the pride of his heart, both he and the inhabitants of Jerusalem, so that the wrath of the LORD came not upon them in the days of Hezekiah [2 Chron. 32:25–26].**

The kingdom of Judah had become very poor during the reign of Ahaz, but now it has again become wealthy.

> **And Hezekiah had exceeding much riches and honour: and he made himself treasuries for silver, and for gold, and for precious stones, and for spices, and for shields, and for all manner of pleasant jewels [2 Chron. 32:27].**

When the ambassadors from Babylon had come, he very foolishly showed them the entire wealth of his kingdom (see 2 Kings 20:12–19). Now, here is God's comment on this episode:

> **Howbeit in the business of the ambassadors of the princes of Babylon, who sent unto him to inquire of the wonder that was done in the land, God left him, to try him, that he might know all that was in his heart [2 Chron. 32:31].**

This may seem like an awful thing for me to say, but Hezekiah should have died when the time came for him to die. Three things took place after God extended his life that were foolish acts: he showed his treasures to Babylon, which will cause great trouble in the future; he begat a son, Manasseh, who was the most wicked of any king; he revealed an arrogance, almost an impudence in his later years. His heart became filled with pride. Second Chronicles 32:25 tells us, "But Hezekiah rendered not again according to the benefit done unto him; for his heart was lifted up: therefore there was wrath upon him, and upon Judah and Jerusalem." You see, it might have been better if Hezekiah had died at God's appointed time.

That is why I want to be very careful. The Lord has spared me and I do not want to do anything to disgrace Him. My friend, this is a wonderful chapter, We have a wonderful heavenly Father.

DEATH OF HEZEKIAH

Now the rest of the acts of Hezekiah, and his goodness, behold, they are written in the vision of Isaiah the prophet, the son of Amoz, and in the book of the kings of Judah and Israel.

And Hezekiah slept with his fathers, and they buried him in the chiefest of the sepulchres of the sons of David: and all Judah and the inhabitants of Jerusalem did him honour at his death. And Manasseh his son reigned in his stead [2 Chron. 32:32–33].

Now I would like to talk a few moments on the subject of revival. I think it is very important for us to note that God is sovereign in this matter of revival. "The wind bloweth where it listeth, and thou hearest the sound thereof, but canst not tell whence it cometh, and whither it goeth: so is every one that is born of the Spirit" says our Lord in John 3:8. Only God can send a revival. God is sovereign in this through the working of the Holy Spirit.

God is not a Western Union boy or a bell-boy. You can't just push a button and have Him come at your command. I hear some folks in their prayers command the Lord to do something. We cannot give commands to God, my friend. Remember the experience of Elijah on Mount Carmel. The prophets of Baal had screamed themselves hoarse and had yelled like fanatics, but they were not able to bring down fire upon the sacrifice. Then Elijah laid the stones in order and he put wood on there and put the sacrifice on it and poured water over it. Then he prayed to God. He was a man of like passions as we are. In effect he said to the Lord: "All we can do is just get the stones together and put a little order into them. We can put the wood here and the sacrifice on it, but You will need to send the fire." Elijah knew the fire must come from God. God responded at that time.

As I write this, there is a spiritual movement in our land. At first I thought it was confined to young people, but I find it also includes young married couples. Young couples are seeing their children growing away from them. They are coming to realize that they must have answers to some of the problems. One young father said to me, "I thought I could always solve my problems, but I need God." Today there is a turning to the Word of God, and I rejoice in it. I see it everywhere.

Very candidly, I never saw that in my ministry in the church. This movement is largely outside the church. I've seen it in meetings that we have had all over this country. Young people, and older ones too, are coming to the conferences. There seems to be a real interest in the Word of God.

There are pastors and some religious leaders who are trying to capitalize on this; so they feed these young people a bunch of garbage. They give them "hard rock" music in place of Bible study. They give them everything but the Word of God. You remember our Lord asked, "If a son shall ask bread of any of you that is a father, will he give him a stone? . . ." (Luke 11:11). And certainly don't give him "hard rock!" Give him the Word of God.

I find them listening to my Bible teaching program, and I have told them, "I'm old fashioned. I teach the Bible just as it is. Why do you listen to me?" One of them said, "Well, we listen to you because you tell it like it is." That's the only way I know how to tell it, and I've been telling it that way for years, but nobody listened. Now they are beginning to listen. Are we on the verge of a spiritual awakening? I am praying that the Lord will send it. I want to be very frank with you; if it comes, He will be the One who will send it. I'm just getting my rain-coat out in case the showers of blessing come. I have never seen revival in my day, and I would really like to see one. Wouldn't you?

Let me present a challenge to you. Why don't you make an inventory of your own personal life? If you want God to move in on your life, ask yourself these questions:

1. Am I honest?
2. Am I truthful?
3. Am I faithful? Can I be depended upon?
4. Am I pure? Am I really pure in this dirty day of filthy pictures and filthy language?
5. Am I dedicated? Am I really a dedicated child of God? Dwight L. Moody heard a man say that the world has yet to see what God can do with a man who is fully yielded to Him. Moody's response was, "By the grace of God, I will be that man." I think Moody was that man and yet, Moody, on his deathbed said, "The world has yet to see what God can do with a man who is fully yielded to Him." Oh, my friend, let's get into the position where God can move through us to give the Water of Life to a thirsty world.

CHAPTER 33

THEME: Manasseh's evil reign

As we have seen, Hezekiah had been sick unto death, but he had prayed to God and Isaiah had prayed with him. He had some sort of boil which may well have been a cancer. God healed him and extended his life for fifteen years. That was a gracious dispensation on the part of God in answer to prayer. But when one looks at this in the full light of the history that followed, one wonders if it was the best thing that could have taken place.

First of all, it was during that fifteen-year period after his life had been spared that Hezekiah displayed the wealth of his kingdom to the ambassadors from Babylon. This opened the door for Nebuchadnezzar to come years later and take the city. He knew exactly where the gold was, and he took it by force. That was the Fort Knox of Israel. No one is attacking Fort Knox today. They tell me that the security there is unbelievable, but the gold is leaking out. The nations of the world aren't able to get it by attack; so they are getting it in another way. Well, that gold in Israel tempted Babylon to come and take it. It had been a very foolish thing for Hezekiah to show that gold to them.

Secondly, you will notice here that Manasseh was twelve years old when he began to reign. This means that this boy was born during the fifteen-year period after God had extended the life of Hezekiah. Manasseh was the most wicked king of all. During his reign there was such godlessness that God had to intervene.

Manasseh was twelve years old when he began to reign, and he reigned fifty and five years in Jerusalem:

But did that which was evil in the sight of the LORD, like unto the abominations of the heathen, whom the LORD had cast out before the children of Israel [2 Chron. 33:1–2].

It's a strange thing, isn't it? Hezekiah was the best king and led the nation in a revival. His son comes to the throne and is the worst king. How can you explain that? I'll let you in on a secret: I cannot explain it.

Around me today things are happening like that which I cannot explain. Periodically I hear of a very fine Christian home with wonderful Christian parents in which a son or a daughter rebels against everything. When one looks at young vagrants across the entire land, one can conclude that they were neglected at home. They saw godless, materialistic parents who were fighting all the time, or they came from broken homes, homes that were centered merely on self and selfishness. I can understand why they rebelled against all that and just walked out. But why is it that a son or daughter will simply walk out of a lovely, Christian home and join the rebellious crowd? I really cannot explain it. I can give two possible reasons, and both of them are feeble.

The first reason is that young people are influenced by the other young people around them. All young people go through a period when they feel that their parents are stupid. I can remember after I had gone away to college I was almost ashamed to come home. They just didn't know enough, you see. That is a period that youth go through.

I have heard other young people tell me the same thing. One young pastor told me how ashamed he was of his dad when he went off to college. But after he had been out in the big bad world and had faced some problems, he returned home for a visit. He realized that although his dad had been somewhat stupid, he had managed to make a good living and had provided a marvelous home for his family. He said that the thing which amazed him was how much his dad had learned in those few years he had been away from home! I think all young people go through such a period, and I can understand that young people are influenced by other young folk who have left home in rebellion. That is one explanation.

Also I have noted that young folk who rebel against a Christian home, especially if they have made a profession of faith, will return to the Lord in time. The king we are looking at here, Manasseh, is an illustration of this.

The reign of Manasseh was evil beyond imagination. It is my conviction that the Shekinah glory, which was the visible presence of God, left the temple. The prophet Ezekiel saw the vision of the Shekinah glory lifted up and removed from the Holy of Holies because of the sins of the people and their rebellion. It moved out to the walls of Jerusalem and waited there. The people did not turn back to God. Then the Shekinah glory withdrew to the Mount of Olives and lingered there. Still there was no movement of the people back to God. So the Shekinah glory was caught back up into heaven. *Ichabod*, which means "the glory has departed," was written over the threshold of the temple. Their house was indeed left unto them desolate.

I know that most expositors feel that the Shekinah glory left the temple during the captivity. I don't feel that is accurate. If the Shekinah glory did not leave during the reign of Manasseh, I cannot see any other period in Israel's history that would cause the glory, the presence of God, to leave. I believe this was the time.

Notice how long this man reigned. He reigned fifty-five years in Jerusalem. This man reigned much longer than others, longer than David, longer than Solomon, longer than his father. Why? Because God is merciful. God is longsuffering. He is not willing that any should perish. After all, God has plenty of time on His hands. He has eternity in back of Him and eternity in front of Him. He is in no hurry, friends. Don't think you are going to push God, or rush Him, or move Him. I hear people say to someone to pray. They say, "If you go right to God, He'll begin to move." Friends, He may and then again, He may not. He will take His time. God is in no hurry. He will give Manasseh ample opportunity to turn to Him.

We are getting God's viewpoint in Chronicles. In 2 Kings 21 we are told of the evils of Manasseh's reign, and here in Chronicles God repeats that he "did that which was evil in the sight of the LORD, like unto the abominations of the heathen, whom the LORD cast out before the children of Israel."

For he built again the high places which Hezekiah his father had broken down, and he reared up altars for

> Baalim, and made groves, and worshipped all the host
> of heaven, and served them [2 Chron. 33:3].

He went into idolatry in a big way. He was as bad as Ahab and Jezebel, and he worshiped Baal as they had done.

> Also he built altars in the house of the LORD, whereof the
> LORD had said, In Jerusalem shall my name be for ever.

> And he built altars for all the host of heaven in the two
> courts of the house of the LORD [2 Chron. 33:4–5].

He introduced right into the temple in Jerusalem the worship of the hosts of heaven: like the worship of Jupiter, the worship of Mercury, the worship of Venus, and the worship of all the stars. In other words, he established the horoscope there. You could have had your horoscope read in the temple in that day.

I'm sorry to say that some churches actually promote this same sort of thing. It is big business today. You can go to any dime store or magazine rack and buy a horoscope. Some folk say it is just innocent fun, but it is not that for a lot of people. They put more confidence in the horoscope than they put in God.

I recall an interview on television some time ago in which an outstanding entertainer made the statement that she had been looking at her horoscope and that she was a Virgo. The girl had been married five or six times and apparently had other affairs, and I would not think she was a Virgo by any manner of calculation! And she felt that when such-and-such a star crossed such-and-such a star, that would be a very important time for her. It is amazing that in our day intelligent people can place so much confidence in the stars.

Manasseh was very much interested in the horoscope. "And he built altars for all the host of heaven in the two courts of the house of the LORD." And he didn't stop with that.

> And he caused his children to pass through the fire in
> the valley of the son of Hinnom: also he observed times,

> and used enchantments, and used witchcraft, and dealt
> with a familiar spirit, and with wizards: he wrought
> much evil in the sight of the LORD, to provoke him to
> anger [2 Chron. 33:6].

He went all the way into idolatry. We are not told how far he went in
causing "his children to pass through the fire." There were degrees.
He could have let them pass through the fire and only get well singed.
Or he could put the baby right down in the arms of that red-hot idol.
You just cannot think of anything as bad as that! This is idolatry, and
Manasseh seems to have gone into it all the way.

Also Manasseh used enchantments and witchcraft and dealt with
familiar spirits (lit., a divining demon present in the physical body of
the conjurer). In our day along with the movement back to God we are
seeing a return to satanic worship.

> And he set a carved image, the idol which he had made,
> in the house of God, of which God had said to David and
> to Solomon his son, In this house, and in Jerusalem,
> which I have chosen before all the tribes of Israel, will I
> put my name for ever:
>
> Neither will I any more remove the foot of Israel from
> out of the land which I have appointed for your fathers;
> so that they will take heed to do all that I have com-
> manded them, according to the whole law and the stat-
> utes and the ordinances by the hand of Moses [2 Chron.
> 33:7-8].

God had promised that if these people would worship Him and be
faithful to Him, He would bless them. Notice what Manasseh is doing
to Judah.

> So Manasseh made Judah and the inhabitants of Jerusa-
> lem to err, and to do worse than the heathen, whom the
> LORD had destroyed before the children of Israel.

> And the LORD spake to Manasseh, and to his people: but
> they would not hearken [2 Chron. 33:9-10].

MANASSEH IS CAPTURED AND THEN RESTORED

You can be sure that when a man or a nation reaches this place, God
will move.

> Wherefore the LORD brought upon them the captains of
> the host of the king of Assyria, which took Manasseh
> among the thorns, and bound him with fetters, and car-
> ried him to Babylon [2 Chron. 33:11].

He was actually taken from his throne and carried captive to Babylon.

> And when he was in affliction, he besought the LORD his
> God, and humbled himself greatly before the God of his
> fathers.
> And prayed unto him: and he was entreated of him, and
> heard his supplication, and brought him again to Jeru-
> salem into his kingdom. Then Manasseh knew that the
> LORD he was God [2 Chron. 33:12-13].

This man had a remarkable experience. I would have given him up,
I'm sure, but God did not give him up. God sent trouble—and plenty
of it—to him. He was carried away as a captive to Babylon. This
should have been a warning to the nation that God was now getting
ready to send them into captivity because of their continual sin. When
Manasseh found himself in real trouble, he sincerely came back to
God. God forgave him and restored him! Yet he was very much of a
weakling, as such men generally are.

When he returned to Jerusalem, he took away the strange gods and
the idols out of the house of the Lord, and he repaired the altar of the
Lord and sacrificed there.

> Nevertheless the people did sacrifice still in the high
> places, yet unto the LORD their God only [2 Chron.
> 33:17].

In other words, the people never did truly come back to God but still
sacrificed in the high places.

Apparently Manasseh reigned all this time. When he was a helpless captive in Babylon, God heard his prayer. This reveals how gracious God is! Here is a son of godly parents who went into sin to the
very limit and then came back to God. That should be an encouragement to parents who are reading this today. Maybe you have a son or a
daughter who has gone the very limit, and you despair that your child
will never turn back to God. I would have given Manasseh up, but
God didn't. God heard his prayer.

REIGN OF AMON

> Amon was two and twenty years old when he began to
> reign, and reigned two years in Jerusalem [2 Chron.
> 33:21].

The evil which Manasseh had done had its effect on this young man,
his son. I can understand why his son went off into evil as he did.

Friends of mine, folk of means, really lived it up until middle age.
They were converted after their children were nearly grown. Then
after they were converted, they had other children who are wonderful
godly children. But the older children have gone the limit into sin.

> But he did that which was evil in the sight of the LORD,
> as did Manasseh his father: for Amon sacrificed unto all
> the carved images which Manasseh his father had
> made, and served them;
>
> And humbled not himself before the LORD, as Manasseh
> his father had humbled himself; but Amon trespassed
> more and more [2 Chron. 33:22-23].

Amon followed in the footsteps of his father in his early days.

CHAPTERS 34 AND 35

THEME: Revival during Josiah's reign

We come now to the last great revival under Josiah. The hour is late. It is five minutes before 12:00 in the history of this nation, and yet God sends revival. This is the last revival to take place before the captivity. Judah has come to the end of the line, and it is amazing that a revival takes place. It follows after the reigns of Manasseh and Amon, two men who really plunged that nation into idolatry and sin. One would think there was no hope at all, but there is always hope. The Holy Spirit is still sovereign in this matter of revival.

I do not know whether we will have a revival in our day or not. Humanly speaking, the nation of Judah could not have revival, but the Spirit of God is sovereign, and God can move in. He can move in today. There is nothing in the Word of God that would preclude that possibility.

One man said to me, "The trouble with you men who believe in prophecy and emphasize the terrible days that are ahead is that you have no place for revival." I disagree with that. My feeling is that he doesn't have any place for revival. The reason I say that is because he and his group are trying to work it up themselves. My friend, you cannot work it up or pray it down. The Spirit of God is sovereign.

Our prayer today should be, "Lord, put me in the will of God." Our prime concern is to make sure that our own lives are right before God. We are not going to get God to do something when our lives are not right in His sight. We need to straighten out our own lives before God. We need to ask ourselves these questions: Am I honest? Am I truthful? Am I pure? There is no use talking about revival as long as we are not getting right in our hearts before God. When we are right with God, then we can look to the Spirit of God to move in a sovereign way, and then we can ask Him to move according to His will.

Now we will look here at Josiah and see that God marvelously used him.

REFORMATION UNDER JOSIAH

Josiah was eight years old when he began to reign, and he reigned in Jerusalem one and thirty years.

And he did that which was right in the sight of the LORD, and walked in the ways of David his father, and declined neither to the right hand, nor to the left [2 Chron. 34:1-2].

You hear people today asking what is right and what is wrong. And you hear some strange answers given. Josiah did that which was right *in the sight of the Lord*. It is what *God* says is right that is right and what *God* says is wrong that is wrong.

Remember that it was God who divided the light from the darkness. You and I cannot do that! We can go into a room and turn on the light switch, and the darkness disappears. We cannot divide it; we can't run a line down the middle and say, "On this side I will put light and on this side I will put darkness." God can do that, and God can say what is right and what is wrong.

For in the eighth year of his reign, while he was yet young, he began to seek after the God of David his father: and in the twelfth year he began to purge Judah and Jerusalem from the high places, and the groves, and the carved images, and the molten images [2 Chron. 34:3].

In the eighth year of his reign Josiah was sixteen years old, and he began to seek God. The spiritual movement today, and the turning to the Word of God, is largely among young people. Although it is not confined to them, they certainly are the majority. I meet these young folks in my conference travels and all around the world. They are interested in the Word of God. Josiah was only sixteen when he began to seek after God. He was twenty when he began his reforms in Judah. You see, revival will lead to reformation.

As I mentioned before, when your sins are forgiven, you will pick up your bed and walk. You will walk away from your sins if you are truly converted. If revival comes in our day, we will not have a divorce problem or a sex revolution. We will see a tremendous change take place. God can accomplish this, and He may do it. This section of the Word of God can be a great encouragement to us.

Josiah was a fearless reformer. After he had cleaned up his southern kingdom of Judah, he went into the tribes of Israel in the north.

> **Now in the eighteenth year of his reign, when he had purged the land, and the house, he sent Shaphan the son of Azaliah, and Maaseiah the governor of the city, and Joah the son of Joahaz the recorder, to repair the house of the LORD his God [2 Chron. 34:8].**

When Josiah was twenty-six years old, he began the repair of the temple. It had fallen into disrepair under the reign of Manasseh, his grandfather, and Amon, his father.

> **And when they came to Hilkiah the high priest, they delivered the money that was brought into the house of God, which the Levites that kept the doors had gathered of the hand of Manasseh and Ephraim, and of all the remnant of Israel, and of all Judah and Benjamin; and they returned to Jerusalem [2 Chron. 34:9].**

"Manasseh and Ephraim" are, of course, tribes of Israel. At this time the northern kingdom had been taken into Assyrian captivity; only a remnant was left in the land. These tribes, which we hear called "lost tribes," certainly were not lost in this day, as they were sending in money for the repair of the temple.

Now the temple was repaired, and they made an amazing discovery.

THE LAW OF MOSES IS FOUND

> **And when they brought out the money that was brought into the house of the LORD, Hilkiah the priest found a**

book of the law of the LORD given by Moses [2 Chron. 34:14].

You see, there weren't many copies in that day. There may have been a few others, but the Word of God had been lost.

> And Hilkiah answered and said to Shaphan the scribe, I have found the book of the law in the house of the LORD. And Hilkiah delivered the book to Shaphan.

> And Shaphan carried the book to the king, and brought the king word back again, saying, All that was committed to thy servants, they do it [2 Chron. 34:15–16].

You may be saying, "I can see that this is going to be right down your alley!" It sure is, although it is not my alley, but God's alley—His Word is very important to Him. Notice what happens.

> Then Shaphan the scribe told the king, saying, Hilkiah the priest hath given me a book. And Shaphan read it before the king.

> And it came to pass, when the king had heard the words of the law, that he rent his clothes [2 Chron. 34:18–19].

Renting (or tearing) his clothes indicated strong emotion. He was dismayed when he heard the Word of God for the first time, because he and his people had strayed so far from God's commands.

> And the king commanded Hilkiah, and Ahikam the son of Shaphan, and Abdon the son of Micah, and Shaphan the scribe, and Asaiah a servant of the king's, saying,

> Go, inquire of the LORD for me, and for them that are left in Israel and in Judah, concerning the words of the book that is found: for great is the wrath of the LORD that is poured out upon us, because our fathers have not kept the word of the LORD, to do after all that is written in this book [2 Chron. 34:20–21].

A return to the Word of God brings revival. Nothing else will bring revival. What is wrong in our day? Why don't we see revival? The reason is simple. The church has neglected the Word of God. Churches have tried every known gimmick and every kind of method. Nothing happens. Revival does not come that way. Revival comes when people return to the Word of God and find out what God has to say.

Josiah is a shaken man, and he wants to know what God is going to do.

> And Hilkiah, and they that the king had appointed, went to Huldah the prophetess, the wife of Shallum the son of Tikvath, the son of Hasrah, keeper of the wardrobe; (now she dwelt in Jerusalem in the college:) and they spake to her to that effect.

> And she answered them, Thus saith the LORD God of Israel, Tell ye the man that sent you to me [2 Chron. 34:22–23].

Now this is God's message to Josiah:

> Thus saith the LORD, Behold, I will bring evil upon this place, and upon the inhabitants thereof, even all the curses that are written in the book which they have read before the king of Judah:

> Because they have forsaken me, and have burned incense unto other gods, that they might provoke me to anger with all the works of their hands; therefore my wrath shall be poured out upon this place, and shall not be quenched [2 Chron. 34:24–25].

God will send judgment just as He promised. However, He has a personal word for Josiah.

And as for the king of Judah, who sent you to inquire of the LORD, so shall ye say unto him, Thus saith the LORD God of Israel concerning the words which thou hast heard;

Because thine heart was tender, and thou didst humble thyself before God, when thou heardest his words against this place, and against the inhabitants thereof, and humbledst thyself before me, and didst rend thy clothes, and weep before me; I have even heard thee also, saith the LORD.

Behold, I will gather thee to thy fathers, and thou shalt be gathered to thy grave in peace, neither shall thine eyes see all the evil that I will bring upon this place, and upon the inhabitants of the same. So they brought the king word again [2 Chron. 34:26–28].

God intends to judge these people, but He will not do it until Josiah is gone.

Then the king sent and gathered together all the elders of Judah and Jerusalem.

And the king went up into the house of the LORD, and all the men of Judah, and the inhabitants of Jerusalem, and the priests, and the Levites, and all the people, great and small: and he read in their ears all the words of the book of the covenant that was found in the house of the LORD.

And the king stood in his place, and made a covenant before the LORD, to walk after the LORD, and to keep his commandments, and his testimonies, and his statutes, with all his heart, and with all his soul, to perform the words of the covenant which are written in this book [2 Chron. 34:29–31].

My friend, let's be very candid and very matter-of-fact and very direct. I believe we could have a revival today, but first there must be a return to the Word of God to find out what God wants us to do. Then I believe there will be and there must be a total commitment to God on the part of God's people. There can be none of this halfhearted service which we see. There can be none of this business of trying to go with the world and trying to go with God. It is impossible to do both. There must be a clear-cut dedication of heart and life to God. When that takes place, the Spirit of God is free to move.

In chapter 35 we have a record of the Passover that was kept. This was a new experience for his generation, and it is interesting to note that Josiah carefully followed the procedure which is written in the book of Moses.

> So all the service of the LORD was prepared the same day, to keep the passover, and to offer burnt offerings upon the altar of the LORD, according to the commandment of king Josiah.
>
> And the children of Israel that were present kept the passover at that time, and the feast of unleavened bread seven days.
>
> And there was no passover like to that kept in Israel from the days of Samuel the prophet; neither did all the kings of Israel keep such a passover as Josiah kept, and the priests, and the Levites, and all Judah and Israel that were present, and the inhabitants of Jerusalem.
>
> In the eighteenth year of the reign of Josiah was this passover kept [2 Chron. 35:16–19].

The Passover is symbolic of the death of Christ. The nation has returned to the knowledge that there must be a redemption made for sins. You see, they had learned about the Passover because they had discovered the law of Moses. This was a tremendous occasion. God says, "There was no passover like to that kept in Israel from the days of Samuel the prophet."

Josiah was the man responsible for this great return to the Word of God. Now we come to the death of this man. Even godly men like this make mistakes—all human beings do.

DEATH OF JOSIAH

After all this, when Josiah had prepared the temple, Necho king of Egypt came up to fight against Carchemish by Euphrates: and Josiah went out against him.

But he sent ambassadors to him, saying, What have I to do with thee, thou king of Judah? I come not against thee this day, but against the house wherewith I have war: for God commanded me to make haste: forbear thee from meddling with God, who is with me, that he destroy thee not [2 Chron. 35:20-21].

Josiah should have stayed home. He had no business engaging in this war.

Nevertheless Josiah would not turn his face from him, but disguised himself, that he might fight with him, and hearkened not unto the words of Necho from the mouth of God, and came to fight in the valley of Megiddo [2 Chron. 35:22].

He refused to stay out of the fight. Now notice what happens.

And the archers shot at king Josiah; and the king said to his servants, Have me away; for I am sore wounded.

His servants therefore took him out of that chariot, and put him in the second chariot that he had; and they brought him to Jerusalem, and he died, and was buried

in one of the sepulchres of his fathers. And all Judah
and Jerusalem mourned for Josiah.

And Jeremiah lamented for Josiah: and all the singing
men and the singing women spake of Josiah in their
lamentations to this day, and made them an ordinance
in Israel: and, behold, they are written in the lamentations [2 Chron. 35:23-25].

Josiah had been a good king and a great king. He had led a tremendous
revival, a great turning to God. But his death ended the revival. Now
God's judgment will fall upon the southern kingdom of Judah.

CHAPTER 36

THEME: *The captivity of Judah*

The days were numbered for the southern kingdom of Judah. Josiah was the last good king of the nation. All the kings who followed him were bad. There was not a good one in the lot. Their evil reigns hastened the judgment of God upon the kingdom of Judah. We are given only a brief word about their attitude toward God and a statement of the main events that brought about the ruin of the nation.

REIGN OF JEHOAHAZ

Then the people of the land took Jehoahaz the son of Josiah, and made him king in his father's stead in Jerusalem.

Jehoahaz was twenty and three years old when he began to reign, and he reigned three months in Jerusalem.

And the king of Egypt put him down at Jerusalem, and condemned the land in an hundred talents of silver and a talent of gold [2 Chron. 36:1–3].

This son of Josiah was deposed by the king of Egypt. He was a rascal and was on the throne only three months. Things are beginning to move quickly now.

REIGN OF JEHOIAKIM

Jehoiakim was twenty and five years old when he began to reign, and he reigned eleven years in Jerusalem: and he did that which was evil in the sight of the LORD his God.

> Against him came up Nebuchadnezzar king of Babylon,
> and bound him in fetters, to carry him to Babylon.
>
> Nebuchadnezzar also carried of the vessels of the house
> of the LORD to Babylon, and put them in his temple at
> Babylon [2 Chron. 36:5-7].

During his reign the king of Babylon comes against the land.

REIGN OF JEHOIACHIN

> Jehoiachin was eight years old when he began to reign,
> and he reigned three months and ten days in Jerusalem:
> and he did that which was evil in the sight of the LORD
> [2 Chron. 36:9].

He didn't last very long—he hardly got the throne warm.

REIGN OF ZEDEKIAH

Zedekiah is Judah's last king.

> Zedekiah was one and twenty years old when he began
> to reign, and reigned eleven years in Jerusalem.
>
> And he did that which was evil in the sight of the LORD
> his God, and humbled not himself before Jeremiah the
> prophet speaking from the mouth of the LORD.
>
> And he also rebelled against king Nebuchadnezzar,
> who had made him swear by God: but he stiffened his
> neck, and hardened his heart from turning unto the
> LORD God of Israel.
>
> Moreover all the chief of the priests, and the people,
> transgressed very much after all the abominations of the
> heathen; and polluted the house of the LORD which he
> had hallowed in Jerusalem [2 Chron. 36:11-14].

CAPTIVITY

Nebuchadnezzar now does more than knock at the door. He pushes over the wall and burns Jerusalem and takes Judah into captivity.

Here is God's explanation:

> And the LORD God of their fathers sent to them by his messengers, rising up betimes, and sending; because he had compassion on his people, and on his dwelling place:
>
> But they mocked the messengers of God, and despised his words, and misused his prophets, until the wrath of the LORD arose against his people, till there was no remedy.
>
> Therefore he brought upon them the king of the Chaldees, who slew their young men with the sword in the house of their sanctuary, and had no compassion upon young man or maiden, old man, or him that stooped for age: he gave them all into his hand.
>
> And all the vessels of the house of God, great and small, and the treasures of the house of the LORD, and the treasures of the king, and of his princes; all these he brought to Babylon.
>
> And they burnt the house of God, and brake down the wall of Jerusalem, and burnt all the palaces thereof with fire, and destroyed all the goodly vessels thereof.
>
> And them that had escaped from the sword carried he away to Babylon; where they were servants to him and his sons until the reign of the kingdom of Persia [2 Chron. 36:15-20].

Now the next verse cites another reason for God's judgment. This is most interesting.

To fulfil the word of the LORD by the mouth of Jeremiah, until the land had enjoyed her sabbaths: for as long as she lay desolate she kept sabbath, to fulfil threescore and ten years [2 Chron. 36:21].

You see, God accomplished a twofold purpose. God always has many things in mind in everything that He does. First of all, they had rejected the prophets. They were living on borrowed time; God would have been justified to have sent them into captivity one hundred years before this time.

It makes me wonder if our nation is not living on borrowed time. How much longer will God put up with our sins? For the nation of Judah, their time had come. There was no more remedy. There is a time when a nation reaches this point. I wonder how close our nation is to this time.

Secondly, for 490 years Israel had not observed the sabbatic years. They had been breaking God's law of the land, which He had given them even before they set foot upon it: "And the LORD spake unto Moses in mount Sinai, saying, Speak unto the children of Israel, and say unto them, When ye come into the land which I give you, then shall the land keep a sabbath unto the LORD. Six years thou shalt sow thy field, and six years thou shalt prune thy vineyard, and gather in the fruit thereof; but in the seventh year shall be a sabbath of rest unto the land, a sabbath for the LORD: thou shalt neither sow thy field, nor prune thy vineyard. That which groweth of its own accord of thy harvest thou shalt not reap, neither gather the grapes of thy vine undressed: for it is a year of rest unto the land" (Lev. 25:1–5). Because of their greed, they have not allowed the land to enjoy its sabbaths. In other words, they had not allowed it to remain fallow every seventh year as God had commanded. They thought they had gotten by with it. For 490 years they had been doing it, then God said, "I'll put you out of the land for seventy years so the land can enjoy its sabbaths." That is the reason the captivity lasted for seventy years. This is quite remarkable.

You see, my friend, God is not mocked. "Be not deceived; God is not mocked: for whatsoever a man soweth, that shall he also reap" (Gal. 6:7).

Notice that the seventy years in exile are passed over entirely. The people are out of the land and out of the will of God. God's clock is not spelled B-U-L-O-V-A or G-R-U-E-N; God's clock is spelled I-S-R-A-E-L, and it runs only while Israel is in the land.

We have seen in this book that although there was a general decline of the nation, there were five periods of revival, renewal, and reformation. There is a striking feature which characterizes each period:

Asa	Return and obedience to the Word of God
Jehoshaphat	Return and obedience to the Word of God
Joash	Return and obedience to the Word of God
Hezekiah	Return and obedience to the Word of God
Josiah	Return and obedience to the Word of God

In each instance, return to the Word of God led to the repentance of the people and the temporary reformation of the nation.

DECREE TO REBUILD THE TEMPLE

Second Chronicles concludes with a bright hope for the future.

> Now in the first year of Cyrus king of Persia, that the word of the LORD spoken by the mouth of Jeremiah might be accomplished, the LORD stirred up the spirit of Cyrus king of Persia, that he made a proclamation throughout all his kingdom, and put it also in writing, saying,

> Thus saith Cyrus king of Persia, All the kingdoms of the earth hath the LORD God of heaven given me; and he hath charged me to build him an house in Jerusalem, which is in Judah. Who is there among you of all his people? The LORD his God be with him, and let him go up [2 Chron. 36:22–23].

This is repeated in the introduction to the Book of Ezra which continues the historical record from this point. It is wonderful to see that although God had sent His people into captivity, He had not forgotten them. How gracious He is!

BIBLIOGRAPHY

(Recommended for Further Study)

Crockett, William Day. *A Harmony of the Books of Samuel, Kings, and Chronicles.* Grand Rapids, Michigan: Baker Book House, 1951.

Darby, J. N. *Synopsis of the Books of the Bible.* Addison, Illinois: Bible Truth Publishers, n.d.

Davis, John J. and Whitcomb, John C., Jr. *A History of Israel.* Grand Rapids, Michigan: Baker Book House, 1970. (Excellent.)

Epp, Theodore H. *David.* Lincoln, Nebraska: Back to the Bible Broadcast, 1965.

Gaebelein, Arno C. *The Annotated Bible.* Neptune, New Jersey: Loizeaux Brothers, 1912–22.

Gray, James M. *Synthetic Bible Studies.* Westwood, New Jersey: Fleming H. Revell Co., 1906.

Heading, John. *I & II Chronicles.* Kansas City, Missouri: Walterick Publishers, 1982.

Jensen, Irving L. *I Kings with Chronicles.* Chicago, Illinois: Moody Press, 1968. (A self-study guide.)

Jensen, Irving L. *II Kings with Chronicles.* Chicago, Illinois: Moody Press, 1968. (A self-study guide.)

Kelly, William. *Lectures on the Earlier Historical Books of the Old Testament.* Addison, Illinois: Bible Truth Publishers, 1874.

Knapp, Christopher. *The Kings of Israel and Judah.* Neptune, New Jersey: Loizeaux Brothers, 1908. (Very fine.)

Mackintosh, C. H. *Miscellaneous Writings.* Neptune, New Jersey: Loizeaux Brothers, n.d.

Meyer, F. B. *David: Shepherd, Psalmist, King.* Fort Washington, Pennsylvania: Christian Literature Crusade, n.d.

Sailhamer, John. *I & II Chronicles.* Chicago, Illinois: Moody Press, 1983.

Sauer, Erich. *The Dawn of World Redemption.* Grand Rapids, Michigan: William B. Eerdmans Publishing Co., 1951. (An excellent Old Testament survey.)

Scroggie, W. Graham. *The Unfolding Drama of Redemption.* Grand Rapids, Michigan: Zondervan Publishing House, 1970. (An excellent survey and outline of the Old Testament.)

Unger, Merrill F. *Unger's Commentary on the Old Testament.* Vol. 1. Chicago, Illinois: Moody Press, 1981. (A fine summary of each paragraph. Highly recommended.)

Wood, Leon J. *Israel's United Monarchy.* Grand Rapids, Michigan: Baker Book House, 1979. (Excellent.)

Wood, Leon J. *The Prophets of Israel.* Grand Rapids, Michigan: Baker Book House, 1977. (Excellent.)